Florida

DIVORCE

5th Edition

HANDBOOK

A Comprehensive Source of Legal
Information and Practical Advice

Gerald B. Keane

Attorney at Law

 Pineapple Press, Inc. Sarasota, Florida

green press
INITIATIVE

Pineapple Press is committed to preserving ancient forests and natural resources. We elected to print *Florida Divorce Handbook 5th Edition* on 50% post consumer recycled paper, processed chlorine free. As a result, for this printing, we have saved:

15 Trees (40' tall and 6-8" diameter)
6,209 Gallons of Wastewater
2,497 Kilowatt Hours of Electricity
684 Pounds of Solid Waste
1,344 Pounds of Greenhouse Gases

Pineapple Press made this paper choice because our printer, Thomson-Shore, Inc., is a member of Green Press Initiative, a nonprofit program dedicated to supporting authors, publishers, and suppliers in their efforts to reduce their use of fiber obtained from endangered forests.

For more information, visit www.greenpressinitiative.org

Inquiries should be addressed to:
Pineapple Press, Inc.
P.O. Box 3889
Sarasota, Florida 34230

www.pineapplepress.com

Library of Congress Cataloging in Publication Data

Keane, Gerald B., 1945-
Florida divorce handbook : a comprehensive source of legal information and
    practical advice / Gerald B. Keane. -- 5th ed.
    p. cm.
Includes index.
ISBN 978-1-56164-402-5 (pbk. : alk. paper)
1. Divorce--Law and legislation--Florida--Popular works. 2. Divorce suits--
    Florida--Popular works. I. Title.
KFF100.Z9K43 2007
346.75901'66--dc22

                                                              2007032490

Fifth Edition
10 9 8 7 6 5 4 3 2 1

Design by Carol Tornatore
Printed in the United States of America

CONTENTS

INTRODUCTION

*D*ivorce is a hard subject. Hard for people to go through and hard for them to understand. Harder still because they need to understand it during the most difficult time of their lives.

This book won't make a divorce enjoyable. But it may make the process tolerable. It is intended to give you an understanding of divorce law as a whole and of the many little pieces that now make it up.

You will not be a legal expert when you finish reading this book. You will, however, be able to assist your lawyer with your divorce. You should be able to understand what he or she is talking about and be able to contribute to your case.

Divorce law is complicated. It gets more and more complicated every year. Laws change, and then cases change ("interpret") those laws. Even marital law specialists, those who read every new case in the field, don't know for certain what a judge will do in a particular case. Divorce law is made up of a fairly intricate framework of statutes upon which case law throws a loose covering; the facts of your case, the approach of your attorney, the philosophies of your particular judge, and even your personality will give your divorce its unique shape.

I can tell you about the laws and I can tell you about how they are being interpreted. I can even guess where the divorce laws are heading. But I can't evaluate the facts of your case (and the facts of every case are different); I can't tell you what approach your attorney will or should take (although I can suggest what characteristics are associated with the better divorce lawyers). I can't list all the trial judges in Florida and rate them. Finally, I don't have the luxury of sitting with you for an hour or so; I can't guess what virtues and vices you bring to your case. But I can and will tell you that your attitudes and apparent credibility will be as important in the results of your case as any divorce law.

For all its complexity, the law of dissolution of marriage is concerned with only a few subjects. Divorce is concerned with support, property, and custody of children.

That makes it seem simple. I can and will tell you how and why support is awarded, whether it is alimony or child support. I can and will tell you about the many forms that support can take and how it can be modified.

I can teach you how property is divided and what property the judge has the power to divide. And I can advise you of the factors used to determine custody of children.

What I cannot teach you is how to apply the equities. And divorce is all about equities. Only a skilled and experienced lawyer, who has handled hundreds of cases and who knows the facts of your case, and who knows you and has questioned your spouse, can even guess how your case will come out.

There are more divorce lawyers working in coffee shops and gas stations than there are behind desks. Everyone you run into who has ever been divorced, or even met someone who has been divorced, will offer to give you advice. They'll know exactly what your lawyer should do and what you should get.

I hope that, after you read this book, you won't be one of those "lawyers" and that you will know enough to know how difficult divorce law is. I hope that you'll know enough to know how little you know. I hope that you will know enough to seek and follow the advice of an expert. I also hope that you will understand that judges aren't computers, that they are evaluating fleeting and elusive hints of what you and your spouse are really like, and that our legal system, for all its faults, is the best and fairest system in the world.

This book is only a guide. It isn't a bible. If you understand the system a little more than you did before you read it, you will become a part of the system, accepting responsibilities and helping it work better. Better for you.

I can't guarantee that you will get justice in your divorce. I can't even guarantee that this book will make it more likely that you will get justice. I can assure you only that you will better understand your divorce, your rights, and your risks. You will be less a victim than a participant.

Florida's divorce laws are unique, as are the laws of the other 49 states. We Florida lawyers like to believe that our laws are more humane and more enlightened than those of most other states. In fact, there is reason to believe that no state, with the possible exception of California, has done more to improve divorce justice. I am proud to practice law in Florida.

No one is fortunate to be going through a divorce. If you must get a divorce, there is no better place than Florida to do so. No better place if you are the husband, the wife, or the real victims, the children.

If you have no children and no dispute about your property or alimony, you can get a simplified divorce. You don't need lawyers and you don't need to fight. Read Chapter 4 if you are able to use that easier way out.

Divorce is always a battle between genders. In writing this book, gender itself became a battle. In fairness to you, the reader, I've used "he or she" in most cases because either gender could be seeking whatever relief I may be discussing; I don't want to create the false impression that only "she" can seek alimony or that only "he" may be the noncustodial parent. I apologize if this makes some parts a little harder to read.

God forbid that you should ever need this book. But, God willing, if you must go through a divorce, I want your case to be as easy as possible. I hope that this book will help you get through it with your dignity intact, your self-respect unshaken, and your respect for our system of justice increased. Good luck.

1

WHAT IS A DISSOLUTION OF MARRIAGE?

What you will learn in this chapter:
- what *no-fault* is all about
- how a divorce differs from a separation
- what the three stages of a divorce case are
- whether your spouse can prevent you from getting a divorce
- why it matters that divorces are heard in courts of equity
- how long your divorce case will take
- what investigation your attorney will do in your case
- why you need an attorney who can and will negotiate
- the best way to resolve your case
- the different types of separations in Florida
- actions for support unrelated to divorce, including URESA
- what an *annulment* is and how it affects marital rights
- the difference between void and voidable marriages
- what a restraining order is and what it does
- how to get protection if you're abused

Clients arrive at attorneys' offices with many questions. Often, the attorney doesn't understand how little the client knows. To be sure that we're all on the same grounds, let me define at the outset certain terms that you need to understand.

What Is a "Dissolution of Marriage"?

A dissolution of marriage means the same thing as divorce, the legal (or judicial) termination of a valid marriage. "Divorces" became "dissolutions" when "no-fault" came along.

The term "divorce" merely means a turning away or going one's separate way and does not essentially carry any implication of fault. Nonetheless, the term acquired so much baggage over the years that some obscure legislator in some forgotten state decided that the new concept of divorce required new terminology. For all practical purposes, a dissolution of a marriage is a divorce, and I use the terms interchangeably throughout this book.

What Does "No-Fault" Mean?

No-fault divorce does not require proof of fault to end the marriage. The petitioner (that is, the party filing first) no longer needs to prove one of the tradition-

1

A *petitioner* is the person who brings the action by filing a *"Petition for Dissolution of Marriage."* He or she is asking, or petitioning, the court for legal help. By statute, the parties in divorce actions are properly referred to as the "husband" and the "wife" and "petitioner" is rarely used in actual cases.

A *respondent* is the person who must answer or respond to the Petition. He or she can also seek relief by filing a "Counterpetition" but that doesn't change him or her from being the respondent.

A *trial* is the court appearance, often in front of a jury, when the evidence is presented and the case decided.

A *hearing* is a court appearance with only the judge present; the term is used for all preliminary appearances in divorces and the trial is usually called the *final hearing* since divorce cases are always tried without a jury.

al bases for divorce, such as mental cruelty, adultery, or physical abuse. Most marriages break up because the parties are incompatible. The other problems are just symptoms of the parties' inability to live together.

Under the old (fault) system, where no adultery occurred, and where there was no mental or physical abuse, or other blame, the respondent (that is, the party who does not start the divorce and, therefore, who "responds" to the petitioner's action) did not have to allow a divorce. If one of the grounds for divorce did not exist, the parties had to collude — that is, lie — about the existence of such grounds in order to get a divorce. No-fault has succeeded in eliminating that shameful exercise. Either party may obtain a marriage whenever he or she believes that the marriage is "irretrievably broken," regardless of who has caused the breaking, if anyone. (A second, little-used basis for divorce is that the other party has been legally adjudged incompetent for more than three years.) No fault divorce means you don't have to point a finger any more; it doesn't mean, unfortunately, that fingers aren't pointed. The reasons are just different now.

What Is the Difference Between a "Lawyer" and an "Attorney"?

The technical difference is that a lawyer is any law school graduate; an attorney is a lawyer who has been admitted to the Bar, that is, is licensed to practice law in the state. In practice, there is no distinction. Even most lawyers (or do I mean attorneys?) don't know the difference. Whether your representative goes by lawyer or attorney, he or she is still the same thing, a licensed member of the Florida Bar. If you have doubts about whether a person is really licensed to practice law, you can call the Records Department of the Florida Bar in Tallahassee for confirmation of membership and good standing. The telephone number is (800) 342-8060 (press 0 at the prompt and then press 4) or go to http://www.floridabar.org and access the "Find a Lawyer" on the bar at the top.

What Is the Difference Between a "Hearing" and a "Trial"?

Some cases go to "trial" and some go to "hearings" or "final hearings." We usually think of a trial as a contest in front of a jury and a hearing as a contest in front of a judge alone. Although dissolution actions are always tried without a jury, the terms "final hearing" and "trial" are used interchangeably.

What Comes Out of a Final Hearing?

A Final Judgment. Or a Decree. Or a Final Decree. Actually, I've rarely heard the latter two terms in Florida. The court's ruling is always called a Final Judgment in our state. I have, however, seen final rulings from other states designated as Decrees.

What Is the Difference Between a "Divorce" and a "Legal Separation"?

Some clients don't want a divorce. They want a "legal separation." There are three situations that could accurately be called a "legal separation": (1) any separation of the parties governed by a written instrument; (2) a separation where the dependent spouse has obtained an order of support unrelated to a dissolution; and (3) a separation where the supporting spouse has obtained an order of how much he or she must pay. Separation is discussed later in this chapter, but it differs from a divorce only in that the technical legal bond remains in place, the partners' property remains jointly owned, and neither party can remarry.

There are many other terms that might be confusing. They may be Greek to you but, in some cases, they're Latin. The glossary at the back of this book will help you.

The Effect of No-Fault

Before no-fault, the central issue in a case was whether there would or would not be a divorce. We still hear people say things like "She won't give me a divorce," which used to mean that the wife wouldn't go along with lying about the existence of a legal basis for divorce. With no-fault, that is no longer an issue. Divorce is now almost a matter of right.

Although the judge could find from the evidence that the marriage is not irretrievably broken, it rarely happens. If there are no children and the allegation in the Petition that the marriage is irretrievably broken is not denied, the judge must enter a dissolution of marriage "if the judge finds the marriage is irretrievably broken." The last phrase seems like such a redundant afterthought that it is clear the intent is that a denial of a divorce should be rare. When there are children or when the respondent denies that the marriage is irretrievably broken, the judge may do any one of four things: grant the divorce, order counseling, delay the judgment for

A *court of law* is one that decides cases primarily involving money. Rather rigid rules govern what that court can and cannot do.

A *court of equity* decides all cases where money is not the primary issue, such as divorces, foreclosures (since the court orders the sale of the home as a way to award money), adoptions, injunctions, etc.

up to three months to allow the parties to reconcile, or take such other action as may be in the best interest of the parties and the minor children of the marriage. Despite these alternatives, few judges will deny the divorce even temporarily unless both parties agree to try to reconcile or to attend counseling. Realistically, like a marriage, neither reconciliation nor counseling will work unless both parties are committed to it.

With fault no longer an issue, there are three issues remaining: child custody (including visitation and support), alimony, and property rights. After judgment, the property rights cannot be litigated again but both custody (and its related issues) and alimony can be modified if circumstances change.

The wife is entitled to change her name upon being divorced. Although she would usually change back to her maiden name or a former married name, the law does not limit her to former names. Jane Doe could choose to become Marilyn Monroe if she chose.

What Is a Court of Equity?

Divorces are decided in a court of equity. You can be excused for not completely understanding what that is; as with many things, even many lawyers don't know what the concept means.

Let me give you a little history on the subject. Almost a thousand years ago, England developed law courts. The judges in those courts decided cases according to previous experience; if a case similar to yours was decided one way a week before, your case would be decided the same way. Thus, the system developed a reliance on precedent (or *stare decisis*). That was good because it made court cases somewhat predictable. What was bad was that the system quickly locked into what matters were decidable; it became rigid and had no method of handling new types of cases. If people had a dispute that didn't fit into something that the courts had previously decided, the parties were, for a time, out in the cold. In desperation, they turned to the king to decide their case. He turned such matters over to the chancery to hear. The chancery was then made up of priests and the like. Since they were not bound by any rigid rules of law, the priests would decide the case on principles of fairness with the procedures influenced by canon law. This developed into an independent system of justice for those unusual cases. Since it relied on principles of fairness or equity, rather than rules of law, it came to known as the court of equity.

The common law of England (the basis for our law) eventually recognized the two separate systems, courts of law and courts of equity. One (the courts of law) was governed by rigid laws; the other wasn't. Since our system is based on the English system, we also started out with two separate court systems.

The distinction between the two courts has long since been abolished in Florida. Theoretically, we have no courts of equity. In fact, we do. Matters that were formerly decided in equity courts are still decided under the same principles. We have only one set of judges and one set of courtrooms. However, a judge will conduct the court slightly differently when sitting on a case in equity than when sitting on a case in law. In equity cases, which include divorce cases, foreclosures, injunctions, adoptions, etc., the judge is not rigidly bound: he or she, in theory, is free to do "equity" as the case may require.

Actually, the "one set of judges and one set of courtrooms" is no longer completely true. The Supreme Court has mandated that each circuit have separate "Family Law Courts," in which all marital cases are heard. The idea is to have the cases heard by judges (who rotate in and out every year or so) who are working exclusively in divorces (and related cases) with the object of giving them familiarity with the law and assuring greater consistency. I think most attorneys would agree that the Family Law Courts have achieved this goal.

One practical effect of being in a court of equity is that your attorney can never be sure what the judge will decide. The judge will decide the case based on a combination of fairness and law. In law, judges must follow the law or risk being reversed on appeal; in equity, judges will only be reversed if they clearly abuse their discretion. A judge can go pretty far before he or she is held to have reached the level of abusing that latitude. Therefore, your attorney will generally advise you what the judge "probably will do" or what your attorney believes the judge "should" do.

How Long Does a Dissolution Action Take?

Except in unusual circumstances, a dissolution action can't be completed in less than 20 days. While some cases take years to complete, the average case probably takes between four and eight months.

The court can allow a divorce in less than 20 days if exceptional circumstances exist. For example, if you were going to become a missionary after the divorce and had to leave for training before the end of the 20 days, the judge would probably agree to have a final hearing in a shorter time. The judge could only do so, however, if your spouse cooperated and filed an answer right away. Obviously

The *Petition for Dissolution*, the *Answer* (or *Response*), and the *Counter-Petition* are all called pleadings. The first part of the case is often called the *pleading stage* because all the pleadings are being filed during that period.

Discovery is the set of procedures your lawyer uses to learn about (or "discover") your spouse's side of the case; your lawyer uses the information gathered in the *discovery stage* to prepare your case for the final hearing.

A *Petition* is the formal written paper that briefly sets out the issues and tells the court and your spouse what legal relief you are seeking.

A *Counterpetition* is the same as a Petition except it is filed by the Respondent, who files it along with an Answer to state the issues as he or she believes them to be and tells the court what relief she/he seeks.

An *Answer* may be to a Petition or a Counterpetition. It is a brief statement of which allegations in your spouse's pleading you admit and which you deny.

Evidence is *discoverable* if it would be admissible in court or if it could lead to admissible evidence.

there can only be a quick hearing if everything is settled before or immediately after filing. In practice, few hearings are held before the 20 days have passed.

Most cases involve three different phases: pleading, discovery, and preparation for hearing. Settlement negotiations often take place during the third phase.

Pleading Stage. The pleading stage usually takes about a month; the Petition for Dissolution of Marriage is filed and the other party has 20 days to answer and counterpetition. Once an Answer or an Answer and Counter-petition are filed, the petitioner has an additional 20 days to answer the counterpetition; since that Answer is usually filed quickly, the pleadings are often in place about 30 days or so after the initial filing.

Discovery Stage. The second stage is "discovery." Once you know from the pleadings what your spouse wants, your attorney can ask for information from your spouse about the issues. There are four common discovery tools, and one less common tool, available to attorneys. They are interrogatories, depositions, requests for production, requests for admissions, and, less commonly, requests for mental or physical examinations.

Interrogatories. Interrogatories are written questions that must be answered within 30 days. Since they are not part of mandatory discovery, they need only be answered if specifically requested. The Florida Supreme Court has approved 7 standard questions (120 or so questions if you count each subpart) your attorney can ask; he can supplement those questions with up to 10 additional questions without permission of the Court.

Requests for Production. The Family Law Rules require the automatic production of certain documents within 45 days of service on the respondent. Your attorney may also subpoena documents and other possible evidence from nonparties. He or she must give the other attorney ten days' notice before he issues such a subpoena unless a deposition is scheduled. This gives your opponent the chance to object if the items sought are not discoverable.

Depositions. Once your attorney has the interrogatory answers and the production, he or she will want to ask your spouse some questions under oath. This is done at a deposition where a court reporter will record the answers. Your spouse's attorney will also be present to protect his or her interests.

Depositions can also be taken of nonparties. Usually, such depositions involve accountants, business partners, or neighbors — anyone who might have information relevant to the case.

Requests for admissions. Final hearings can sometimes be shortened if the issues can be narrowed in advance. Your attorney can send requests for admissions to your spouse demanding that he or she admit the truth of certain facts. If those facts are admitted (or no response is made), those facts can be submitted to the court at the final hearing as true without further proof. Although effective in other types of cases, requests for admissions are rarely used and even more rarely effective in divorce cases.

Requests for Mental or Physical Examinations. If the physical or mental health of either party is put at issue by the pleadings or discovery evidence, the other party can ask to have that party examined. You cannot seek a mental or physical examination without his or her health being made an issue by either your spouse's pleadings or by the facts of the case. If either party asserts disability or poor health in order to get or avoid support, there may be an issue which justifies an examination. If your spouse has a history of erratic behavior or has recently been hospitalized for a serious illness, his or her health is an issue and you may obtain the right to have your spouse examined. Such examinations are less common than you might think.

Discovery can often take months. Because depositions must wait for interrogatory answers and production, they cannot be going on at the same time. The minimum reasonable full-discovery period is probably about two and a half months; four months is not unreasonable.

Hearing Stage. Once the pleadings are set and discovery is completed, your attorney must make final preparations for trial (final hearing). The pleadings and discovery have provided enough information to do this. By this time, your attorney will have seen all the evidence, probed into that evidence at deposition, evaluated your spouse's demeanor and apparent credibility, and, just as importantly, seen you testify at deposition. Your attorney will use all of that information to evaluate your chances at trial and to prepare questions, legal research, and evidence for the final hearing.

Settlement Negotiations. This is when your attorney should make a settlement offer and negotiate it with your spouse's attorney. Your case can be resolved in one of two ways: by trying the facts and letting the judge decide or by coming to a compromise by settling on all issues. A settlement is the best possible resolution; a trial, even one that ends in your favor, is the worst.

Once the issues are clear and the facts are known to both sides, the attorneys can work together to find a middle ground that is acceptable to both sides. Take note that I said "acceptable." To resolve disputes, compromises must be made; you must give up certain things to get others. For example, you might give your spouse the house and get more alimony. Or you might be willing to pay the outstanding bills in order to pay less alimony.

Historically, the attorneys would try to negotiate the issues in the case between themselves during informal conversations, usually over the telephone. That practice has given way to mediated negotiations, which I will discuss later. Although there is no reason why the attorneys shouldn't be able to resolve most issues in most cases without the time and expense of mediation, you will find that mediation is almost automatic (and, often, Court ordered) in your case.

Sometimes, when the parties are mature and reasonable, and the attorneys are capable of working well together, the attorneys and clients may meet together in a settlement conference.

If a settlement is reached, one of the attorneys will draw up a "settlement agreement," a formal statement of the exact terms that you agreed upon. The exact language must often be negotiated back and forth; sometimes, new aspects of the issues become apparent in reviewing the proposed agreement. When all the language and all the terms are agreed upon, both parties sign the agreement and the case is submitted to the judge at a short (usually less than three-minute) hearing.

Any attorney worth hiring should be willing to negotiate in good faith; if yours won't, you have the wrong attorney. Settlements save money for the clients, generally leave both parties more satisfied, and almost always make future contact between the parties more amicable.

While negotiations are going on, the trial date is being scheduled. A "notice for trial" is filed that advises the court that the matter is ready to be set for trial. In response, the judge will enter an order proposing three or four alternative trial weeks during the next several months.

> A *Settlement* is an agreement on all the issues of the case that is reduced to a written document called a *settlement agreement*. If accepted by the judge, it becomes part of the Final Judgment.

In some jurisdictions, judges' calendars are booked several months in advance and it can take some time to get a trial scheduled. Many judges overbook trial weeks with the reasonable expectation that many, if not most, of the cases will settle before they have to be tried.

Settlement will almost always shorten the time to complete a case. This time savings, along with the avoidance of the risks any trial presents, is a major reason why all cases should be negotiated in good faith. Although negotiations can start early in a small or uncomplicated case, negotiations must usually await completion of discovery.

If the parties agree to settlement terms, the final hearing can be held very soon, usually within a week to ten days. The hearing in a settled case takes only about three minutes.

Separation

There was a time when people didn't get divorces. For many reasons, emotionally estranged spouses lived apart and never divorced. They were separated and, in many cases, they obtained "legal separations."

For years, people came and asked me about legal separations, and I told them, somewhat accurately, that we had no such thing in Florida. No judge issues anything called a "writ of legal separation" or a "legal separation decree." I told them what I could do for them, call it what they may. People continue to use the term so I've given up; I'll call it a "legal separation," too. That's what this section is about.

A legal separation, for our purposes, is any separation that is evidenced by some writing which gives it legal structure or import. There are three procedures or types of separation, two judicial and one nonjudicial, which achieve that result. These include actions for support, actions to determine one's duty for support, and separation agreements.

Separation Agreements. Separation Agreements are by far the most common form of legal separation, mainly because they are almost always used in settling a divorce case. The parties' agreements are put into a written contract, and the contract usually, but not always, later becomes part of the Final Judgment.

Until a Final Judgment is entered, if ever, a separation agreement can be enforced in the same manner as any other contract. This creates one of the rare times when a court of law (which decides contract actions) is simultaneously a court of equity (which, as we've said, decides divorce cases). This occurs because, although the action may be to enforce a contract, the contract in question is one of such importance to the state that the court would have discretion to enforce it equitably. If the terms were unfair to either party, the judge could modify those terms to achieve equity.

A separation agreement, whether agreed to on the way to a divorce or as an alternative to a divorce, should address the same matters that are decided in divorce actions, except for the divorce itself. It must provide for custody and support for any children, and support for a dependent spouse. If used to facilitate a divorce, it must also provide for property division.

Separation agreements are governed by much the same considerations as apply to nuptial agreements. (A nuptial agreement, covered in Chapter 14, is nothing more than a contingent separation agreement.) The parties can agree to almost any terms acceptable to both as long as both are acting freely and with reasonable understanding of their rights. They do not, however, have complete liberty, especially concerning the children. But as long as both parties disclose their assets, income, and immediate prospects, and they enter into the agreement while each is represented by an attorney of his or her own choosing, the agreement will be presumed valid and it will be very difficult to overturn. An agreement can be modified by the Court if substantial changes have intervened between the execution of the agreement and the attempt to incorporate it into a judgment. This occurs very rarely.

Benefits of Settlement Agreements. There is one big advantage of settlement agreements: the parties will more likely abide with agreed terms than with imposed terms. For this reason, and because judges hate to try divorce cases, the law favors settlements.

Actions for Support. Florida law provides two separate support actions. One empowers a dependent spouse (or one with dependent children) to petition the court for support. The other is the converse: the party liable to pay support can ask the court to set the amount. Both actions may be filed without seeking a dissolution of marriage.

If you are abandoned by your spouse and are in need of support for yourself or your children, you can file an action for support. In that action, the judge can make provision for alimony, child support, use of property, and payment of bills.

If you or your spouse have moved out and you are having difficulty agreeing upon how much you should provide for support, you can file an action to have the court set your support obligation. Like an action for support, the judge can enter a judgment covering any matters related to support, such as use of the house and cars, in addition to setting alimony and/or child support, assuming the relief is sought in the pleadings.

Independent support actions are relatively rare. If the marriage has deteriorated to the level where a court must impose support on one spouse or the other, the marriage is undoubtedly lost. Except for unusual religious reasons, which arise more rarely every year, there is simply no reason not to sue for dissolution. An action for support is no simpler and costs no less even though the divorce is not at issue. In any event, when an action for support is filed by one party, the other invariably counterpetitions for dissolution of the marriage. In those rare cases when a party seeks support independent of a divorce, the court has exactly the same power to determine child care and support issues. It is not clear that the court has any jurisdiction over property in such cases but most courts would, if asked, make arrangements for use of the property. The court does not have authority to divide property owned jointly in such cases.

The most common independent action for support is a UIFSA action, that is, an action under the Uniform Interstate Family Support Act. UIFSA is a law that has been enacted in essentially the same form in every state in the United States to enable spouses to enforce support against a spouse living in another state. The details of that act are covered in Chapter 9, Enforcement.

Finally, there is a cost-free way to enforce a child support obligation. All citizens, whether receiving welfare or not, have the right to have the Department of Revenue represent them in collecting child support. In fact, while the price is right, the fact is that you often get what you pay for. The attorneys doing the work are terribly overworked and do not have the time to do the discovery and other investigation to be effective. In some cases, however, the circumstances of the case and the diligence of the Department of Revenue attorney can produce very satisfactory results.

Annulment

Annulment is the judicial determination that no valid marriage exists. That sounds simple but there are many complications. First, the law strongly favors marriage and presumes that a marriage is valid. In seeking an annulment, you must overcome that presumption.

There are "void" and there are "voidable" marriages. A marriage is merely *voidable* if the parties can take steps after the ceremony to validate the marriage; continued cohabitation is the most common means of validating a marriage. If it

A marriage can be annulled if it is *void* or if it is voidable. A void marriage is one that can never be made a valid marriage. A *voidable* marriage is one that can be validated after the ceremony.

is *void*, there is nothing the parties can ever do that would make it a legal marriage.

Fraud or deceit in identity or procedure may render a marriage voidable. For example, if you claimed to be someone else, or if you convinced your girlfriend that the ceremony was not a marriage ceremony, the marriage would be voidable. She may, on the other hand, ratify (make legal) the marriage by continuing to cohabit after learning the facts.

This type of fraud is in contrast to fraud in the inducement, such as a woman falsely claiming that she's pregnant, which does not render the marriage voidable (or void).

Duress may render a marriage voidable. A "shotgun wedding" results in a voidable marriage that can, like one resulting from fraud, be ratified by continuing to cohabit after the duress is relieved (i.e., after the shotgun is put away).

Incestuous marriages are those between parent and child, brother and sister, aunt and nephew, and uncle and niece. It is not incestuous for an adoptive brother and sister to marry. An incestuous marriage would seem to be void since it clearly fits the description of a marriage that could never be validated no matter what the parties did, but the law is not always what you think it is. Incestuous marriages are, strangely enough, not void, but voidable.

A bigamous marriage is void. If either party is married to another at the time of the new ceremony, the new marriage is bigamous and void. The law makes bigamy difficult to prove by presuming that, between an earlier and a later marriage, the later marriage is valid and the earlier one terminated. If you're the one asserting a prior existing marriage, you have the burden of proving that the earlier marriage was never terminated. Proving a negative is almost impossible, but the law does give some relief. It doesn't require proof that the marriage was not dissolved in all possible places, only in those places where the spouse was legally entitled to seek a dissolution.

Bases for Annulment. A marriage may be annulled for any of the following reasons:

· undissolved prior marriage (void);
· incestuous marriage (voidable);
· either party under age (voidable);
· mental incapacity, whether through disease or intoxication (voidable);

- physical incapacity (inability to engage in the sexual act) (voidable);
- lack of intent (jest or formal marriage only) (voidable);
- duress to the extent that one party was deprived of the ability to independently formulate the intent (voidable);
- fraud or concealment, providing no consummation has taken place (voidable).

That last basis, fraud, includes some interesting distinctions. First, if you can prove that your spouse married without intending to ever consummate the marriage, your marriage is voidable. If, however, your spouse never consummated it but you can't prove he or she intended not to consummate it at the time of the wedding, the marriage is legal and binding.

Likewise, lying about your prior but undissolved marriage(s), chastity, or parenthood may make the marriage voidable. On the other hand, as stated above, an outright false assertion by a woman that she is pregnant in order to force a man to marry her is not a sufficient basis for annulment.

Defenses. A marriage that is voidable may be ratified, that is, made legal, once the basis for the annulment is discovered and corrected. For example, if you were so intoxicated at the wedding that you didn't act voluntarily, you may later ratify the marriage by staying with your spouse. Likewise, if you find that your new husband lacks the ability to consummate the marriage, you must act promptly to annul the marriage or you will be held to have ratified the marriage.

In order to get an annulment, your grounds must be corroborated by another person. That's usually easy enough when the grounds are lack of mental capacity, but how on earth could you prove that your spouse will not (and never intended to) consummate the marriage if he or she won't admit it? Of course, if the wife is a virgin and a court-ordered examination confirms this fact, that would prove her nonconsummation; but her husband would still have to prove that she intended, at the time of the marriage, never to consummate it.

Support during Annulment. The court has the authority to make the man support his "wife" (or a woman support her "husband") and their children, if any, during any action for annulment, but the court cannot order any further alimony if the marriage is annulled.

Property rights and the parties' rights with respect to their children can be handled in an annulment action in the same way as in a dissolution proceeding.

Restraining Orders
A restraining order and a temporary injunction are much the same thing, each

An *injunction* is a court order that a party do or not do something.

A *restraining order* is a court order that someone not do something, usually until the court can hear the case more fully.

serving temporarily to stop someone from doing something that may be harmful to another. I will use the terms interchangeably.

There are several uses for restraining orders in dissolution actions. They can prohibit one spouse from beating the other, one spouse from going to the marital home, harassment at work or through friends, nuisance telephone calls, one spouse from following the other, etc. Note that I do not say "prevent" or "protect" because all the order can do is put the power of the court behind the prohibition. If the spouse violates the order, he or she can be held in contempt of court and punished. That's the idea, not the practice. In practice and excepting only spouse abuse injunctions (where the courts are very strict), the courts will only reluctantly impose any punishment for violation of injunctions.

Abused Spouse Injunctions. The Florida legislature has created a procedure for abused spouses, former spouses, anyone related by blood or marriage, or anyone who is or was living in the same dwelling, as if a family, and someone having a child with an alleged abuser to obtain injunctions very simply. Since the procedure permits entry of the temporary injunction without the other side being heard, it can easily be abused. While spouse abuse remains a serious problem, this procedure has served to encourage another form of abuse, abuse of the legal system. There must be a better, more enlightened, way to deal with this issue.

To obtain an abused spouse injunction, the petitioner, usually a woman, merely tells the deputy clerk of the circuit court that she needs an injunction against getting beaten. If the petitioner has enough money, he or she must pay the filing fee plus a fee for sheriff's service. If insolvent, he or she gives an affidavit to that effect and gets the services free.

Upon the fee being paid (or the insolvency affidavit being signed), the clerk has the petitioner (the abused spouse) fill out a form stating why protection is needed and whether other relief is appropriate, such as exclusive use of the house, temporary custody of the children, temporary support, or mandatory counseling for the abusing spouse. After the petitioner has sworn to the allegations, the clerk then brings the "Petition for Injunction for Protection Against Domestic Violence" to a circuit judge and has the judge enter the injunction, giving such protection as the Petition indicates is appropriate. The judge never even sees the petitioner at this stage.

The judge is required to set a date as soon as possible (but, in any event, within 15 days because the temporary injunction expires after 15 days), when the parties can appear and the accused spouse can defend himself or herself. At that hearing, the judge will also consider an award of temporary support if it is requested in the Petition. Once the Court rules on making the injunction permanent, he/she has the option of referring the parties, if it presents no danger, to a certified family mediator to resolve the incidental issues of use of the home, custody, child support, and alimony. If a Final Judgment of Injunction Against Repeat Violence is entered and served, the spouse is bound to obey it. If the order is disobeyed, the court can, and is likely to, jail the spouse, especially if the violation is great. This is in contrast to the handling of most domestic cases; the difference, I suspect, is that there is more of a criminal, as opposed to a domestic, aspect to these proceedings.

No one can argue with the idea of making it easy for a battered and abused person to get protection from the law. The problem is that such a summary procedure, with no adequate due-process safeguards, effects such a major change in people's lives. The procedure is seen by some as nothing more than an invitation to use the law to punish one's spouse.

Many petitioners withdraw their petitions before the scheduled hearing. The initial injunction is good for 15 days and it dies on its own if the petition is withdrawn. If the petitioner fails to appear for the scheduled hearing, no further action is taken and the injunction expires 15 days after it initial entry.

I suspect that the underlying premise of the law may be wrong, the premise being that beatings are an acute problem that must be dealt with without delay. The evidence seems to show, however, that most marital beatings are a chronic problem, not one that suddenly arises. Does that mean that a spouse should remain subject to being beaten again? Obviously not. It means that a long-existing problem should be dealt with using a procedure requiring adequate notice to the spouse, even notice of only a few hours. In acute cases, where the threat of violence is immediate, immediate and strong protection should be used. The current procedure fails to differentiate between the two situations.

A true spouse-beater doesn't deserve better than this sloppy law. Due process wasn't developed to protect the guilty (although it often does); it was developed to protect the innocent. But this law is too often used precipitously, to the detriment of both parties and of the marriage. Few marriages, even otherwise saveable marriages, survive the use of an abused spouse injunction. I strongly urge an abused spouse to talk with an attorney before seeking an injunction. If the situation truly requires an injunction, you will get it; if it doesn't, you might be able to save your marriage.

Temporary Restraining Orders (TROs). Temporary restraining orders, when used properly, are one of the quickest and most efficient methods of getting a case

Contempt of court is any affront to a court. Willful misconduct in the presence of the judge is *direct contempt.* Any action taking place outside the judge's presence is *indirect contempt.*

Civil contempt and *criminal contempt* refer to the penalty. *Criminal contempt* results in a straight penalty, fine or jail time just like any other crime. *Civil contempt* results in an ongoing penalty, such as jail time or a per diem fine, until the party complies with the court order.

under control. When one spouse is at a significant disadvantage to the other, whether physical or psychological, the weaker spouse can be prevented from fairly seeking his or her rights in the case because of the intimidation of the other.

The most common problem is that the two spouses cannot safely and quietly live in the same house while they are fighting each other in court. Sometimes they can, but that's unusual. Either party can petition the court, as part of the dissolution action, for exclusive use and possession of the house. No court should dispossess either spouse from the house unless living together presents real danger to either party or their children; either physical or emotional peril could justify ejecting one of the parents. In fact, if either side testifies to danger, the court will almost always err on the side of caution; the judge will order one spouse out of the house.

The party who will suffer least from the expulsion should be removed. The wife will usually be permitted to stay, especially if she keeps the children, unless she has relatives in the area who can take her in or unless the house clearly belongs to the husband.

The decision to expel one party from the house is usually made on terribly insufficient evidence since it is difficult to get more than 15 minutes for such hearings. That decision, however, could have long-term effects on the disposition of the property. It establishes a status quo and creates a heavy burden on the other spouse to prove that he or she is ultimately entitled to the house.

Other temporary restraining orders are less damaging. If either spouse asserts harassment, threats, excessive telephone calls, etc., and the other side denies any such conduct, the wise judge will usually not try to decide which party is truthful; instead, the judge will enter a mutual restraining order that prohibits both parties from such future conduct.

A TRO can also be used to prevent one spouse from taking the children, depriving the other of use of a car, taking money out of a bank account, or selling any property. Its scope is very broad, limited only by the need to be protected from immediate harm.

Enforcement. A protected spouse may enforce a restraining order in two ways.

If the other side is violating it in an ongoing manner, the protected spouse may seek civil contempt by filing a motion for contempt. If the violation was a one-time incident, the remedy is through criminal contempt proceedings. Although criminal in nature, the prosecution of criminal contempt is generally handled by the party's civil attorney. The terms "civil" and "criminal" refer only to the procedures used and the form of the penalty, not the nature of the violation.

The difference between civil and criminal contempt is that civil contempt is usable only to compel compliance. The violator who has been held in civil contempt gains release from jail by doing what he or she was ordered to do. The violator is said to have the "keys to the jail" in the sense that he or she has the power to end the incarceration. Criminal contempt, the purpose of which is to "vindicate the authority of the court," results in a straight sentence (or, more rarely, a fine) that must be served regardless of present compliance.

Let me give you some examples. If the husband were ordered not to park his four-wheel drive Bigfoot at the house but he did so in defiance of the court order, the court could sentence him to jail for up to 30 days or until he agreed to remove the vehicle. On the other hand, if he were ordered not to go around the house or bother the wife and he came over and threw a cement block through the sliding glass doors, the wife would get little satisfaction from his promise not to do it again; in that case, by using criminal procedures, the wife could obtain a conviction for criminal contempt and the husband might be sentenced to jail for a specified period of time, usually 10 or 30 days. He would probably also be ordered to have the doors repaired.

This is one area where, I believe, the Family Law Court system has made a big difference. Because they see so many abuses of judgments and rulings on an ongoing basis, the Family Law judges are far more likely now than in the past to send a violator to jail.

2

CRISIS TIME: CROSSING THE THRESHOLD INTO DIVORCE

What you will learn in this chapter:
- what you should do if a divorce is looming
- whether you can take money from a joint account
- when you should tell your spouse you are going to divorce him or her
- why you shouldn't try to force the filing spouse to talk about the divorce
- what information you need right away if you are served
- how to find the right lawyer quickly
- whether you can negotiate fees
- why price is of secondary importance
- how to protect assets
- why you should call your best friend when you need to talk
- why keeping your dignity intact is important

A divorce may be the most traumatic event in your life. And no part of the divorce is more difficult than the beginning, especially if you are an unsuspecting spouse. Let's look at what happens and what you can do about it. This chapter deals with a hypothetical couple, the Egzits. The wife petitions for divorce and the husband becomes the respondent. If your case is the opposite, please try to reverse the roles here.

Petitioner's Side

First, let's view the divorce from the perspective of the wife (I. Wanda Egzit) who wants out of a bad marriage. She is undoubtedly confiding in her best friend and is getting a lot of advice, some of it good. The best advice she can get is find a good lawyer *now*.

Assuming that she reads Appendix A ("Choosing and Dealing with Lawyers") in this book, she will have chosen a good and competent lawyer. We'll call him Mr. Shane. She makes an appointment to meet with him in his office. She tells Mr. Shane that she wants a divorce and gives him some of the background. We hope that the lawyer first inquires about the children, their ages, health or emotional problems, and how they relate to both parties.

Next, Mr. Shane will probably get a general overall picture of the finances:

value of the house, incomes of both parties, liquid assets such as bank accounts and stocks, etc. He might ask about the relative ability of the parties to find alternative housing in the area.

Finally, after he understands the marital situation, Mr. Shane will probably advise Mrs. Egzit how to protect the existing assets. The most vulnerable, after the children, are the bank and brokerage accounts. They need to be preserved, not raided. Any attorney who tells a client to raid the accounts and take the assets is doing a disservice to his client and the marriage. There may be a fine difference, but there is nothing improper about taking control of the assets so that they are available for the court's ruling.

In most cases, Mrs. Egzit can justifiably transfer half of all liquid assets into her own name. If her attorney feels that either she may be awarded more than half by the court or that her husband will dissipate the rest to make himself a pauper, Mr. Shane might advise Mrs. Egzit to take control of all of the assets. In such an event, however, immediately after the action is filed, both the attorney and Mrs. Egzit have a duty to disclose the conserving action and to assure that the assets are made available for the court's later disposition.

Some attorneys will give long-range, divorce-planning advice: build a nest egg by diverting money from the marriage in small amounts that won't be noticed. Rarely is that fair or proper; there are times, however, when it is necessary. For example, if Mr. Egzit tightly controlled the family money and left nothing in the control of Mrs. Egzit, she might need the protection the savings could provide. (My problem with the whole idea is that Mrs. Egzit shouldn't be staying in a sham marriage for any length of time just to build up an account; if it has reached the stage where she's started to squirrel money away, it's already time to get out.)

Mrs. Egzit has now taken half of the bank accounts (not interfering with the money needed to pay bills) and half of the brokerage accounts. She has made sure, if her husband is unstable, that both she and the children will be in no danger when Mr. Egzit is served. She will remain in the house, unless there is the possibility that staying there puts her or the children in danger.

Her attorney is about to file the action and will soon serve Mr. Egzit. Does she tell her husband? The only issue is danger. If there is danger that he will become violent, she doesn't tell him anything. She makes sure that she and the children are in a safe place when the process server finds him.

In most cases, however, she should tell him soon before service, usually the night before. (When we look at Mr. Egzit's side of this divorce, we'll see why this should be done.) She shouldn't tell him any sooner, unless the parties have been working together toward an amicable divorce, because of the danger that he might start arranging finances, etc. to her disadvantage.

Respondent's Side

It's rarely a happy time when your spouse wants a divorce. Sometimes it's a relief when the spouse files but, in most cases, divorce is a devastating blow to one's life, one you won't recover from for quite some time.

As we know, in this case Mrs. Egzit wants out. Her husband, Don N. (for Nawanna) Egzit, feels differently. Although the marriage has problems, he loves Wanda and their two children. He knows that Wanda hasn't been happy but he doesn't know she is about to file against him. On Sunday night, just before going to bed, Wanda tells Don that she has seen a lawyer and that he will be served in the morning. Naturally, he is very hurt, confused, and hostile. What should he do? First, Don must accept one reality of life: He has no right, legally or morally, to make Wanda stay with him. Marriage is a relationship at will under Florida law; a marriage will last only as long as both parties want it to last. Don cannot force Wanda to change her mind.

He can, however, encourage Wanda to change her mind. Don can talk to Wanda about their problems and see if they can find solutions that might work. If Wanda refuses to discuss reconciliation, and she is likely to refuse, Don won't gain anything by forcing her. As hard as it might be, discipline during this crisis time is very important. Don must accept Wanda's right not to discuss the matter at this point.

Under no circumstances should the respondent argue, make threats or, worst of all, use violence. It is important to find out what she has told the children and start right away to work together in their best interests. If the children have not yet been told, work out a plan for handling it. Make a joint decision, if you can, about when and how the children should be told.

Don should find out who Wanda's attorney is and what Wanda's plans are for the marital home. Does Wanda expect to continue living there? Does her attorney plan to have Don thrown out right away? Wanda knows the answers to these questions and she might be willing to tell Don, if the two of them can talk about it. Don's attorney will need to know as much as possible about these issues at the first meeting so that they can be dealt with immediately.

Managing the Crisis

If you are about to be served in the morning, your mind is going to be racing and you probably won't sleep much. Think about how you are going to find a lawyer. If you are the unsuspecting ambushee we are postulating, you haven't read this book in advance and don't know how I recommend finding an attorney. (See Appendix A for some guidance.) Assuming you are wise, however, you will think of the name of any (good) lawyer you have ever dealt with, so that you can call that lawyer in the morning and ask who he or she recommends to represent you.

If you don't know any attorneys, try to think of someone you know who has recently gone through a divorce. You can call that person for information about his or her lawyer as well as about the opposing attorney in that case. One or the other might be just the lawyer for you. You must, despite your racing mind, ask the right questions: Was he or she knowledgeable, caring, skilled, available, reasonable, etc.?

It is important to pick the right lawyer for you, not for your friend. Your friend may have been very satisfied with a particular lawyer but the answers to your questions may convince you that this lawyer is not the one for you. Follow your instincts on that, although your instincts may be pretty messed up these first few days. Don't get a "bomber" (a very aggressive lawyer) just because you are hurt and frightened. Especially with children involved, a bomber might be the worst possible lawyer for you.

If you don't find a lawyer in any of these ways, look in the telephone book under "Attorneys." Go to the heading for "Marital and Family Lawyers." In that column, you will find all of the lawyers who are willing to accept a divorce case; but be aware that not all of them will be experts, or even highly experienced, in the field. Look for lawyers who are board certified in marital and family law. Board certified lawyers are those who are certified by the Florida Bar as having extensive experience and knowledge in divorce and related practice.

Not all good marital lawyers are board certified. But all board certified marital and family law attorneys are likely to be good marital lawyers, so pick one who is board certified.

As soon as you can, call the lawyer you picked. Ask if you can speak with the lawyer personally. If he won't speak with you and his secretary can't give you an appointment within 48 hours, go on to another attorney. That might be a sign that this lawyer won't be available to you during your case. Being busy is as much an attitude as a fact. Truly busy attorneys will fit their clients in when the clients need them; those who *think* they're busy will never be able to find the time for you. (It's just another example of the old saying: if you want to get something done, ask a busy person.)

On rare occasions, the right attorney will not be able to help you as quickly as you need. But, in those rare cases, the office will help you, trying to work out after-hours meeting times or identifying your immediate needs so the attorney can take some holding action in the meantime. If the attorney is familiar with you and is willing to represent you, his or her secretary might, for example, get enough information from you so that the attorney can make a call to your wife's attorney to delay a hearing or your removal from the house.

It is important to ask about fees when you contact an attorney's office. If his or her fees are out of your range, it is best to find out right at the beginning rather than waste your and the attorney's time.

What you're looking for is concern and service. When concerned enough, your attorney's office will find a way to help you.

Now you are finally talking to the attorney. It may be 45 minutes after you called or it might be the next day. Your first task is to make sure this is the attorney for you. You'll be interviewing the lawyer as much as he or she is interviewing you.

First conferences vary considerably from attorney to attorney. In general, however, what you want to do is tell your attorney, as briefly as possible, your situation. The lawyer may let you talk or may want to control the conference by having you only answer questions. I would suggest that you might be a little leery of attorneys that overcontrol you and the conference; they think that, from the very first moment, they must start preparing you as a witness. That's fine except the attorney is forcing you onto his or her agenda and treating your needs and problems as less important than what he wants.

Let's say that the facts of your situation are pretty simple: that your wife wants a divorce after twelve years and three children; that you both work; that your assets are the house, two cars, a bank account, and a small investment account; and that you are about to be served. Your attorney is likely to immediately ask you why the marriage is in trouble and whether you believe it is irretrievably broken. From there, your needs and your lawyer's style will shape the meeting.

Don't forget to ask about fees early in the conference. Attorneys don't really like to talk about fees, especially if you are an emotional wreck. Good attorneys don't want to be callous, and talking about fees, while it is beneficial to both of you, certainly creates the impression that the lawyer is more concerned about his or her needs than your problems. Help your lawyer and yourself by asking, by making it part of your agenda.

Once you have your lawyer and know the fees you have to pay, go out and find the money to pay him the required retainer. Don't leave your lawyer hanging, and don't make your lawyer your banker. Borrow the money wherever you can but don't have unsettled fees intruding into your relationship with your lawyer.

Your lawyer's fees will not usually be negotiable. Lawyers establish their hourly rates and their minimum fees by comparison with the other attorneys in your town. They have an idea of what they are worth to their clients and you are unlikely to convince your lawyer that he or she should reduce the fee just for you. There is room for compromise, however, if you have little money but your spouse has significant money available. In that case, your attorney knows that he or she might be able to have the court order your spouse to pay your initial retainer. The willingness of courts to award temporary fees varies from area to area.

It is difficult for you to know if your attorney's rates are higher or lower than those of other attorneys in town. The best way to find out is to ask your lawyer. Comparison is relatively easy among board certified attorneys since there are usually only a few in town and a comparison among them is meaningful. Comparison is not as meaningful for non-certified lawyers since those attorneys don't meet any defined standard of competence in this field of practice. Is your lawyer quoting you the rates of attorneys who are more competent or less competent? There's no way to tell.

One word of caution: Don't hire your lawyer based on his price. You wouldn't buy the cheapest parachute you could find, nor would you hire the cheapest brain surgeon. You shouldn't hire the cheapest lawyer either. There's a reason a lawyer is cheap, even if you can't see it right away. On the other hand, you shouldn't necessarily hire the most expensive lawyer. Some attorneys overprice themselves. (See Appendix A for further discussion of fees.)

Once you've hired a good lawyer, you shouldn't need this book for anything but general information anymore. On specific points, you will listen to your attorney and follow his or her advice. But, let me just mention a few more points.

First, protect your assets as best you can. Don't raid the bank account but make sure you move enough out of the checking account to pay the immediate bills. If you have a savings or investment account, take whatever action you can to protect them from being raided by your spouse.

If it's obvious that you're going to be leaving the house, make arrangements for where you will live and for installation of a telephone. These things sound easy when you're not going through a divorce; they can be overwhelming in the midst of the wreckage of your marriage. The only way to deal with these matters is to try to be systematic; write everything down and set a schedule to take care of things.

Let me give you some very important advice: call your best friend and tell him what has happened. You need someone to help you through this. You can be sure that your wife is confiding her worries in someone, and it is helping her. You must have someone who can listen to you and who can help you in the ordinary decisions you will have to make.

Don't let your friend give you legal advice; he's not there for that. And don't try to make your lawyer into your best friend. First, although your lawyer will be concerned about you and your case, you simply can't afford what it will cost to pour out your feelings to him or her. Second, your lawyer is not qualified to deal with your emotional problems; counselors are generally far cheaper than lawyers anyway.

Your attorney is going to advise you not to threaten, hassle, or bother your wife. Don't call her to annoy her; don't go to her work place. Don't steal things from the house when she's not there. By all means, and at every opportunity, see the kids. But don't let the kids be an excuse for you to badger your wife.

You won't feel very masculine during this initial period: your wife has symbolically castrated you and now I'm telling you not to assert yourself with her. You feel like a victim and I'm telling you just to take it.

I'm not telling you to be anything but an adult. And that's the hardest thing to do during the first few days and weeks. You'll want to strike out and make her hurt as much as you hurt. Believe me, there's not a human being who doesn't hurt very badly during a divorce, regardless of who files. Some people are just better at hiding their feelings. And, without a doubt, it is usually easier for the one who wants the divorce than it will be for you.

In the long run, for your self-respect and for your position in the case, you are miles ahead if you act like an adult. And that doesn't mean that you don't stand up for yourself, your children, and for your hard-earned assets. You fight, as much as you need to fight, in the proper way and at the proper time.

It is not easy to keep your head when all others around you are losing theirs. When you keep your dignity and self-control when everyone, especially your wife, expect you to come apart, you are gaining control of the situation. If she can push the buttons and cause you grief, figuratively and literally, she's in control and will probably control the whole case.

There is only one thing that you will certainly still have when you come out of a divorce: yourself. Keep that intact. Conduct yourself in a manner that will make your children proud of you and, more importantly, make you proud of yourself. Divorces are rough on egos. Make sure that, no matter what happens, you can look yourself in the mirror after the case is over and have some respect for the person looking back at you.

It doesn't matter whether you are the husband or the wife. Divorce is hard on both and usually harder on the respondent, the one filed against. If the husband files instead of the wife, the positions of the parties are reversed from what appears in this chapter but the advice is the same.

I'm back to my earlier message: there are some things that you can't control. Accept that and deal with what you can control. Keeping yourself under control is the first step; choosing a good lawyer is your second step; following your lawyer's advice is the third. If you can take the first step, the second and the third will probably follow.

3

DISSOLUTION PROCEEDINGS

What you will learn in this chapter:

- how a divorce is started
- what papers are filed with the court
- what happens at a temporary hearing
- what *discovery is*
- what can be enforced by the court
- what a pleading is
- what counties you can file in
- how and why your spouse is served
- what injunctions do
- how temporary support works
- what happens at the final hearing
- what a settlement is and how it helps YOU
- who prepares the judgment
- what role the judge plays in the hearing
- what happens if you don't answer after being served
- who pays the attorney's fees
- what happens if you disobey a court order
- what remedies exist for non-payment
- the difference between civil and criminal contempt
- the best advice in four sentences

Dissolving a marriage is no fun for anyone. The steps that must be taken are painful and the procedures sometimes seem designed to inflict the maximum suffering upon people who are already strained to their limits by the breakup.

Knowledge of the how and why of it all won't eliminate the pain, but it may lessen the feeling that there's no end to the suffering. This section deals with a combination of procedural steps and substantive laws; the two are so tied together that an explanation of one without the other would be meaningless. Let's start with a road map, the bare-bones procedures from beginning to end.

Basic Steps

All divorces start in the home and most of them move to a lawyer's office. When the lawyer has the basic facts, he or she prepares a "Petition for Dissolution of Marriage." The petition is the formal paper that tells the court what the petitioner wants. The petition and a summons are the papers that are served on the respondent at the beginning of the case. A summons is a court order to appear in the action or else lose the right to be heard in the case. The service of those

A *Petition for Dissolution of Marriage* is the formal paper filed with the court that starts the divorce. It recites the basic facts of the marriage and advises the court what relief the petitioner wants.

A *summons* is a paper that is served on the respondent along with the Petition. It states that the respondent is now subject to the court's jurisdiction and that a response must be filed within 20 days or the respondent's right to be heard in the action will be cut off.

A *petitioner* is the party starting the action.

A *respondent,* when used, refers to the party not initially filing the action. In divorce cases, the parties are usually referred to as the *husband* and the *wife* since both parties are generally seeking relief and the terms *petitioner* and *respondent* have little meaning.

Jurisdiction is a complicated term. As used here, it means the power and authority of the court over the parties, their children, and/or their property. It can also refer to the geographical area over which the court has authority or to the nature or amount of relief over which a particular court can exercise its authority.

papers, by hand delivery to the respondent by the sheriff or the process server, is what gives the court jurisdiction over the respondent.

Once served, you must get a lawyer immediately since you have only 20 days in which to respond to the petition, either by motion or by answer and counterpetition. The petitioner (we will assume that the petitioner is the wife and that you are the husband in order to keep this outline simple) will usually ask for a hearing for temporary relief within a short time after filing. If the temporary relief she seeks includes support for herself or the children, she must attach to her notice of hearing a financial affidavit setting out her income, expenses, assets, and liabilities (See Appendix C).

At least two days before the temporary hearing, you (the husband) must also provide a financial affidavit as well as the previous year's tax return, W-2s, etc. if the return has not yet been filed, and pay stubs for the previous three months. The judge will use the affidavits and other evidence presented at the hearing as bases for making a temporary ruling on such matters as custody of and support for your children, use of the marital home, alimony, and injunctions. The temporary ruling will remain in effect only until the end of the case, but it is very important since it often influences the ultimate ruling the court must make on the same issues.

The next step is called *discovery*. Both sides are permitted to make formal inquiries into the facts and positions of the other side through oral or written depositions, interrogatories, requests for production, and requests for admissions. Once the facts are in hand, the case is ready for trial. The judge will set a case management conference upon notice from one of the attorneys that the case is ready to be tried. At the case management conference, the judge will require the attorneys to choose a final hearing date from several available and designate a mediator if one has not already been chosen. The attorneys estimate how long the trial will take and request that amount of time from the judge.

At the *final hearing* (sometimes called the trial), the final step, all the evidence is presented to the judge so that he or she can enter an appropriate judgment.

This summary leaves out two major parts of a dissolution case. One is settlement negotiations, which can take place both before and after the case is filed. If the negotiations are successful, the case can be submitted to the judge at a very short hearing on the settlement terms, which saves everyone time, money, and anguish. The other part is the enforcement proceedings that generally ensue from temporary orders.

Enforcement is accomplished by motions to the court that say, in effect, "She's not letting me see the kids," or "He's not paying support on time." Such motions are seldom satisfactorily resolved, not always because the judges

An ***affidavit*** is a written statement of facts that is sworn to and notarized.

A ***deposition*** is the questioning of a witness under oath that takes place other than in a courtroom. The answers are recorded by a court reporter and can be later typed out in transcript form. The purpose is twofold: to learn the position of the other side and find out what facts are known to him or her, and to pin the witness down to those facts so that he or she cannot later claim other facts to be true.

Interrogatories are written questions that must be answered under oath. Generally, a standard set of around 110 questions (stated in 7 groupings), prescribed by the Supreme Court, are used in divorce cases. They are used to learn background information before a deposition is taken.

A ***request for production*** is a formal request to the other party to produce objects, usually papers and documents, for inspection and, perhaps, copying.

A ***request for admissions*** is a formal request that the other side admit that certain facts are true and not in dispute. It serves to limit the issues that the court has to decide.

Discovery is the general term that is used for all of the above methods of getting information from the other side.

A *pleading* is a paper filed with the court to recite the essential circumstances of the case and the relief sought. Since the term includes *answers* and *responses*, it also means any paper responding to the recitation of the facts and circumstances. The only *pleadings* are a *petition* or *complaint*, the *answer* or *response*, *counterclaim* or *counterpetition*, and *crossclaim*.

Attorneys sometimes erroneously refer to any paper filed with the court, such as a *motion*, as a *pleading*. A *motion* is any paper filed with the court that is not a *pleading* which asks the court to take action.

don't do their jobs but usually because the issue is before the judge because one of you has not been abiding honorably by the temporary ruling.

An important thing for everyone in a divorce action to remember is that, in the heat of a divorce, the parties often detest each other. The attorneys tend to adopt their clients' positions and harbor the equivalent, if less deeply felt, hostilities toward the other side. But all of us, including the parties, the attorneys, and the judge, should constantly remind ourselves that two people who have been married to each other for any length of time are, very likely, impaired by equivalent disabilities. Another, but less helpful, way of saying it is that they might deserve each other.

A colleague pointed this out to me one day, and I have never since approached a case without seeing the opposing party, whether good or bad, as a possible reflection of my client. I don't identify with my clients any less, but I now appreciate how my client may look to an objective person like a judge. The value of this wisdom to an attorney involved in a case is short-term. The value to the client is lifetime if he or she can be persuaded to accept it.

Right to Counsel. If adequate money is available, both parties are entitled to be represented by an attorney, and this is particularly important if child custody is at stake. The court can, and usually does, award attorneys' fees from the more able to the less able party to ensure that both parties have access to competent representation. The award can be made at the end of the case or, early in the case, by an award of what is called "suit money."

Legal aid, generally through a lawyer's referral service, provides attorneys willing to do pro bono (free) legal work to needy clients. However, these attorneys will sometimes not provide divorce representation unless there is reason to believe that the case involves violence. A divorce is like elective surgery; there are less radical legal proceedings that serve the essential needs of the parties, including simply separating from the spouse and obtaining an order of separate maintenance.

Place of Filing

In Florida, one of the parties must be a resident of the state for at least six months before filing for divorce in this state. Thus, a non-resident can file for divorce in Florida if his/her spouse is a resident. Residency begins when you move to the state with the intention of staying permanently. If you move out of the state during the action, your spouse could use that as evidence that you were never truly a resident, but the move itself will not terminate jurisdiction if you were truly a resident when you filed.

Because they frequently move, members of the military are given special residency privileges. If a serviceman is stationed in Florida, he/she is considered a resident for the purposes of bringing any action, including a dissolution action; a serviceman, otherwise a resident of Florida but stationed elsewhere, does not have to be present in the state during the previous six months to file for divorce. A serviceman who wants to keep Florida as a permanent residence while stationed elsewhere generally indicates his or her designation by obtaining a Florida drivers' license and by registering to vote in the state.

For all practical purposes, the petition can only be filed in the county where the parties last lived as husband and wife. If you live in Florida but your spouse doesn't, you can bring the action in any Florida county. Even if you both live in Florida, the case can be filed in any county if your spouse doesn't object; for reasons of privacy, prominent people sometimes agree to litigate their divorce away from their home county.

Petition. Although the language of a dissolution petition is often technical, the three essential allegations are that a marriage exists, that it is irretrievably broken, and that you've resided in Florida for at least six months. The petition may also include requests for custody, alimony and/or child support, partition of real or personal property, the right to special equities, equitable distribution, and attorney's fees. The petition must include whichever of these are appropriate, for the court can only rule on matters presented to it through the petition or counterpetition, or, on occasion, through other issues tried by consent.

Service. There are three ways for a Florida court to obtain jurisdiction to dissolve your marriage. The first and most common is for a sheriff or a process server to serve the respondent personally, whether he or she is found in Florida or, after having lived in the state during the marriage, has moved to another state.

The second means is by the respondent personally appearing in the case. A *personal appearance* is any conduct, such as filing an answer, which acknowledges that you are participating in the case. If you file any paper in the case, you have submitted yourself to the court's authority and will be bound by its rulings. Parties often appear without being served when the parties have reached agreement before the action is filed. In such cases, the petitioner will file the action and send a copy of the petition in the mail to the respondent, who will then file an answer (and thereby appear in the case) to give the court jurisdiction to enter a judgment on the agreement.

The third way is service by publication. If the respondent can't be located or if he or she lives outside the state, the respondent can be served by a notice of the action published in the local newspaper (that is, local to where the action is filed). A copy of the Petition must then be sent to the respondent's last known address. This method is a last resort since service by publication gives the court jurisdiction only over the marriage, the children if they are in Florida, and any property in Florida that is listed in the notice. It does not give the court jurisdiction over the respondent's person and, without that, the court cannot order alimony or child support.

Answer and Counterpetition. The respondent's answer or response must admit or deny every allegation in the petition. Failure to deny any of the allegations constitutes an admission unless the answer asserts lack of knowledge, which is treated as a denial. If the respondent files no answer, he or she can be defaulted, that is, denied the right to defend, except on issues in which the court must determine amounts, such as child support, alimony, and custody matters. I'll go into that later.

Most respondents file a counterpetition for dissolution along with their answer. They do this to present their own demands to the court and also to prevent the petitioner from controlling the case. By control, I mean that, if you don't counterpetition, your spouse can arbitrarily dismiss the case if things look bad. This could even occur at the final hearing if the petitioner thinks the judge is going to rule against him or her on important points. As you sit there feeling smug, the petitioner's attorney could announce that he or she is dismissing the petition, and, unless you've filed a counterpetition, the case is over and you are back at the beginning again. But, if a counterpetition has been filed, the case can go forward regardless of the dismissal.

Injunctions. Let me deal with injunctions very briefly here. Injunctions order people to do or not to do something. In marital cases, they are used:
   · to remove one spouse from the house (in theory only available if his or her

continued occupancy presents actual danger to the other spouse);
· to prohibit harassment or violence by one spouse against the other (sometimes entered against both parties mutually except in the case of domestic violence injunctions);
· to prevent the sale or other disposition of marital property until the court can rule on it;
· to assure the use of a particular car by one spouse;
· for anything within the wildest imaginations of oppressed parties.

One who violates an injunction is in contempt of court and could (but almost never does) go to jail for it.

Domestic violence injunctions are obtained in a separate proceeding (and case) but are often joined with the divorce action later. When a domestic violence injunction is violated, the victim must contact the clerk's office in the county where the injunction was issued. That office will take an affidavit from the victim and forward it to the state attorney's office for prosecution, usually as a first degree misdemeanor (punishable by jail time up to one year).

A writ of *ne exeat* ("do not leave") is really just another form of injunction. It forbids a party to leave the state or to remove the children or property from Florida. Its main use is to assure that the party will be available to pay support.

Necessaries during Action. Historically, the husband was liable, by law, for debts incurred by his wife for "necessaries," that is, the basic needs of life. That included housing, food, medical treatment, and clothing. This is no longer true. Unless the husband signs something that makes him liable, he has no liability for debts taken on by his wife for any reason. Wives have never been liable for their husband's debts.

Final Hearing (Trial). Now comes the trial, which may be a full-blown hearing before a judge (or, increasingly, before a magistrate) or it may be a three-minute hearing at which you go through the formalities of having your settlement agreement incorporated in the judgment.

Final judgment is entered soon after the trial. Once the judgment is entered, you would think the case would be over unless one of the parties appeals. However, even without an appeal, a dissolution is never completely finished

> A *magistrate* is a non-judge appointed by the chief judge to take testimony in a case and make findings of fact in writing that the judge then bases a judgment or order on. The *magistrate* is always a lawyer.

until no more obligations exist between the parties. It goes on and on and on until one day, there is no more support to pay and no more visitation to arrange, and it just quietly dies.

All marital cases are tried in front of a judge or a magistrate. Although these hearings are public, rarely is anyone except the participants present. The judge can only exclude the public when extreme circumstances require.

The petitioner has the right to go first and put on all of the evidence support-ing his or her side, including witnesses and documents. The respondent's attorney can cross-examine all of the petitioner's witnesses and then put on the respon-dent's witnesses, who are, of course, also subject to cross-examination by the peti-tioner's attorney. Finally, the petitioner may put on witnesses to rebut the evidence presented by the respondent. A court reporter is usually there to record all testi-mony during the trial.

Because of discovery before the final hearing, there are seldom any surprises during the hearing itself. At the end of the case, the attorneys are permitted to argue the case; after the arguments, the judge can either announce his or her rul-ing immediately or take the case under advisement and rule at a later time. The judge may want more time to review his or her notes, the evidence, and the law before deciding the case, or the judge may just be trying to avoid an emotional scene between two highly charged parties.

Final hearings are often a three-ring circus. Sometimes, both attorneys walk out scratching their heads, usually because the judge decided the case on a factor that they never considered important. Sometimes the judge is right and sometimes not. While the judge may be objective, he or she lacks the considerable back-ground in the case that both attorneys have; it's therefore easier for the judge to get distracted by a detail that, if he or she were more fully informed, would be rec-ognized as irrelevant. That's the risk of letting a judge decide a case.

If at all possible, the parties should settle their case before going to final hear-ing. Certainly, they have more knowledge of the background and what's best for their children. If they are not blinded by bitterness, they are in a far better posi-tion to resolve the issues fairly. If they have settled, the final hearing is held with just the petitioner and his or her attorney present to establish the basic elements needed to obtain a divorce: residency, existence of a marriage, separation, that the marriage is irretrievably broken, and that the parties have resolved all property rights by agreement. If the agreement is not patently unfair, the judge will then enter a judgment that incorporates the agreement. With a settlement, the only evi-dence that must be corroborated is residency. Florida law now permits a petition-er to corroborate residency by a valid Florida driver's license, a Florida voter's registration card, or the testimony or affidavit of a third party.

Entry of Judgment. Although appellate courts have reservations about the practice, judges themselves don't generally prepare Final Judgments, or orders for that matter. After the judge has ruled, one of the attorneys, usually the prevailing one, reduces the ruling to writing and sends it to the judge for entry. To ensure that the judgment is accurate, a copy is sent to the opposing attorney and he/she is given a reasonable period to object. If no objection is made, the judgment is signed by the judge and filed in the clerk's office. Copies are sent from the judge's office to both attorneys.

The preparation of a judgment (or order) is one of the most adversarial acts in a dissolution case. The task of the prevailing attorney in preparing the judgment is to reduce the judge's ruling to a writing that is accurate, complete, and defensible. By defensible, I mean that it should reflect all the findings that will enable it to withstand an appeal. Since judges sometimes don't dictate every finding to be put in the judgment, the attorney may have to assume all findings of fact that are necessary to support the judge's ruling and to include those findings in the judgment. For example, if the judge awards custody of the children to the wife, the judgment should contain a finding that it is in the children's best interests that the wife have primary residential care. Even though the judge may not have expressly stated such a finding when he or she asked the attorney to prepare the judg-

A *settlement* is a resolution of all of the issues in a case by agreement; it avoids the need to try the case. When a case is settled, one of the attorneys drafts a *settlement agreement* which, when all of the language is acceptable, is signed by both parties. The agreement is then submitted to the judge at a very short hearing and, if approved by the judge, is made part of the Final Judgment. The *Final Judgment* or *judgment* is the paper signed by the Judge that closes the case (except for later disputes, called *post-dissolution* matters).

A *judgment* is really just a form of an *order.* The only distinction is that a *Judgment* ends the case (at least until post-dissolution disputes arise) while an *order* decides only an aspect of the case. There will generally be just one *judgment* in a case, but there may be many *orders.*

In deciding a divorce case, a judge serves two roles. First, the judge evaluates the evidence and determines what the facts are; the judge's determination is referred to as the *findings of fact* or simply *findings.*The judge then applies the law to those findings and makes his or her rulings. Most judgments contain both findings of fact and rulings; some contain only limited findings of fact. Some rulings cannot be made unless the findings of fact are recited. For example, lump sum alimony cannot be awarded unless the judgment recites that the judge found special justification for the award.

A *default* is both the failure to file an answer and the name of the order that cuts off the respondent's right to file an answer later. It may be entered by the clerk if no paper whatever was filed; it must be entered by the judge if some paper has been filed but no answer.

When an order or judgment has been erroneously entered, either party can seek to have it voided, or *vacated*. If an order is *vacated*, it is the same as if it were never entered.

A *contempt proceeding*, more often simply called *contempt*, is the general term used to describe the filing of a Motion for Contempt and the hearing on that motion.

A *motion* is a request that the court take action. It is usually in writing but some motions, especially ones concerning evidence, are made orally in open court. A *motion for contempt* is, of course, a request that the court adjudicate the other party in contempt of court.

A *supplemental petition* is the paper that must be filed to request that a part of the Final Judgment be modified. In general, it must allege that a substantial change has occurred since the judgment was entered.

Your attorney will always refer to any unpaid support as *arrearage*, that is, the amount of money that is in arrears.

ment, it is essential to the ruling and should be included in the judgment. The judge will have the opportunity to review those findings before signing the judgment.

I know that this all sounds strange, but notwithstanding what the appellate courts think, I can assure you that this procedure results in the best judgments.

Defaults

If you fail to respond to the petition, that is, you default, and if there are no issues involving support, your spouse can then go to final hearing without any further notice to you. If there are money issues or issues related to the children, you must be given the right to defend on the amount. Theoretically, you cannot be heard to argue any other point.

Defaults are not that common where there are significant issues. Furthermore, in most cases where a default is entered, a judge will be most liberal in vacating it and permitting you to respond.

Attorney's Fees and Costs

The court can order one of you to pay some or all of the other's attorney's fees and court costs. Usually the husband, often the better employed, is the one ordered to pay all or some of the wife's fees. The amount he is ordered to pay is not necessarily what the wife may have contracted to pay her attorney but rather what the court decides is reasonable. The amount may differ because the judge finds that a different hourly rate should apply or that the husband should pay only a part of her fees. An order of partial payment is, in fact, by far the most common. Until 1993, an application for attorney's fees had to be supported by the testimony of an expert witness; that is no longer required.

The fees can be ordered to be paid directly to the attorney, who can thereafter enforce the fees in his or her own name. The usual means of enforcement is by contempt proceedings, which is allowable because the fees are in the nature of alimony. Fees are enforceable as alimony because they are the payment of a bill on behalf of the wife that she is unable to pay herself; in effect, they are part of her support. (That does not mean that it is treated as alimony for tax purposes.)

> *Attachment* is the seizure of your property by the sheriff to pay a debt. *Garnishment* is the seizure of your wages from your employer before you are paid, also to pay a debt. To do this, the court must issue either a *writ of attachment* or a *writ of garnishment*, as appropriate, to empower the sheriff to make the seizure.

Name Change

The wife is entitled to change her name at the time of divorce. Although a woman who makes the change usually returns to a former or maiden name, I know of no law that prevents her from having the court change her name to a completely new one. The husband cannot prevent the wife from continuing to use his name after the divorce and the judge cannot order it; it is completely up to the woman.

Enforcement/Modification

After the judgment is entered, either party can ask the court to enforce or to modify the judgment by filing a motion (to enforce) or a supplemental petition (to modify).

When a party seeks modification of child support, the supplemental petition can be filed in the county in which either party lived when the judgment was first entered, or resides on the date of application, or where the agreement (if there was one) was signed, or where the judgment itself was entered. Child custody can be modified where the judgment was entered or in any county where the child or either parent resides. Any supplemental petition to modify must be served upon the respondent by a process server.

You can seek enforcement in either the county where you live or where your spouse lives. You may seek to have your spouse held in contempt, seek entry of a judgment for unpaid support, or have your spouse's property or wages seized. Sometimes, both parties seek to enforce different aspects of the judgment in the same proceeding. (See Chapter 6 regarding automatic judgments for unpaid child support.)

Contempt Proceedings

There are two types of contempt, civil and criminal. Civil contempt is coercive, forcing you to do something which you are capable of doing. Criminal contempt is punitive, punishing you for something you did that can't be remedied. Most enforcement proceedings are civil in nature; you ask the judge to send your spouse to jail if, after being given reasonable opportunity, he or she still won't, for example, allow you to visit the children. If your spouse seeks civil contempt for your failure to pay support, the judge will usually give you ten days to pay what you owe, or at least a part of it, depending on your ability to pay; if you don't pay the amount ordered, sentence you to serve up to 30 days in jail. Even if you are actually put in jail, you can purge yourself and get released by paying the purge amount (the amount, up to the amount of all arrearage, that the court finds the respondent has the present ability to pay). That is the nature of civil contempt: you are given the "key to the jail cell" since the power to get released is in your hands.

A sentence for criminal contempt does not include the "key to the jail cell." When the judge says 30 days, you'll serve 30 days. Criminal contempt is usually used when you have willfully decreased or eliminated your ability to pay support. If you were to appear in court on a civil contempt charge and announce: "Sorry, Judge, but I just quit my job. I can't pay nothin'," the proceeding would be stymied. You no longer have the ability to comply and a sentence for civil contempt would be improper. At this point, the judge must convert the proceeding to criminal contempt to accomplish anything. The judge must advise you of the charge, of your right to counsel, of your right to have counsel appointed for you if you cannot afford one, and of the new hearing date. In Florida, a typical sentence for criminal contempt is also 30 days. And, as I said before, you're there for 30 days. Period. There is no opportunity to pay up or take any other action to get out immediately, as would always exist for civil contempt. Or it could be longer; a judge could, under severe circumstances, impose a sentence for as long as six months.

In a civil contempt proceeding for failure to pay support, you are presumed to be capable of paying the overdue amounts. The existing order or judgment has already found that you have the ability and that presumption continues until you prove otherwise. Thus, your spouse will make a prima facie (sufficient) case for contempt as soon as nonpayment is proved. You must then prove inability as a defense. In the absence of proof of inability the court can rely upon that presumption in setting the purge amount and sentencing you to jail.

Your spouse may also seek a judgment for back support payments.

Previously, a party could obtain either a contempt ruling or judgment, but not both. Once he or she obtained a judgment for the arrearage, the right to seek contempt ceased to exist. Now both can be obtained in the same proceeding. Even while you may be sitting in jail on a civil contempt sentence, your spouse can be executing on the judgment in the same way that he or she could execute for any other type of judgment. The sheriff can seize and sell any of your nonexempt property up to the amount of the judgment. If the arrearage is paid through a levy, your spouse would be entitled to be released.

In Florida, a support payment becomes vested, that is, becomes the property of the recipient party, on the date it is due; the court has no power, after that date, to excuse or forgive that payment. The court only has three options for willful nonpayment: hold you in contempt (civil or criminal, depending on whether you have the present ability to pay), enter judgment (with or without a finding of contempt), or, under extreme circumstances, refuse to do anything. The court can refuse to enter judgment or hold you in contempt only if, considering all of the circumstances, it would be clearly inequitable to do so. In such an event, your spouse would still be technically entitled to the payments, and they would continue to accrue, but he or she would have no way to collect them until the circumstances changed. It is rare for a judge to refuse to enforce support.

Florida law also provides attachment and garnishment, in an enhanced form, for collecting support payments. In fact, the court can order a continuing writ of garnishment against your income. In effect, this is little used today because of the ready availability of payroll deductions (see Chapter 6).

Foreign decrees have separate procedures for their enforcement. Those procedures are covered in detail in Chapter 9.

Final Notes

The basically simple concepts of equity have become frighteningly complex. Judges still try to decide cases fairly and properly and, if the evidence is properly presented, they have a reasonable chance of doing that. However, if the evidence is sloppy, if one of the parties is obnoxious or unruly, or if one them otherwise manages to offend the judge, the case is not quite so likely to be decided correctly. None of those circumstances is likely to develop if both sides are represented by competent attorneys. Judges don't like divorce cases, and unrepresented parties just make it harder for the judges. The best advice that a couple contemplating divorce can get from this book can be summarized in four sentences:

1. Try to be fair and reasonable with each other.

2. Protect the best interests of your children at all costs, even at the expense of your own interest, if necessary.
3. Hire two good and ethical lawyers.
4. Follow their advice.

4

SIMPLIFIED DISSOLUTION OF MARRIAGE

What you will learn in this chapter:

- when you can and should represent yourself in a divorce
- what procedures you must follow
- where you can get the forms you need

Many marriages end early, with no property, no children, and no real issues. The parties just want out and they want to do it as quickly and simply as possible.

Until 1984, there was no easy way to get out. The Petition for Dissolution had to be in the proper form and only lawyers knew how to put it in the proper form. And lawyers are expensive, especially for people who have no property.

Recognizing the need for a simple system that would serve the needs of those people who neither need nor can afford an attorney for their divorce, the Florida Bar proposed to the Supreme Court what came to be called "simplified dissolution of marriage."

Necessary Circumstances

In 1984, the Supreme Court authorized the use of the simplified dissolution of marriage procedure. Now, if there are no children (and the wife is not pregnant), if all property rights are settled between the parties, and if both parties are willing to go to court together, the marriage can be ended simply, quickly, and inexpensively.

Procedure

To use the simplified procedure, you go to the clerk of the circuit court (civil division) and get the necessary forms. These forms are reproduced in Appendix F.

The clerk can assist you in filling out the forms but cannot give you legal advice. The forms are very simple. The Petition for Dissolution has only seven

39

Eligibility for Simplified Dissolution:

• no children;
• no dispute about property or debts;
• both parties will voluntarily appear in court.

blanks, the important ones being for your names and the date and place of your marriage. If you have property, you list on a separate form which property and which debts go to whom and fill out a simple financial affidavit. A wife can indicate on the Petition if she wants to return to a former name. Although no rule or case prohibits the payment of alimony in a simplified dissolution action, the instruction book approved by the Supreme Court states that neither party can receive alimony in a simplified dissolution action.

Proof of Residency

No other paper is needed. Residency can now be corroborated through a valid Florida driver's license or a Florida voter's registration card. If neither of you have a license or voter's registration card, you can get a sworn affidavit from someone who knows you have lived in Florida for more than six months. If you prefer, you could have that person testify in court to your residency.

Final Judgment

After filling out the forms, you bring the forms to the clerk and pay the filing fee. He or she will assist you in setting a final hearing. On the day of the hearing, you and your spouse will go back to the courthouse and appear before a circuit judge. Neither of you will have to testify unless, after examining the petition, there is need for some clarification.

Twenty days after filing of the Petition (and, if you divided property and debts, the settlement agreement form) and you have appeared before the judge, a Final Judgment is automatically entered and mailed to you.

The good part is that the procedure is cheap, fast, and painless. The bad part is that unrepresented parties are inundating the court system and botching their divorces. Family law judges cite this as the biggest problem they face and some are seeking to find ways to encourage the local bars to assist in some manner. Special offices established to assist these unrepresented parties have, so far, been unable to make the situation much better.

I doubt that it makes any difference, but the forms are bad. The Petition form seems to be adequate but the forms used in simplified dissolutions for the settlement agreement and the Final Judgment both contain glaring errors. For example, despite being in the rules for more than five years, the settlement agreement still recites that "irreconcilable differences" have caused the breakdown of the marriage; that's the California standard for a dissolution, not Florida's.

In Appendix F, I include the forms for a simplified dissolution with mistakes uncorrected since they are Supreme Court forms and should always be used exactly as issued. If you think that you qualify to use them, make preliminary preparations before going to the clerk's office and then fill the forms out under the direction of the clerk.

Dissolution Kits

In its considerable commitment to making it easy for laymen to file their own divorces, the Supreme Court has made dissolution kits available through the clerk's offices of each county. The kits cost as follows:

> Simple Dissolution: $8.25
> Divorce with property but no children: $13.50
> Divorce without property or children: $15.35
> Divorce without children: $19.65

The filing fee of $352.50 must be paid. There is no waiver or reduction for destitute applicants. Most, if not all, counties have a "Self-help Coordinator" to assist litigants without an attorney prepare and file their papers. There is no charge for that service.

5

CHILD
CUSTODY

What you will learn in this chapter:

• why custody is the most important issue
• what *shared parental responsibility* means
• whether mothers are still given preference
• what standard decides all custody cases
• what factors the court will consider in awarding custody
• what contact means
• how contact guidelines make visitation easier for both parents
• how grandparents can get visitation rights
• how a guardian ad litem can help the judge decide custody
• how interstate custody battles are handled
• why the UCGJA may not be the governing law

Child custody is the central issue in family-law practice. Nothing is more difficult and nothing is more important. If you win on every other issue and you and the children lose on this one, you've lost the war. "Winning" means doing what is best for the children, not necessarily getting custody yourself.

Historically, children (and their mothers) were treated as personal property. Since only the male could own property, he would always get custody of the children when a separation or, more rarely, a divorce occurred. The pendulum swung completely the other way in the last couple of centuries as women gained dignity and their nurturing skills were better appreciated. It became virtually impossible for a father to win custody. Society has changed again and, with it, the law.

New Concepts

Recent law, specifically the laws dealing with the notion of shared parental responsibility, has retreated a little from the concept of custody. *Shared parental responsibility* refers to the sharing by both parents in the important decisions about the children after the divorce. Nevertheless, even while the parties share "parental responsibility," provide "primary residential care," and exercise "contact," the law retains the term "custody." In the framework of modern thinking, custody means where the children primarily live.

About 50 years ago, case law established the principle that, all things being equal, the mother of a child of "tender years" would get custody since she was "best fitted" to provide the affection, care, and early training such a child needed. This came to be called the "tender years doctrine." Children as old as ten years of age were found to be of tender years. In theory, it no longer matters since the legislature has statutorily overturned the tender years doctrine. As we will see, both parties are to be given equal consideration in custody determinations, regardless of the age of the children.

But despite the abolishment of the tender years doctrine, the vast majority, approximately 90%, of the visiting parents are fathers. Although my comments will apply equally to either parent visiting children, I will refer to the father as the visiting parent to make the discussion easier to read.

General Considerations

In custody matters, there are three realities: (1) the court has very broad discretion; (2) the wife usually (but now not always) wins; and (3) the primary (and almost only) consideration is the "best interests of the children." Keep that last one in mind; everything else is secondary. All the statutes and all the cases only provide guidelines for the best interests. Sometimes, parties and courts get wrapped up in the details and forget the objective. If the best interests standard is always kept in mind, and the details are regularly weighed against that monolith, the case can be kept in perspective.

Now, let's see if you were paying attention. The first two realities are the court's broad discretion and the wife's advantage. Can you tell me why? Of course you can: because they are perceived as promoting the best interests of the children. If you didn't immediately come up with that answer, you had better reread the last paragraph. Everything in this section concerns that standard and how it is reached. Think "best interests of children" as you read this whole section and you will always be in touch with the essence of custody matters.

Because divorce courts have very broad discretion, they are not held to rigid rules that may bring results contrary to the best interests of the children. Judges are permitted to decide, under the unique facts and circumstances of each case, what is best for those children.

Mothers usually get custody because society perceives that women are better equipped by nature to provide the nurturing and care that children need. Women don't always win custody but they do start off with a psychological presumption in their favor (and that is, as we will see, contrary to law).

Despite the court's discretion and the reality of a woman's advantage, there are many considerations that apply to custody determinations. Let's get specific.

Split custody means that the children of the marriage don't all live together; the father may have the son and the mother the daughter.

Divided or joint custody (sometimes called rotating custody) means that neither party is designated as the primary residential parent and the child lives approximately equal time with both parents.

Policy Factors. The law expressly requires the court to decide custody matters in accordance with the best interests of the children. It also recites a public policy of frequent and continuing contact with both parents after a divorce and of both parents sharing in parental rights and responsibilities.

In an attempt to be nonsexist, the law says that fathers must be given the same consideration as mothers in deciding who provides the primary residence for the children, regardless of the age of the children. This law is supposed to eliminate the presumption in favor of the woman. While it is certainly good law and accurately recognizes the developing skills of many fathers, equal consideration is not a reality. I do not believe that even the younger judges, many of whom are modern, involved fathers or liberated women, take that mandate literally. I am sure that they try, but I see no evidence that any father enters a custody battle on an equal footing with the mother. A mother will generally lose only if she is either unfit or conclusively less fit than the father.

I am not certain that the presumption in favor of the mother represents bias or merely the realistic presumption that the woman has generally been the primary caregiver. If there is evidence that the father has been the primary parent to the children, his chances of getting custody are significantly increased.

Split custody, the placing of siblings with different parents, is strongly disfavored. The courts feel that the trauma of the divorce is bad enough without separating the children from each other. Split custody is extremely rare. It is more commonly allowed, but still unusual, with older children.

Dividing custody by giving each parent equal time with the children is also disfavored by the law as confusing to the children. Despite this, a new (1997) statute now authorizes the court to order "rotating" custody if the court finds that it will be in the best interests of the children. That change has made little or no difference. Few courts will award rotating custody.

Shared Parental Responsibility. Both parents are equally responsible for rearing their children. Courts are directed to order shared responsibility unless it would be detrimental to the children. If, in a particular case, one parent is better qualified to exercise a specific aspect of child-rearing, or if the parties wish to have one parent have sole control over a particular aspect of raising the children, the judge can give responsibility for that aspect to that parent. The court may divide the responsibilities in any manner that is in the children's best interests. Sole parental responsibility may be awarded, with or without visitation, when the court finds that shared parental responsibility would be detrimental to the child. Sole parental responsibility is awarded in only the most extreme cases, generally only in cases where the parties are totally unable to work together for the benefit of the children.

A parent's handicap should not usually deprive him or her of sharing in parental responsibility to the extent possible. A handicap might limit or alter visitation aspects, such as requiring supervision if the father were to be a severe epileptic.

The court considers evidence of spouse abuse as evidence of detriment to the children. The law even says that if "the court finds that spouse abuse has occurred between the parties, it may award sole parental responsibility to the abused spouse and make such arrangements for visitation as will best protect the child and the abused spouse from further harm."

The responsibilities that the parents share include where the children will live, how and where they will be educated, and who will provide medical and dental care. Both parents are entitled to equal access to school, medical, and dental records for their children.

Specific Criteria. In deciding who will have primary residential care of the children, the court must consider the following factors in determining the best interests of the children:
- which parent is more likely to allow frequent contact with the other parent;
- what love and affection exist between the parents and the children;
- the capacity and disposition of the parents to provide the children with the necessities of life;
- the length of time the children have lived in a stable, satisfactory home and the desirability of maintaining it
- the permanence, as a family unit, of the existing or proposed custodial home;
- the moral fitness of the parents;
- the mental and physical health of the parents;
- the home, school, and community record of the child;
- the reasonable preference of the child, if the child is deemed capable of giving such a preference;
- the willingness and ability of each parent to facilitate and encourage a close and continuing parent-child relationship between the child and the other parent;
- any other factor considered by the court to be relevant.

This list is helpful to attorneys and judges in narrowing down the factors that are most important in each case. The last, "any other factor," gives everyone the latitude to raise other issues that do not fit neatly into the statutory categorizations.

You will note that the fault concept raises its specter in the consideration of "moral fitness of the parents." Even if mudslinging is irrelevant in every other part of the case, it is certainly relevant in custody battles. Even there, however, the moral unfitness of a parent is only relevant if it affects the welfare of the children.

Roles under Shared Parental Responsibility

The primary residential parent is still very much the custodial parent of old. The mother has the children with her most of the time. She makes most of the day-to-day and emergency decisions. She receives support (in most cases) and purchases the necessities of life for the children from that support and her own contributions. Shared parental responsibility intrudes into her domain only in two major areas: more and freer visitation and more sharing in decision-making.

The father has the opportunity to remain a closer parent than before the law changed. Although not a completely equal partner, he shares in decisions about his children; he sees them more; and, ideally, he gets the satisfaction that they grow up as his cultural and moral fruit instead of just carrying his genes and dissipating his money. He is not a complete partner because the custodial parent will generally get her way when the parties cannot agree.

Current laws don't solve all custody problems, but they represent a healthy change from the former practice of treating the children as personal property and the father as an outcast. A mother might still abuse the relationship between her children and their father and a father might still ignore his obligations to his children. That's sad enough without having the law reinforce that conduct by making a father feel like an outsider.

Visitation (Contact). The terms visitation and contact are interchangeable. They both refer to the time that the children spend with the nonresidential parent. The law strongly encourages frequent and continuing contact between the children and the father.

While visitation was long viewed as a father's right or privilege, we now recognize that it is the children's right also; they badly need their father in their lives. Since the central issue in custody matters is the best interests of the children, visitation must be arranged on the same consideration, even if that works to the detriment of one (usually the father) or both parents. Accordingly, the mother cannot cut off visitation if the father does not pay since that would just punish the children further. Likewise, a father cannot refuse to pay support just because he is being denied visitation.

Some judicial circuits have developed "contact guidelines" that provide the minimum contact that a father should have with his children. Although formerly developed by committees of family lawyers, the trend is to include judges and even psychologists in the development of appropriate guidelines. Once the judges adopt the guidelines, they are generally applied in every case unless unusual circumstances exist, such as significant distance between the parents or unusual work hours. Initially, the guidelines were intended to be minimums that applied no matter what and caselaw requires the judge to take evidence in every case and fashion contact to suit the

A *judicial circuit* is a grouping of counties served by the same circuit judges. There are twenty judicial circuits In Florida, with several serving only one county and with one serving seven counties.

A *cause of action* is a term used to mean both the right to bring a suit and the suit itself. In the context of grandparents' visitation rights, the cause of action is "independent" in that it is not brought in the parents' divorce action and thereby dependent on the existence of that case.

particular circumstances of each case. Nevertheless, in the vast majority of cases, unless an agreement is reached for a different schedule, the judge will impose straight "guideline" contact. That being so, it is a rare custodial parent who willing to agree to more liberal contact voluntarily, especially considering the negative impact more liberal contact can have on the child support payable. (See Chapter 6 for a discussion of child support.)

Sarasota currently has contact guidelines that were largely shaped by the influence of psychologists on the committee. They clearly reflect the psychologists' view of the best-interests-of-the-children standard, much to the detriment of the non-residential parent. Contact between that parent and the children, especially very young children, has been severely limited to assure the children with the security that a single place of residence provides. In the ebb and flow of competing interests, these guidelines most probably represent the high water mark of the academic view of children's rights. Fathers' rights advocates are displeased that the father's rights have been so completely subordinated to the perceived rights of the children. It is my understanding that many of the underlying premises of the psychologists' arguments (such as, that a baby will be damaged if he/she is away from the mother for several hours at one time) are being rebutted by more recent studies. In all likelihood, the extremes that these guidelines present will ebb and be replaced by guidelines which recognize that the best interests of the children are served by respecting a balance of the best interests of every member of the family and encouraging greater contact with the father. As history has shown, today's enlightenment is often seen tomorrow as quaint naiveté.

Now that I've told you that the best interests of the children always control decisions about the children, let me contradict that. We all know that grandparents

A *stipulation* is merely an agreement between the parties, sometimes oral and sometimes written, that certain facts are true or, more commonly, that certain rulings can be made without dispute.

A *guardian ad litem* is an advocate for the children. He or she is not a guardian in the ordinary sense of having custody or control over the children themselves but is rather the guardian of their rights and interests before the court.

are great for kids. They may spoil them a bit but, ah, what the heck. Florida law has, until recently, always been very pro-grandparents, even creating a separate cause of action for them to get visitation. That is no longer true. Grandparents' rights, and the rights of children to have contact with their grandparents, have been completely eliminated in Florida by the Supreme Court. Grandparents have no rights because the mandating of visitation contrary to a parent's wishes conflicts with the hallowed relationship between a parent and a his/her child. The Supreme Court ruled, and rightly so, I believe, that parents have a constitutional privacy right that is violated by any statute giving grandparents independent visitation rights. Sometimes tough cases make bad law; sometimes they just illuminate unavoidable conflicts of interests. While we may all be in favor of grandparents seeing their grandchildren, we must also defer to a parent's right to decide if that is best.

Restrictions upon Visitation. Restrictions are sometimes placed on visitation. The most common one, usually by agreement between the parties, is that neither spouse have a member of the opposite sex spend the night when the children are in the house. The court cannot forbid either parent from having overnight guests unless there is specific evidence that it would damage the children.

The courts sometimes restrict the use of alcohol and/or drugs while the children are present. To avoid the obvious implication of such a restriction, courts often make the order mutually binding upon both parties.

More restrictions result from agreements than from contested actions. In the give and take necessary to achieve a settlement, a party is more willing to give the other some minor restriction in exchange for some perceived concession from the other. Note that the contact guidelines contain some rules that could be perceived as restrictions; most guidelines will contain similar language.

Custody Battles

The hearts and souls of millions of children lie scattered on the fields of custody battles. And the parents, scanning the littered field, shake their heads in bewilderment. Few ever take responsibility; it's always the other spouse's fault. On the positive side, and there isn't much that is positive, is the fact that bitter, expensive, and emotionally exhausting custody battles could be evidence that parents love and want their children. I have never seen a divorce where neither party wanted the children — an occasional problem child, yes, but never all the children. I know that custody battles are sometimes just a means of punishing or controlling the other spouse, but I'd like to believe that occurs in far less than half of the cases.

Courts have a lot of trouble deciding custody cases. That's one of the reasons that mothers continue to have a big advantage. Since each party generally testifies about how good he or she is as a parent and how mediocre or unfit the other is, the judge generally needs the assistance of outside witnesses.

Any outsider who has a lot of contact with the children can be of help to the judge. One of the best witnesses is the child's teacher. The teacher sees the child almost every day, often sees the interest that one parent or the other shows, and sometimes sees the results of one or both parents' actions toward the child. Even when a teacher is available to testify, the judge often still needs additional help. That's where outside experts come in.

Social Investigation. It's a rare judge who wants or will take sole responsibility for making a custody decision. It's simply too important and complex a question to depend upon the brief, seething, and nervous testimony of two emotionally distraught people. The judge can get help from a guardian ad litem or a parenting evaluator. Either party may petition for the appointment of a guardian ad litem or evaluator when a custody battle looms. Even if neither party seeks it, the judge may appoint a guardian ad litem or parenting evaluator to obtain information not available in the courtroom. The guardian/evaluator can talk to the parties informally. He or she can solicit the opinions of neighbors and friends. Most importantly, the guardian can talk to the children about seemingly irrelevant and inconsequential matters that permit the children to express their feelings about their parents and surroundings without being put on the spot. There's nothing worse than asking a child which parent he or she prefers. Informal input from the children is the best way to help the court on that issue without the children feeling responsible for the outcome.

In the absence of a guardian/evaluator, the judge will rarely have any true impression of the preference of the children. Although the children's preference is a statutory consideration, most judges will only reluctantly allow a child to testify on that issue, even with the parents out of the room.

Like everyone else, experts are subject to bias and their reports rarely resolve the issue completely. They help and that's enough. The judge must still make the

decision, and even with the investigator's report and with all of the statutory standards, it is rarely definitively clear what is in the children's best interests. That is
why the psychological (and often unconscious) presumption in favor of the mother so often decides the case.

Guardians ad litem are volunteers. There is no charge for having one on your
case. That's the good news. The bad news is that, because guardians are not
trained professionals (although they do receive some training), the quality of
guardians is uneven. There are many who are bright, insightful, and conscien-
tious; there are some who do not reach such high standards. Since you generally
cannot choose who will serve as the guardian ad litem in your case, there is some
small risk that the guardian's involvement in your case could unfairly prejudice
your rights or those of your spouse.

Parenting evaluators are, on the other hand, mental health professionals and
better qualified to make objective recommendations. Although guardians ad litem
are not paid for their services, parenting evaluators are paid and, being professionals, do not always come inexpensively.

Avoiding Custody Battles. I have good advice regarding custody battles:
avoid them. Instead, get joint counseling. Talk it over with friends and relatives.
Agree to mediate the issue. Most of all, despite the difficulty, speak with your
children's other parent. Love your children and act accordingly. If you can't avoid
the battle, use an attorney who cares more about your children than the large fee
a custody battle often creates. I believe that in a custody battle, ethics require that
the attorney's first client be your children. If you start doing things that are hurting your children, the attorney has to have the judgment and the courage to oppose
you. If your attorney doesn't know that he or she represents your children first and
won't give you assurance at the start that your children will be protected even
from you, you have the wrong attorney. Even if your children are independently
represented by a guardian ad litem, your attorney should always keep in mind
what is in your children's best interest while still advocating your rights.

In this area, more than in any other, you must get a good lawyer.

Mediation

Mediation is covered in greater detail in Chapter 12. I just want to point out here
that the judge has the power to require the parties to submit to mediation whenever custody, primary residence, or visitation are contested. The judge doesn't
have to but will usually do so in the hope that he or she can avoid deciding the
issue.

The mediator can be someone employed by the court and available at nominal

cost to you or merely someone appointed (or selected by you and your spouse)
for a particular case. The process that is
used will substantially conform to that
described in Chapter 12.

Mediation is the process of structured
negotiations using a trained neutral
third party to keep the negotiations
focused on the Issues rather than on
the hostilities between the parties.

If the mediation is successful and
the contested issue resolved, the mediator draws up a mediation agreement for
the parties and their attorneys to review.
Upon everyone's approval, it is submitted to the judge. If the judge finds it
acceptable, it is entered, usually as part

A *consent order* is no more than an
order presented to the court on the
stipulation that it is acceptable to
both sides.

of a Final Judgment of dissolution. When the mediation agreement deals with
some but not all of the issues and other issues are still being litigated, the judge
may enter a temporary order until the case is finished. The consent portions of any
temporary order and of the Final Judgment are enforced in the same manner as
any other order or judgment.

Any information obtained from the parties in the mediation process is
absolutely privileged and may not be disclosed without the written consent of all
parties to the mediation. The privilege of both parties against disclosure of any
such information applies regardless of the success of the mediation.

This privilege is an admirable aim but it is an illusory protection. It fails to give
an honest person any protection. Any statement made during the mediation is privileged, but the honest person, later asked the same question under oath, whether in
deposition or in court, will give the same answer. Thus, once any damaging disclosure has been made in mediation, the same disclosure can easily be elicited outside
the process despite the privilege. Once the other spouse has the information, he or
she can find a way to use it; the only restriction on its use is that statements made
only in the mediation process are not directly admissible in court.

Mediation only works if both parties are open and frank. Unfortunately, I
have to advise my clients going through court-ordered mediation to be very careful about making any statement that could possibly be used against them. I'm not
sure that mediation can work with that restraint. Despite this, there is some opti-
mism about the program. The court-provided (i.e., inexpensive but only available
to relatively low-income families) mediation service in Sarasota is reporting a
success rate of about 50% to 60%. Private mediators claim a 90% success rate. I
would like to believe that even where a consent order is not reached, the mediation has other benefits to the parties that show up in other aspects of the case or
in the later relationship.

The full title of the act is too much of a mouthful to use in negotiations between attorneys or argument to the court. Your attorney will, therefore, usually refer to it as the *UCCJEA* or often still the *UCCJA*.

Res judicata means that an issue that has been litigated between two parties, with a court decision entered on the merits, is forever decided between them and cannot be litigated again.

A *writ of habeas corpus* is an order issued by a court directing the respondent to bring the child before the court and justify why the respondent holds that child. If the respondent has no legal right to have the child in that state, the court can take the child from the respondent and arrange for the other parent to come to the state for the child. The process is very quick and efficient, and it is probably the most common means of getting a child back.

Uniform Child Custody Jurisdiction and Enforcement Act

Like all uniform acts, the Uniform Child Custody Jurisdiction and Enforcement Act is full of good intentions. Unlike most of the others, the UCCJEA performs adequately. For now, let's see what the UCCJEA is all about. Massive interstate migrations made the Uniform Child Custody Jurisdiction and Enforcement Act necessary. As children and their divorced parents crossed state lines to find new homes, it became essential that states cooperate in protecting their citizens from child-snatching, unauthorized removal, and refusal to return the children after visitation. Since cooperation was difficult while each state applied its own rules and standards, it became essential that some uniformity be established. Florida was one of the worst states in respecting other states' judgments and decrees.

Uniformity became available in 1968 when the UCCJA was drafted. Since then, every state has adopted the act in roughly the same form; Florida adopted the law, basically without change, in 1977. For 25 years, the UCCJA reigned until it was replaced by the UCCJEA, passed in Florida in 2002.

The law is directed toward eliminating the following evils:

· child-snatching, unauthorized removal, and refusal to return after visitation;
· forum shopping and endless relitigation of the custody issue;
· custody determinations in states foreign to the child's home and to the evidence on the issue;
· the excessive cost of obtaining evidence from distant states;
· destruction of the concept of *res judicata* in custody cases.

Basic Rules of the Act. The structure of the law is very complicated, but it does rather simple things. First, it establishes (not completely successfully) which single state has jurisdiction over the trial of a child's custody. Second, the UCC-JEA provides procedures for obtaining any necessary information from other states. Third, it requires all other states to recognize and enforce a state's judgment or order. Finally, it provides how and when another state may acquire jurisdiction over the child for modification of the initial award.

The UCCJEA is a procedural and jurisdictional act rather than a substantive one. That is, it does not establish or limit rights but provides rules for determining where a case should be heard. For this reason, the details of the law are not important to the layperson. It is enough to know that the basic idea of the law is that the state that should try the case is the one with either (1) "home state" jurisdiction or (2) maximum access to evidence about the issue. The "home state" is the one in which the child has lived with one or both parents for six months immediately before the proceeding (or in which the child lived, and one parent still lives, within six months of the start of the proceeding and from which the child is absent because of removal or retention by one parent claiming custody).

As you see, the law seeks to ensure that the state with the maximum contact with the child has jurisdiction as opposed to another state with minimum contacts.

Because the best interests of the children must always be paramount, the UCCJEA does provide some escape from its rigid rules. The most important escape clause is the emergency jurisdiction provision. Under it, for example, a Florida court can assume jurisdiction if the child is actually present in the state and needs immediate protection by the court. This might occur where a deranged, drug-abusing, or child-abusing parent has the child in this state; even though Florida might not be the home state, it could intervene to take whatever action is necessary to protect the child. Generally, Florida's intervention in such circumstances would only be temporary, until the case could safely be turned over to the more appropriate state.

Limits of the UCCJEA. One interesting (and possibly troublesome) effect of the law occurs under certain circumstances: if, for example, a Florida resident files for dissolution of marriage from his wife, who has lived with the children in another state for the last six months, the local court would have no jurisdiction over the children even if the wife were to submit herself to Florida's jurisdiction. The Florida court would have jurisdiction to award child support since that requires jurisdiction over the parent but, since the UCCJEA requires that a state have jurisdiction over the child in order to deal with custody, it would not have jurisdiction to make any ruling on custody.

The law does create other problems. Suppose the wife in the previous example told her husband that she needed some time to think and returned with the children to live with her parents in New York. As the end of the six months approaches, the husband would be put in the awkward position of either filing an action for dissolution or of demanding that the children be brought back. Unless he could show that Florida was the most convenient forum, in the sense that most of the evidence on the issue of custody was here, New York would become the home state at the end of the sixth month.

New York would not, however, become the home state if the wife wrongfully removed the children from the state. It is unlikely that Florida would lose jurisdiction if a Florida court had awarded temporary custody to the husband before the wife left or if the court had ordered her not to remove the children.

The UCCJEA does not provide any means for enforcement, such as contempt actions, since, like child support, contempt orders depend upon jurisdiction over the parent. This is not as big a problem as it seems. If Florida entered a valid order requiring that the children be returned to Florida, New York should enforce that order by any means available in that state, including issuing a writ of habeas corpus.

The law could not hope to answer all the questions presented by the complexity of the relationships between parents, children, and states. Naturally, there are some questions left unanswered. And, naturally, different states answer some of those questions in different ways. As one small example, the law requires that Florida cannot exercise jurisdiction if a case is already ongoing in another state. That other state will either find it is the appropriate state or defer to Florida if it finds Florida is the right place. Does Florida defer to Oklahoma when that state has accepted jurisdiction despite clear evidence in Florida that Oklahoma has improperly taken the case? Under those facts, one judge followed the dictates of the law and declined to hear the case; the appellate court reversed him, admonishing him to make his own decision about the propriety of Oklahoma's jurisdiction.

The appellate court probably relied upon the portion of the UCCJEA (which was then controlling) which gives the trial court discretion to decline jurisdiction if it is "just and proper under the circumstances." Obviously, the courts of the many states can find many and diverse reasons to exercise jurisdiction under that language.

Parental Kidnapping Prevention Act

Potentially more important than the UCCJEA is the Parental Kidnapping Prevention Act of 1980. This federal law is aimed at the same abuses as the UCCJEA and addresses them in substantially the same manner. As a federal law, however, it preempts any state law on the same subject, namely, the UCCJEA. Let me state that a different way; when the PKPA of 1980 and the UCCJEA overlap, the UCCJEA effectively ceases to exist. Since they substantially overlap, the UCCJEA has substantially ceased to exist, at least, in theory. Surprisingly, neither judges nor attorneys have addressed this issue very vigorously. It rarely comes up in appellate opinions and I am unaware of any cases in Florida that have thrown out a judgment under the UCCJEA as being without force in light of a conflict with the PKPA. Possibly the key conflict centers on the essential issue of jurisdiction: the UCCJEA provides no priority between the two main standards (home state and most convenient forum) while the PKPA gives the home state absolute priority. Thus, if a state were to assume jurisdiction for any other reason except that it was the home state, its judgment or order would be, under the PKPA, without force and no other state would have to defer to that ruling. As you see, except where jurisdiction is exercised by the home state, the UCCJEA is technically a lame duck.

It appears, from the few cases on the issue, that the courts are avoiding any recognition of the conflict between the UCCJEA and the PKPA. Maybe the PKPA is just another law that attorneys and judges will ignore or work around. So far, they have done just that. The PKPA has some big advantages over the UCCJEA in that it provides:

· the Federal Parent Locator Service to assist in finding a missing parent or child;
· the Fugitive Felon Act for parental kidnapping when the state treats such an act as a felony (as Florida does);
· the services of the FBI to investigate parental kidnappings.

The effectiveness of these advantages of the PKPA depends on the willingness of the State Attorneys in Florida to take parental kidnapping seriously. They have not done so to date, preferring to distance themselves from domestic matters. Their future cooperation is essential to federal assistance.

6

CHILD SUPPORT

What you will learn in this chapter:

- why some payers prefer alimony to child support
- who must support the children
- whether your standard of living after divorce makes any difference
- whether there can be child support without a divorce
- the different forms of child support
- how child support has been standardized
- whether a remarried wife can keep exclusive use of the home
- how mortgage payments on the house are credited
- why some child support never ends
- how support is paid
- how income deduction orders work
- how automatic judgments for child support work
- how and when child support can be modified
- whether a court can order automatic cost of living increases
- who gets the IRS exemption
- how arrearage affects title to real property

Were it not for custody, child support would hold center stage as the most important aspect of family law. In some ways, child support is more difficult because the best interests of the children seem more easily lost. The issue becomes a monetary battle between the parents rather than a provision for the children. Whatever the husband pays, the wife doesn't; $5 extra out of the father's pocket is $5 more in the wife's. For this reason, the issue is more like alimony than a child-related issue. In fact, in one sense, child support is more difficult than alimony because alimony payments are deductible by the payer for income taxes and terminate upon remarriage; since child support is not deductible and must be paid even if the wife remarries, it is often seen as alimony without any of the palliatives.

Historically, only the father had to support the children. If able, he was required to pay the full amount of the children's needs. That has changed. Now, both parents have an equal duty to support the children.

Awarding Support

In awarding child support, the court formerly had broad discretion. That is no longer true. Now, the amount of child support is set by the statutory guidelines and

> *Process* is the term used to include the pleading and the summons. The *pleading* informs the respondent what the law suit is about, and the *summons* advises the respondent that he or she is subject to the court's power and that he must answer it within 20 days.
>
> *Service* is the formal delivery of process on the respondent. Since it is important to be able to prove that process has been served, the law requires either a deputy sheriff or an authorized process server to make the service; he or she must then file a sworn statement with the court that the respondent was properly served.

the judge can only deviate by more than 5% upon a written finding (or a specific finding in the record) of why the guideline amount would be unjust or inappropriate.

The judge must, however, follow some rules. The first rule is that the judge must have jurisdiction over the nonresidential parent (I'll use "father" or "husband" for simplicity, although everything I write would apply to a nonresidential mother/wife) to order him to pay support. This means that the husband must be served personally with process. (See Chapter 3 for more details about service of process.) If the court only has jurisdiction over the wife, the marriage, and the children, it cannot order child support. Being a court of equity, however, the court could possibly find a way to subject the husband's property to cover the child support even if the husband were not actually served.

Determining the Amount of Support

The amount of child support should be the amount the child needs limited by the ability of the parents to provide. For example, suppose a child reasonably needed $250 per week for his or her support; the court could not order the parents to pay that if their total weekly income were only $200. Likewise, if the parent had $600,000 per year coming in, the court could not make that parent pay $25,000 per year as child support if the child's needs were only $12,000 annually. However, need is a relative standard based on the standard of living during the marriage. Some children need piano lessons and private schooling; for other children, neither would ever be considered a *need*.

The standard of living in the marriage is a factor in setting the amount of child support. If the children went to private school while the family was together, that will probably be considered a need after the divorce. Both parents obviously thought that such schooling was appropriate and were willing and able to pay for it. That schooling could, however, be eliminated if the divorce, or any other circumstance, makes it impossible for the parents to pay for it after they split.

Suppose now, however, that a father, after leaving the family, earns substantially more money. Are his children entitled to share in his prosperity or are their needs limited to what they had when he was poorer? The answer is that they will share in his prosperity and will no longer be held to the standard of living the family enjoyed before he prospered.

The court can impute income (that is, assign an amount of income to a parent that he or she does not actually have) to a parent who is either unemployed or underemployed. For example, if a father who was a doctor decided to take a couple of years off and become a bricklayer, his earning capacity as a doctor could be used in determining his ability to pay child support. The court would find that he had the ability to pay child support as if he were still practicing medicine.

Support without Divorce
Child support can be ordered where no divorce is involved. The father of an illegitimate child can be ordered to pay support. Most of these cases are handled by the Department of Revenue as a means of recovering Aid for Families with Dependent Children paid to unwed mothers.

A wife who is separated from her husband can obtain child support without filing for dissolution; likewise, a separated husband can have a court set his obligation for child support without filing for divorce. Essentially, these proceedings are part of what is commonly called an action for "legal separation." They are relatively rare.

Adopted Children
An adopted child is treated in all ways the same as a natural child. A husband who adopts a child, either his wife's by a previous marriage (stepparent adoption) or a child from completely outside the marriage, has the same obligation to support that child as he would for a natural child.

Stepparent's Income/Obligation
A stepfather has no obligation to support his stepchildren. For this reason, if the ex-wife remarried, her new husband's income should not technically be considered in deciding whether child support needs to be changed. In practice, however, it becomes a factor under two circumstances. The first occurs in two-income families. The income of the ex-wife (that is, the mother of the children) is more available because her new husband is providing some or all of the family's needs. For this reason, the ex-husband has a right, in a modification proceeding, to know how much the new husband makes or, at least, how much he contributes to the family expenses. Since there would not yet be a new husband during the divorce, the income of a new spouse could only be a factor in a modification proceeding;

but the income of a boyfriend living with the wife during the divorce could be considered by the court in determining how much she can contribute to the children's needs.

The second circumstance arises when the ex-wife stops working as a result of a remarriage. It would be patently unjust to allow her to impose the entire burden of supporting the children on the father. Under these circumstances, the courts are reluctant to simply impute income to the wife; rather, they may permit the ex-husband to discover the new husband's income and fashion a child-support award in consideration of that. I guess the theory is that the wife, as a homemaker and spouse, becomes, in a sense, a partner of the new husband and she shares as co-producer in the new husband's income.

Children of Artificial Insemination

A child born of artificial insemination performed with the husband's permission is conclusively a legitimate child. This is true whether the husband's sperm or a stranger's sperm is used. The father has the same obligation to pay child support for such a child as one conceived naturally.

Settlement Agreements

Most divorces are resolved through settlement agreements. The parties agree on all of their rights and obligations, including child support, and present the agreement to the judge for incorporation into the Final Judgment. Although few agreements are rejected, the parts of the agreement that relate to the children are subject to the approval of the court.

Since the children cannot negotiate for themselves, the husband and wife are under certain limitations about agreements concerning the children. The parties cannot permanently waive child support; even if a wife agrees to waive child support, she can still seek support in the future. If such a waiver has been approved by the court, that waiver is far more likely, but not very likely, to be enforced. In the absence of adoption of the child by a replacement parent, the court probably cannot finally and absolutely terminate child support. Because it is a court of equity, it can always do what is necessary to protect the best interests of the children, including voiding its own previous order terminating all future obligation for child support.

Forms of Child Support

Child support is payable in many forms. The most common, of course, is periodic payments. But it may also be in the form of insurance; medical, dental, or religious expenses; school tuition; the cost of summer camp; or use of the marital home. Any conceivable need of the child could be payable by the father as a form of child support. Why, you might ask, would a court ever approve a waiver? A court might do so if the father provided substantial consideration in substitution for periodic support, such as conveying his interest in the house so that the child could live there.

Periodic Payments. Periodic child support is usually paid weekly, monthly, or bimonthly, according to how the husband receives his pay. Sometimes agreements or judgments recite that the payment is "in advance," but such a recitation is the exception rather than the rule; as a result, neither party generally knows if the payment is for the last two weeks or for the next two weeks. This only becomes important when the support is terminated for some reason. For example, suppose payments were made on the 15th day of each month and a child turned 18 on the 15th. Would the payment be due on his birthday? Obviously, it would if the payment were in arrears but would not if the payment were in advance. There is no decision which states that, in the absence of a statement about whether payments are in arrears or in advance, what period the payments cover. Obviously, the way to avoid the problem is to state in the order or agreement which it is.

Periodic payments had always been awarded based on a very arbitrary evaluation of the child's needs and the parents' (or, until recently, the father's) ability to provide. Local jurisdictions have long tried to use support guidelines, with some success. In 1987, to eliminate variations and to provide some predictability, the legislature enacted statewide guidelines. See pages 65–66 for further discussion of this.

Insurance. Insurance can be used for child support in several ways. First, if the non-residential parent has health insurance available at a reasonable cost under a group plan through his or her employer, the court must direct, in its order for child support, that health insurance be provided for the child. ("Reasonably available" means that the insurance is available to either party at a reasonable rate under a group policy.) The requirement that health insurance be provided if available is consistent with the common law duty of the father to provide the necessaries of life for his dependents. The obligation to provide health insurance through an employer or union can be enforced through service of the order on the employer/union if the parent required to provide the coverage fails to provide proof of coverage within 30 days of receiving a copy of the notice.

By statute, the court can, but isn't required to, order the husband to purchase or maintain a life insurance policy or bond to secure the child support award. The court can, in the alternative, order the husband to secure the child support with suitable property; for example, the judge could impose a lien on any real property or stock holdings the husband owned to assure that the child support is paid. If the husband wanted to sell that property, he would have to substitute other acceptable security. All of this said, however, case law limits the court's ability to require life insurance or other security to cases in which there is a special need, such as the payer has a health problem that makes it unlikely he will be around to pay child support for the child's whole minority.

Dental insurance is becoming more commonly required. Since the coverage is now typically provided in group policies, it is usually made part of the child support.

Use of Home. There is rarely enough money to go around when people divorce. Sometimes the judge has to find some other way to ensure that the children are taken care of. One of the ways is by leaving the children in the marital home. Unless the home is awarded to the wife outright, the husband will usually have a one-half interest in the property. When minor children are involved and the house isn't the husband's only significant asset, the wife sometimes (but increasingly rarely) gets exclusive use and possession of the house until the last child reaches majority, dies, or is otherwise "emancipated" (no longer considered a child). Whether the exclusive possession can continue after the wife remarries is not clear. There is authority both ways. I believe that each case must be decided using the standard of the best interests of the children. If the exclusive use and possession automatically terminated upon remarriage and the children suffered as a result, that result would seem to punish the children for the remarriage. On the other hand, no husband is going to be happy having his half of the house used by his replacement.

During the wife's exclusive use of the home, the mortgage payments may be made by the husband, by the wife, or by both, depending on ability. When only one party makes the payments, he/she gets no credit for the reduction in the mortgage unless the agreement or judgment so provides. In deciding what credit should be given in the judgment, the Court must consider such factors as exclusive use/possession, whether alimony covers the payments, child support, the value of the use, the lost value to the other, tax implications, and the effect of capital gains upon sale.

Duration of Payment

Although it seems like kids grow up too fast, child support seems like it goes on forever for the payer. It doesn't. Generally, child support stops when the child reaches age 18, marries, or otherwise becomes emancipated. It also stops if the payer dies, the child is adopted or dies, or, under certain circumstances, if the child's independent income is sufficient for his or her needs.

The husband can agree to pay child support beyond age 18 and the court will enforce it. In many cases, he would agree either to pay for college or pay child support as long as the child remains in college. The only way that can happen is by agreement; the court can't order it. The court can, however, extend child support beyond 18 years of age if the child is dependent, still in school, and reasonably expected to graduate before his/her 19th birthday.

An agreement providing for child support has to be worded very carefully. For example, suppose the agreement provided that, "notwithstanding the child having reached 18, the father shall continue to pay child support until the child completes high school (or college)." Even if the child married, the child support would continue unless another provision specifically stopped it upon marriage.

Some agreements, but not many, provide that the death of the father does not terminate child support and that his estate shall continue to pay it until the occurrence of one of the specified events (turning 18, emancipation, etc.). For such (rare) cases, child support after death will usually be provided through life insurance or an annuity rather than having the estate set aside money for the future payments. Insurance, often decreasing term, is the most common way of providing for the support.

If the child is physically or mentally disabled such that he or she is not self-supporting even though over 18, the court can order that support continue so long as the disability continues. A child can be emancipated by becoming fully employed and evidencing no intention to turn over his or her wages to the parents, by leaving the home of both parents and refusing to be subject to their direction, and several other ways. Likewise, for some purposes, joining the armed forces or being arrested serves to emancipate a child. In each case, the child's emancipation lets the payer petition to end the support payments.

Remember that neither the court nor the parties can terminate support without any possibility of reinstatement while the children are alive, under age 18, unmarried, etc. Notwithstanding any such ruling or agreement, the court has the inherent authority to order support if the children need it.

How Payment Is Made

Child support must be paid through the Florida Disbursement Unit unless both parties request, and the court finds it in the best interests of the children, that the payments be made directly to the wife. The vast majority of new child support is paid in that manner.

Payment through the Disbursement Unit serves several purposes. First, it creates a record of payments which is admissible in court without need of any witness to authenticate it. Second, it avoids direct contact between the parties where

An *affidavit* is a statement in writing under oath that is notarized by a notary public.

A *default* is any failure to do what is required. In this area, it is the failure to make child-support payments; concerning pleadings, a *default* is, first, the failure of the respondent to answer within 20 days and, second, the formal document entered by the clerk or the court, upon the respondent's failure to answer and the petitioner's request, that cuts off the respondent's right to answer late.

that might be troublesome. Finally, the structure is also a little intimidating to the father because he knows the record is being kept and it may thereby encourage more regular payment. There are fees for payments through the Disbursement Unit, however. The cost is almost always borne by the father. The fee is 4% of each payment with a minimum of $1.25 and a maximum of $5.25. If the payments are initially made directly to the wife by agreement and the father is late or in default with a payment, the mother may file an affidavit with the court stating the fact of the default and her wish to have future payments made through the Disbursement Unit. She must send a copy to the father. Fifteen days after receiving the affidavit, the clerk will notify both parties that future payments must be made through the Disbursement Unit.

Income Deduction Orders. In 1984, the legislature adopted a procedure for income deduction orders. The idea is great and has worked well despite the procedure specified by law. The law presumes that such an order is necessary and directs the judge to require that all child support (and alimony) be deducted from the father's paycheck unless the court finds, upon "good cause shown," that it shouldn't become effective until the direct payments become delinquent in an amount equal to one month's support.

The law is a little cumbersome. When income deduction is ordered, the court must furnish the father with a written statement of his rights, remedies, and duties, which must include:

- all fees and interest which will be imposed;
- the total amount of income generally to be deducted and the amount that will be deducted until any arrearage is paid;
- that the order applies to any paychecks he receives from his current employer and future employers during the period of support;
- that a copy of the order will be served on his employer(s).

When the court defers the effect of the income deduction order and the husband goes into arrears an amount equal to one month's support, and the wife seeks an income deduction order, the father can contest it only with regard to the amount of support payable, the amount of arrearage sought, or his identity. Once the order is effective, the employer must be provided a notice which instructs the employer to deduct the specified amount from the next paycheck more than 14 days away and send it within two days to the clerk; warns the employer that he or she will be liable for the amount not deducted plus attorney's fees, costs, and interest if the deduction is not made, and authorize the employer to deduct an additional $5 for the first deduction and $1 for each deduction thereafter. The notice must also advise the employer that the deductions must be made until further notice from the court, or until he no longer provides income to the father. When the father is no longer on the payroll, the employer must notify the wife of the father's last known address and the father's new employer; the employer is subject to a $250 fine if it fails to do so.

The employer is also subject to a $250 fine if he or she discharges, refuses to employ, or takes disciplinary action against a father because of an income deduction order. The fines increase to $500 for any subsequent violation. All fines are payable to the wife. The employer can be sued by the father for discharge, refusal of employment, or disciplinary action. If the suit is successful, the employer must pay the lost wages and benefits plus attorney's fees and costs.

The income deduction order has priority over any other legal processes under state law pertaining to the same income. If there are two separate income deduction orders for the same employee, the employer must contact the court for further instructions.

If the wife (or girlfriend, as is often the case) is an IV-D case (welfare recipient), income deduction orders apply in favor of the welfare agency in much the same way. In addition, income deduction orders can be used across state lines.

Automatic Judgments. Under a law effective for all payments due after July 1, 1988, a judgment is entered automatically for all late payments. When a payment is 15 days late, the clerk must send a notice to the paying parent that a judgment will be entered unless he or she contests the entry; the payer can only contest it on the grounds that there is no delinquency, that the amount noticed is wrong, or that he or she is not the person they are after. If no motion is filed or if the payer's motion is denied, the delinquent amount (plus costs and a $5 fee) becomes a judgment and a lien on the payer's real estate in that county. It remains a lien until the support-receiving parent or the clerk files a satisfaction of judgment.

Attachment/Garnishment. Traditional methods of attaching or garnishing salary can also be used to enforce child support (and alimony) payments. Those procedures sometimes have a little more teeth in support enforcement. Their uses are discussed in Chapter 9.

Uniform Child Support Guidelines

The legislature decided in 1987 that all children in the state are equal, that is equal relative to their parents' income. The current guidelines start at combined available income of $7,800 and go up to $120,000. (Above that income, the child support increases by a percentage of the excess: 5% for one child, 7.5% for two children, etc.) They provide a percentage increase for incomes over that amount. The guidelines establish the amount of support due for up to six children.

The guidelines are three pages long in the statutes (longer in this book), with more than half of the text explaining how to apply them. All things considered, they are as simple as they could be. (See Appendix E for the child support table excerpted from these guidelines.)

The law defines what is income. Basically, income is anything received from work, disability, worker's compensation, unemployment, pension, social security, alimony, investments (including rentals and trading in property), royalties, trusts/estates, reimbursed living expenses, and recurring gains derived from dealings in property. If the parent is voluntarily unemployed, the court must impute income, that is, assign an amount of income to that parent according to what he or she might be making if working. Welfare payments are not included.

Before applying the guidelines, the income is reduced by income tax deductions (adjusted to ultimate filing status, allowable dependents, and income tax liabilities), FICA (or self-employment tax), mandatory union dues, mandatory retirement payments, health insurance payments (excluding children's coverage), and court-ordered support for other children. Once the working income is determined for both parties, they are combined. The total preliminary support necessary for the appropriate child is found on the guideline chart, along the line to the right of the combined figure. To that is added the cost of the children's health insurance and 75% of any day care expenses. The father's obligation is the same percentage of the resulting support total as his income is to the combined income figure.

This sounds harder than it is. Look at the support chart in Appendix H and follow this calculation. Suppose the net income for the husband is $2,000 and for the wife is $1,000; assume also that they have three children. On the chart, you will find, across from $3,000 (the combined income), that the total preliminary support obligation is $1,252 for three children. If we assume that health insurance for the children costs $200 per month and day care is $400 per month, the total support obligation would be $1,752 (that is, the $1,252 plus the insurance cost and 75% of the day care cost). Since the father makes two-thirds of the income (that is, $2,000/$3,000), he must pay two-thirds of the support or $1,168 (two-thirds of $1,752). If the husband is already paying the health insurance through his employment, he would continue to do that and pay the wife $968 through an income deduction. Combined with the $20 insurance premium he is paying directly, he is meeting his obligation for $1,168.

The court can adjust the support obligation for special circumstances, such as extraordinary medical, psychological, educational, or dental expenses; independent income of the children; if the father has to pay alimony in addition to child support; the ages of the children; special needs traditionally met in the family; the amount of time the father spends with the children; the total assets available to everyone involved; and any other adjustment necessary to achieve an equitable result. The existence of debts is one of the factors that might require an additional adjustment. The court may order the primary residential parent to execute a waiver of the IRS exemptions for the children so that the paying parent can take them or just make an adjustment for the benefit the wife gets from taking the exemptions. If the guidelines would require the husband to pay more than 55% of his gross income for child support, the court can adjust the obligation for that alone.

Both parties must file a financial affidavit showing income and deductions used for child support calculations within 45 days of service of the Petition for Dissolution upon the respondent. Subject to the court's power to adjust the amount for appropriate reasons, the support guidelines are mandatory. Requiring the use of the guidelines has effectively eliminated the need to negotiate or litigate the amount of child support. The guidelines would also seem to eliminate the uncertainty about the amount payable when one of two or more children reaches majority. For example, if the total support payable for two children were $1,200.00 per month, it is unrealistic to merely cut that in half when the first reaches majority. Since the mandated guidelines will provide the appropriate amount of support for one child, that should control over any possible suggestion that a straight proportional amount of support be eliminated.

Everyone benefits from the relative certainty that the guidelines provide. Now, unless alimony is still not settled, the child support issue is usually resolved before the final hearing.

Modification
As we have seen, a child support award is never final as long as the child remains a minor, is unemancipated, and so on. (See pages 61–62.) The award can be modified, either decreased or increased, if there is any substantial change that makes the existing amount inappropriate. Some of the changes that, if substantial, could justify a modification include changes in the child's needs, in either parent's ability to pay, or in the child's assets or income. A detailed of discussion of modification appears in Chapter 10.

To avoid having to return to court every few years, parties sometimes seek to have child support increase automatically with the cost of living. For a while, such clauses were commonly found in settlement agreements. Now they are extremely rare.

Cost of living adjustments, commonly called COLAS, cannot be ordered by the court. They are considered to be speculative and unsupported by evidence that a child's needs and, more importantly, a father's ability to provide will increase at the same rate as inflation. Because of that reasoning and the restriction on court orders, a mother has no bargaining position for such a clause in a settlement agreement. If the parties do agree, however, they are probably enforceable, although I would expect the court to exercise its discretion in each case to see if the provision is fair and necessary.

Reporting Use of Child Support

The court that initially entered a child-support order can require the wife to report to it how she uses the child support.

In practice, courts rarely require wives to report on child support. When husbands ask for it, courts generally see this as an attempt to continue some control over the wife. They are very reluctant to give the husband that control, feeling that any parent who is fit to have custody has to be trusted to use the money for the child's benefit. There are probably many exceptions to that presumption, but that doesn't make it likely that a court is going to agree and require the report in any particular case.

Income Tax Exemption

Since 1985, in the absence of an agreement to the contrary, the parent with custody of the children for more than half the year is entitled to take the exemption for the children on his or her tax return. The law seems to state that the parent with custody must waive the right to the exemption each year to transfer the exemptions to the other parent. Many agreements condition the execution of such an agreement upon the paying spouse being current in support payments. Florida law specifically authorizes the court to order a party to transfer the exemption for periods that the paying parent is current in his obligation.

A parent taking the exemption now must state, on his return, the Social Security number of the other spouse to enable the IRS to confirm that only one parent is taking the exemption. Presumably, with the current black-and-white rule and the easier verification, double-dipping will be far rarer; now, except for the confusion about whether annual waivers must be made, there can be no doubt about which parent is entitled to the exemption.

7

ALIMONY

Alimony is not a four-letter word. Most ex-husbands just tend to use four-letter words in the same sentence with it. Alimony is probably the most emotionally charged word in the law. It actually means "nourishment" and the idea seems fair enough. But who can blame a man for hating to pay alimony, no matter how justified it is?

There are three types of alimony: permanent-periodic, rehabilitative, and lump sum. I could add temporary alimony, which is awarded until a Final Judgment is entered, but it differs from permanent-periodic primarily in its temporariness; some of the minor ways in which it differs are discussed in Chapter 3. And I could add "bridge-the-gap" alimony but that is just rehabilitative alimony for which the recipient did not provide prove a specific need; it is, as the title says, just to bridge the gap after the divorce. All alimony is measured by the same standard: the payer's ability and the recipient's *need*. Evolving law has, however, put meanings on those words that sometimes make them unrecognizable.

Either party may be entitled to alimony. Although there are now occasional awards of alimony to husbands, I will assume for our discussion that the wife is the petitioner for, and the recipient of, alimony since that still reflects the reality in the vast majority of cases. You will note that, even after the marriage is dissolved, the parties are still properly referred to as the "husband" and "wife" by the law; the initial pleadings must use those designations and all subsequent pleadings must continue to do so.

The most hated of all alimony (by husbands, not by wives) is permanent-

Criteria for alimony:

- the parties' standard of living during the marriage
- the duration of the marriage
- the age and physical and emotional health of each party
- the parties' financial resources
- when applicable, the time necessary for the recipient to acquire sufficient education and training to enable her to find appropriate employment
- the contributions of the parties to the marriage
- all sources of income available to either party

periodic; let's deal with that first.

Permanent Alimony

The reasons for awarding permanent-periodic alimony (which I will just call permanent alimony hereafter) will vary from case to case. It will always be based on need and ability. It might be awarded because the wife, as a result of advanced age or bad health, is unable to support herself. Phrased another way, it is an award of regular income to the spouse less able to support herself of the means to have sustenance and the necessities of life.

In determining a proper award of alimony, the court must consider all relevant economic factors, including, but not limited to, the seven factors listed above.

The next-to-last factor, contributions to the marriage, was purposely made vague. It is not limited to financial contributions. Judges should evaluate the overall contributions, both financial and emotional, that enhanced the marriage.

Sometimes, courts can simplify even complex statutes. The Supreme Court, in what is probably the most important case on alimony, reduced the list to the duration of the marriage, the standard of living enjoyed during the marriage, and the value of the parties' respective estates. It would be nice if it were really that simple.

One thing that makes alimony a difficult subject is the tremendous latitude that courts have. An alimony award cannot be reversed unless no reasonable man could take the view the court did. Considering the range of people that our society is inclined to recognize as reasonable, that is wide latitude — so wide, in fact, that alimony awards are virtually irreversible. Let's look at the statutory considerations and see what they mean in practice.

Standard of Living. This consideration seems to fly in the face of the traditional, bottom-line standards of need and ability to pay. In fact, it doesn't, as long as you change the meaning of "need." Defined very narrowly, need covers the basic things essential to survival in our society: clean housing, adequate food and clothing, medical care, and dependable transportation. Remembering that we are in a court of equity, would it be equitable to expect a man worth millions and earning $300,000 per year to provide his ex-wife with no more than the man earning $24,000? Clearly, the answer is no.

In all fairness, neither party should go from prosperity to poverty as a result of the marriage. So, if we understand "need" to include everything reasonable for someone in that station in life, as judged by what existed during the marriage, the ability and need standard is not violated. This is true even if "need" includes a $400,000 house, a Mercedes, and $8,000 in spending money each month.

The only way to "do" equity on the need/ability-to-pay issue is to look to the standard of living that the husband provided during the marriage. If that standard creates high needs, the husband with the ability to provide those needs will be ordered to continue to provide them. This is especially true where the wife's efforts and contributions have enabled the husband to pursue his career and have denied the wife the opportunity to develop hers.

Duration of Marriage. To some people, a two-year marriage seems interminable. Permanent alimony will ordinarily not be granted unless there is a long-term marriage.

There is no set rule for determining if a marriage is a long one. As a rule of thumb, most attorneys consider a marriage under five years to be a short marriage and permanent alimony is rarely available. A marriage of around ten years is a medium-length marriage, and permanent alimony will be available only under special circumstances. Anything approaching 20 years is clearly a long marriage, and, unless the wife is young and very marketable, she starts with a presumptions that permanent alimony is appropriate.

The age of the wife is really the big factor here. If the parties married at age 21, the wife would only be 41 when a 20-year marriage ended. She would generally be seen as young, still having substantial job prospects in her future, especially with some training. On the other hand, if she were 35 when they married, the 20-year marriage would probably entitle her to permanent alimony.

In itself, the duration of the marriage will not determine whether permanent alimony is awarded. It may be awarded in some marriages under five years and will not be awarded in some 25-year marriages. The duration of the marriage is just an element that adds or subtracts from the weight of all the other factors rather than being decisive in itself.

Age and Health. Obviously, these are very important factors. A 40-year-old wife in good health will probably not get permanent alimony while a 66-year-old disabled wife will almost certainly get it. Nothing impairs a wife's ability to support herself more than bad health; and the next worse thing is age. Bad health is a physical problem, while advanced age is probably more a psychological problem in the sense that few employers will hire a woman in her middle sixties, however well-qualified she may be.

On the other hand, the age and health of the husband must be taken into consideration. If he is in his sixties and has health problems, the court is unlikely to award permanent alimony to his 45-year-old wife even if they were married 25 years, unless he's very wealthy, or unless his old age is secured through generous pensions, or unless some other contributing factors exist. Let's look at some of the others.

Financial Resources. This is purposely a vague term meant to include income from all sources as well as assets. The court may consider the net worth of both parties as well as their income in determining that alimony is appropriate. To make that clear, the legislature has added the seventh criteria: all sources of income available to either party.

There is some case law which holds that a wife cannot be expected to deplete her capital assets to support herself. Consider this situation: The wife has real estate holdings worth over $2 million but no income; the husband has no assets but earns $400 per week. I cannot believe that, under those circumstances, any alimony would be awarded. Both parties' assets must be considered in a court of equity.

We must keep in mind the balancing that is going on between ability and need. A super-wealthy man who, if he dug deep, could afford $20,000 per week, will not be held to pay that as alimony if his wife cannot justify a need for it, and few could ever justify it even under "need" as we defined it above. Using that definition, the standard is the wife's reasonable needs up to the husband's reasonable ability to pay.

To the extent that an inheritance produces income, it may be considered by the court in determining the husband's ability to pay alimony. Even were it not income-producing, it is a financial resource that the court could look at. This is especially true for lump sum alimony, discussed later in this chapter.

Sometimes the financial resources do not exist in a strictly monetary sense. Take, for example, a young doctor who, planning a divorce, gives up his practice and goes to work cutting lawns. Will his income as a weed-whacker be used to determine his financial ability? (Remember this is a court of equity.) Of course, it won't.

The judge is permitted to impute income to an underemployed or unemployed husband. Thus, if the wife could prove that the average doctor in her husband's specialty and with his experience was earning $350,000, the judge would use that to determine the husband's ability to pay. This concept of imputed income has done a lot to keep divorcing men working in their most lucrative field.

Pensions, including federal and military pensions, and other forms of retirement security may be considered by the court in awarding alimony. The military has gone to great lengths to make it easy to have a portion of pension payments sent directly to the ex-wife when awarded by a state court. Disability income may also be considered.

Basically, if something has any value, now or in the future, it may be considered in determining an appropriate award of alimony.

Contributions to the Marriage. The "contributions to the marriage" standard is a two-edged sword. There are positive and there are negative contributions to a marriage. Contributions do not have to be either income or property.

The contributions of a good and dedicated mother, wife, and homemaker are considered to be equivalent to whatever the husband brings in financially. A wife's contributions to building the career of the husband are also a major factor, whether she sent him through medical school or merely provided a beautiful and gracious home in which he could entertain business clients.

"Contributions to the marriage" is even more vague than "financial resources." The intent is that the court should consider any form of contribution to the marriage and assign it some value in weighing whether and how much alimony should be awarded. The law has come a long way in recognizing the contributions of women outside the workplace.

A widow who remarries can permanently lose her widow's benefits as a result of the marriage. Women have sought to have that loss considered in the alimony determination when the new marriage fails. The courts have rejected that position and that is likely to continue. In a similar vein, an appellate court, in 1996, rejected consideration of the alimony the wife gave up to marry the husband.

Marital misconduct is a negative contribution to the marriage. For years, that term was restricted to adultery, but the law is giving it a little broader meaning today. Although there is even one case which includes a wife's constant nagging as a form of marital misconduct, the term still means adultery in most contexts. Historically, marital misconduct could be used against a wife seeking alimony but could not be used against the husband for any reason except to explain the wife's conduct. That exception allowed a wife who had been a marriage-long victim of a philandering husband to explain a minor retaliatory mistake. This exception prevented the husband from minimizing his alimony exposure based upon her relatively insignificant misconduct. Equity wouldn't tolerate that and allowed the wife to mitigate her misconduct by showing what brought it about.

Notwithstanding a statute which dictates that adultery may be considered, some courts, including the Florida Supreme Court, have held that the adultery of either party is not a proper consideration in determining alimony unless it depleted the marital assets or income or it increased the needs of the wife. An example of how misconduct may increase the wife's needs might be where the wife suffered unusually because of the husband's adultery and developed emotional or physical problems as a result. Certainly, any court would consider any form of marital misconduct, including spouse abuse and excessive gambling, where it affected the family's finances. Even in those cases, however, the court's focus for alimony determination should be on the financial effect and not the misconduct itself. (Although not usually included in the term "adultery," homosexual activity is considered a form of marital misconduct which might also be taken into account in an alimony determination, but, again, only to the extent that it had detrimental financial impact.)

Since the divorce itself creates financial stress in most cases, it could be argued that adultery should always be a factor in alimony considerations whenever it breaks up the marriage. When it doesn't cause the breakup of the marriage, adultery is generally not a factor in terms of alimony. In general, this argument doesn't generally make adultery admissible in the absence of significant and direct financial impact. It is safe to say that most courts will not hear evidence of adultery without compelling evidence that the adultery and financial losses were inextricably related.

Even when adultery is a factor, the identity of the spouse's lover is not discoverable; that is, the name of the lover does not have to be disclosed to the other side. Of course, if the spouse denies the adultery, you have the right to know the alleged lover's name to continue your investigation. As you can see, there is a certain logic in that; if the adultery is admitted, there is no need to know the lover's name except to harass him or her.

Sources of Income. This consideration is no more than a clarification of the financial resources criterion already there. I don't think it adds anything to the judge's consideration.

Alimony vs. Property Settlement. The distinction between alimony and a property settlement can be important. A significant difference between a property award and alimony arises if either party were to die. Alimony stops on the death of either party, but an uncompleted property transfer becomes a claim against the deceased spouse's estate and, to the extent assets exist, must be completed before others receive anything from the estate.

Finally, property awards are unmodifiable. Unlike alimony–which is deductible from the payer's income and included in the recipient's income for tax purposes–once the amount of a property award is set, it can never be changed.

Allocation: Alimony vs. Child Support. Permanent alimony ends upon the death of either spouse. It also ends if the wife remarries. This factor is what once made it difficult for a wife with children to decide how to allocate payments between child support and alimony. (Child support is not deductible by the husband nor taxable to the wife.) Although she would usually like to allocate as much as possible to the children because of the tax advantage, she knew she would lose that as the children reached majority. On the other hand, if she remarried, she lost all the alimony immediately. Now, as a result of the child support guidelines, there is much less negotiation on the allocation; child support is pretty much set in stone in every case and alimony is negotiated on its own merits. (Keep in mind, however, that alimony must be determined before child support is calculated since the alimony payment is deductible by the husband and is included in the wife's income for child support calculations.)

Modification of Alimony. By its nature, a periodic alimony award is never final. It is always subject to change when there is a substantial change in the circumstances of either party that affects needs or ability. Automatic adjustments in alimony awards, such as having it increase each year according to the Consumer Price Index, have generally been overturned on appeal since the husband's ability will not necessarily grow with the CPI. If the award is tied to both an index, which presumably relates to the wife's increasing need, and the husband's salary increases, it has a better chance of being upheld. In general, courts do not like automatic adjustments. The parties can, however, agree to almost anything, and, unless clearly unreasonable, it will be incorporated into the judgment without significant risk of reversal on appeal.

Postmortem Alimony. Life insurance can be ordered by the court, or provided by agreement, to give the wife security if the husband should die early. The policy itself can be awarded to the wife as lump sum alimony (assuming it has some surrender value) and the premium payments awarded as permanent alimony. Obviously, the wife would have to pay taxes on the premiums. The authority to order life insurance was enacted by the legislature to overcome a long list of cases which prohibited such an award as a prohibited postmortem award of alimony. The statute initially failed to dissuade the courts from their ongoing legislating; only recently did the Florida Supreme Court finally tell the court system that the legislature meant exactly what it said and that life insurance can be used to provide, in effect, postmortem alimony.

Other Protections. The court can make other provisions to protect alimony, such as placing a lien on the husband's property or requiring him to post a bond. These are intended more to protect against his dereliction than his death.

If the court has sufficient reason to believe that the husband is about to leave the state with the intention of avoiding his alimony obligation, it can issue a *writ of ne exeat* (literally, "He shall not leave"), which effectively prevents the husband from taking off. He is arrested on the writ and is not released until he posts a bond sufficient to meet the court's requirements.

Palimony. Although the term was coined over 30 years ago and its significance disappeared almost immediately, "palimony" still comes up in conversations. This is particularly true because traditional households have continued to decline. The term refers to a nonmarital right to be supported becasue of promises or implied promises arising in a nonmarital relationship. The term is catchy but the concept comes down to nothing more than a contract right: "Did A enter into a contract for consideration to support B?" The best summary of the status of "palimony" is that there is no such thing anywhere in the country.

Misused Alimony. The payment of alimony gives the husband no control over the wife and no control over how she spends the money. Some husbands have tried to eliminate or reduce payments on the grounds that the wife was using the money for drugs or alcohol and not for the intended purpose. Consistently, the courts have overlooked the wife's misuse, reinforcing the idea that the husband has absolutely no say in the use of alimony by the wife.

Permanent alimony has made a comeback. The decline in alimony awards during the eighties has stopped and permanent alimony again is common. In all likelihood, we will never return to the frequent alimony awards of the sixties and seventies, but the overreaction of the courts to the feminist movement now also seems to be history.

Since rehabilitative alimony is so important, let's look at that.

Rehabilitative Alimony

Rehabilitative alimony is kind of like training wheels on a bike. It gives the wife time to get her balance before the wheels come off. Sooner or later, they will be taken off (unless there is a modification, but that's a later story).

Rehabilitative was the stylish alimony of the eighties. It serves the needs of all segments of society, recognizing that, given time, women can compete economically; at the same time, it allows the husband to see that his alimony obligations will soon end. Not soon enough for some husbands, perhaps, but at least there is an end.

Rehabilitative alimony is designed to help the wife regain a previously existing ability for self-support or to enable her to acquire an ability that would have existed but for the marriage. It presupposes an undeveloped or lost ability to support herself. In practice, rehabilitative alimony is the name given to any alimony of relatively short duration; usually, it is intended to give the wife time to rehabilitate herself, but sometimes, in the past, it was just the court's way of saying, "I recognize that the breakup of your marriage has been very difficult for you and it might take you a while to get yourself back together." Now, the court can give **"bridge-the-gap"** alimony for exactly that purpose. The difference between the two is that rehabilitative alimony can only be given if (1) there is reasonable evidence that the wife can or will be able to support herself in the future, and (2) she presents a plan that will enable her to become self-supporting; bridge-the-gap alimony requires nothing more than the judge thinking that the woman needs it.

Rehabilitative alimony can be periodic or lump sum. When it is periodic, it differs from permanent alimony essentially only in its duration. When it is lump sum, it doesn't differ at all from any other lump sum alimony except that the judge says that its purpose is to rehabilitate the wife. Since I deal with lump sum alimony in the next section, I will consider only periodic rehabilitative alimony here. Keep in mind, however, that when the judge decides to characterize lump sum alimony as rehabilitative, he or she is considering the same factors as in periodic alimony but is also finding that a lump sum payment is the better way to pay it.

To refresh your memory, reread the list of criteria used to determine an alimony award given at the beginning of this chapter. Since rehabilitative alimony is for a different purpose than that of permanent alimony, be aware that, although the criteria are the same, the emphasis must be different. Simply stated, "the time necessary for either party to acquire sufficient education and training to enable him or her to find appropriate employment" is the heavyweight. "Contributions to the marriage" is the featherweight.

Although husbands much prefer rehab alimony, as it is often called, to permanent, it should, in theory, be more painful for its short duration. Here's why: permanent alimony is intended to supplement whatever minimal capacity for self-support the wife has; rehab alimony presumes that the wife will spend the alimony period acquiring skills rather than working to her maximum capacity. Of course, in many instances, the woman retrains herself by working her way up through lower-paying jobs during the rehabilitative period. In those cases, the amount should not differ from permanent alimony. In cases where the wife will obtain formal schooling or training, however, the bite should be bigger than with permanent alimony.

Although rehab alimony is not necessarily intended to assure that the wife will attain the same standard of living as she enjoyed during the marriage, a higher standard of living during the marriage will almost always result in higher rehabilitative alimony.

The duration of the marriage is a factor in rehab alimony. In considering that the wife has a capacity to support herself that was lost or diminished as a result of the marriage, the court must consider how long she was out of the job market. A wife of one year might be entitled to a brief period of rehab alimony, if any, while a wife of 20 years might receive three or more years of rehab alimony. But since a combination of factors determines alimony, a marriage of short duration might yield an equally long rehab period if the contributions and the interruption of career are significant. For example, if a woman quit college after her sophomore year and worked to pay for her husband's remaining two years of schooling, she would certainly have a good argument for two years of rehab alimony to finish her own education.

As pointed out in the section on permanent alimony, the fact that the marriage is long-term does not guarantee that permanent alimony will be granted. If rehabilitative alimony is granted, the amount awarded would also undoubtedly be higher, if only because people married a long time usually have a higher standard of living than shorter-term married people.

If an equitable distribution of the property is made, rehab alimony can be used to protect the wife's property. Without the alimony, the wife might have to deplete the property to support herself, thereby making the distribution a charade. The interim support will allow her to preserve her assets while finding a way to support herself.

If the wife is given alimony so that she can go to school, her alimony would not stop just because she dropped out of school. The husband would have to show that, for some other reason, the rehabilitative alimony is no longer needed.

One interesting aspect of rehab alimony is that the wife's remarriage does not, of itself, terminate the alimony obligation. Such a termination may, of course, be effectively agreed between the parties in a settlement agreement. The remarriage may also bring about a termination of the alimony if the wife's new circumstances mean that she no longer needs the rehabilitation. For example, if the wife remarried a wealthy man, she might give up her efforts to retrain herself; or if she remarried the owner of a lumberyard and started working there along with him, it might be hard to justify the need for the first husband to pay alimony.

Rehabilitative alimony can be awarded along with permanent alimony. If the evidence shows that the wife's rehabilitation will never be complete, the court can award a larger amount of alimony during the rehabilitative period with an automatic adjustment downward at the end of that period. In such a case, the rehabilitative period would be used to increase the wife's earning ability and the permanent alimony would then supplement her still insignificant income to allow her to have the appropriate standard of living.

Like permanent alimony, rehabilitative alimony can be modified. Although modification in general will be covered in greater detail in Chapter 10, let me make some important points specifically on modification of rehabilitative alimony. First, rehabilitative alimony can be extended or converted to permanent alimony as well as changed in amount during the original projected period. If the wife wants to extend it, however, she must seek the extension before the last payment is due. Once that date passes, and in the absence of some specific retention of jurisdiction to award alimony in the future, the court loses jurisdiction to make any ruling that bears upon alimony. When it's gone, it's gone. Note that the period for modification is the prescribed payment period and not just the period during which payments are made; thus, if the husband were ordered to pay for 30 months but he paid all of it off at the end of 15 months, the wife would still be able to move to modify until the 30th month.

In seeking an extension of rehabilitative alimony, the wife must show that, despite diligent efforts to rehabilitate herself, she has been unable to do so. The burden is on her since the award creates a presumption that she can rehabilitate herself and that, at the end of the period, she would be rehabilitated. If she proves that she just couldn't do it, she may seek either an extension or a conversion to permanent alimony. Both modifications are possible but not very common. The husband's assurance that his alimony misery will end is sometimes just a mirage.

Lump Sum Alimony

I happen to think that lump sum alimony is a dinosaur that just hasn't been buried yet. Let me explain why. Equity courts have very broad discretion, but it isn't unlimited. One limitation used to be that a divorce judge could not make a property division for the parties; if the property was titled in one party's name, usually the husband's, there was nothing the judge could do to give the wife any of that property. The judge could give her a lot of alimony, if the husband had substantial income, but no property. A stupid rule of law.

Judges and lawyers have no respect for stupid law. They find ways to get around it, while always deferring to the principal of *stare decisis* (the idea that precedent, a previous decision, must control subsequent cases). It is often done through a legal fiction, using one valid concept to serve an entirely different function.

If the truth be told, lump sum alimony was invented to divide property when judges weren't allowed to. One day, some bright judge who knew that justice (but not the law) demanded that the wife be given some property, suddenly said, "I know, I'll call it alimony!" The judge probably fished around for a little while for names: sudden alimony, one payment alimony, instant alimony, and, ah, lump sum alimony. I doubt the judge thought that the label would fool the appellate court; it's unlikely that it did. The judges up there probably winked at each other and agreed that while it smelled and looked like a property division, it must be alimony because that is what the trial judge called it.

The reason the trial judge came up with lump sum alimony, the reason that the appellate court winked at the charade, and the reason its use spread and lasted for decades is that the trial judge did justice and equity where the established law gave him no way to do it. The need for this legal fiction ended, at least in Florida, in 1980 when the Florida Supreme Court issued the landmark case of *Canakaris v. Canakaris*. Relying upon a lower appellate court decision issued six years earlier, the Supreme Court established the principle of equitable distribution. Under equitable distribution, a court can treat all property acquired during the marriage as "marital assets" and distribute it between the parties according to their respective contributions to the marriage. It no longer matters how the title was held. It was a great decision and one that effectively eliminated the need for lump sum alimony.

But lump sum alimony did not die. It changed, adapted, if you will, and filled another previously unseen need in the law. The lump sum alimony that I discuss here is the modern version, the post-*Canakaris* form.

Installment Payments. Contrary to its name, lump sum alimony does not have to be paid in a lump. It can be made payable in installments, but unlike periodic alimony, it cannot be modified. Once the amount is set, that's exactly what the wife gets. (Sounds a bit like property division, doesn't it?)

Criteria for Lump Sum. We start with the same seven factors (eight if we count "any other factor necessary to do equity and justice") that apply to all alimony. (See list on page 69.) To support an award of lump sum, however, the judge has to find "justification" for lump sum payment. *Canakaris* recited the formula simply as need, ability, plus justification. Despite the questionable history of lump sum, some of the justifications that developed for its use seem compelling even in this cynical age: to end a hostile relationship (rather than prolong it with payments every week or month), to give the wife some security where the husband is sick or old, to meet a particular need the wife has for instant cash (such as pressing debts), and to counter the fact that the husband is a spendthrift and would not keep up his payments. For these and any other grounds that a reasonable man could have, alimony can be awarded in lump today. Because we are still always in a court of equity, the justifications can be as unlimited as circumstances and the imagination can provide.

Limitations. There are some constraints, however. First, the trial court cannot award lump sum when the parties' assets are limited and the husband has a demonstrable ability to make his payments, such as through disability or pension. He cannot award a nest egg amount, that is, an amount that is obviously intended to be invested so as to produce sufficient income for the recipient to live on.

Recognizing both the historical and modern rationale for lump sum alimony, one appellate court reversed a lump sum award where the wife had neither a need for support nor an entitlement under equitable distribution. Even a legal fiction can't be upheld just because the judge didn't like the husband.

Modification/Termination. Lump sum alimony is a vested right, that is, one that cannot be modified once awarded. Nor can it be terminated, even by the death of either party. Although a court has no inherent power to modify or terminate lump sum, it can do so if the parties agree in a settlement agreement. Generally, any agreement between the parties that is neither immoral nor unfair will be enforceable through the court, even if it conflicts with what the law would allow the judge to do in the absence of the agreement.

Source of Lump Sum Alimony. Lump sum alimony can be payable from either marital or nonmarital assets. There must be a special reason or great need to make it payable from nonmarital assets. This is the big advantage that lump sum alimony has over equitable distribution, which, as you will see in Chapter 8, can only be made with marital assets (assets acquired during the marriage).

One of the most common assets awarded as lump sum alimony is the marital home. It is available, usually needed by the wife, and justified by the need of the wife for continuity, if not for any other reason. As we have seen, the court cannot give the wife the house if it is the parties' only significant asset since this would strip the husband of all of his assets. Under those circumstances, the husband lacks the ability to provide alimony in that form. There is some authority, however, for exactly the opposite result: in one case, the husband was found to lack the liquid assets to pay permanent support and the trial court was upheld in giving the wife virtually all their assets. Conflicts like that always arise because of the peculiar facts of the cases which require different awards to achieve justice.

Combination Awards

Alimony can be awarded in any combination of permanent, rehabilitative, or lump sum. The award of one does not preclude the award of another or of the other two. So long as the overall award is equitable, there is no error in mixing them together.

The court has to be careful about retaining jurisdiction over alimony. The court has jurisdiction as long as any periodic award is payable. But the court does not retain jurisdiction by an award of lump sum, even if it is payable in installments, unless (1) the court expressly retains jurisdiction to award alimony in the future, or (2) the parties have stipulated in their agreement that the court will have continuing jurisdiction to award alimony in the future. Since the agreement is always incorporated into the Final Judgment, the stipulated jurisdiction becomes part of the judgment itself. The express retention of jurisdiction by the court to award alimony in the future is usually done when the wife is not disabled from supporting herself at the time of the divorce but, as a result of an existing progressive illness, will likely become disabled in the foreseeable future.

8

PROPERTY AND PROPERTY DIVISION

Property division has never been easy for the courts. In fact, until 1980 judges had no power to impose a property settlement on the parties; if the house was in the husband's name, the judge could (theoretically) do nothing for the wife. If property was in joint names, the judge could, if asked, partition it (that is, have it sold and divide the proceeds). For untitled property, such as the pots and pans, it was first come, first served.

Considering that divorce cases are heard in a court of equity, this was not a good state of affairs. Judges did what they could. For example, some judicial genius invented "lump sum alimony." Using that fictional form of "alimony," the judge could award one party the house without technically violating the law against making a property division.

Sure, it was a fraud, but it did effect a certain amount of justice and equity. The problem was that some judges never got the knack for using lump sum alimony to divide property. As a result, the chances for getting a fair and reasonable property division depended very much on the particular judge hearing the case.

Things dramatically improved in 1980 when our Supreme Court "recognized" (that's a respectful euphemism for "judicially legislated") the concept of *equitable distribution*.

Equitable Distribution

Under the concept of equitable distribution, record title to the property no longer matters. If the property was acquired during the marriage from funds or efforts related to the marriage, the property is a "marital asset" and could be divided between the parties according to their contributions to the marriage. A wonderful and fair idea but, as you will see, full of hidden trap doors and secret passages that don't appear at first glance.

> *Equitable distribution* is the legal concept of dividing property accumulated during the marriage according to the contributions of the parties rather than who holds title (record title).
>
> *Judicial legislation* is law established by the courts rather than the legislature. Under United States and Florida law, the legislature is empowered to make the law and the courts can only interpret or explain that law. In fact, more important law seems to be made in the courts than in the legislature.

Equitable distribution is similar to the concept of *community property*, such as California has. Under community property, all property accumulated during the marriage is owned equally by the parties.

Under equitable distribution, the property must be divided equitably, not necessarily equally. The law does require the court to begin with the premise that the distribution should be equal unless there is a justification for an unequal split based upon the relevant considerations.

"Contributions to the marriage" is one of the considerations. This factor is of almost no importance now. The judges start with the presumption of an equal division and almost never deviate from it. It would take extreme circumstances to bring this factor into play.

Equitable distribution has been a major revolution in making divorces more fair. It is far better than the previous fiction of lump sum alimony. Until 1980, one domineering party, usually the husband, could keep all property, including bank accounts, in his sole name. The court could do nothing, except to use lump sum alimony, to equalize finances. Equitable distribution has given the courts the tool to thwart that practice.

On the other hand, equitable distribution has also effectively preserved nonmarital assets. "Nonmarital assets" are assets that are clearly unrelated to the marriage, such as property owned before the marriage, gifts from family or friends, or inheritances. Continuing the legal developments of the mid-seventies, equitable distribution returns those assets, so long as they were still identifiable, to the person who brought them into the marriage. (One exception: If the court wants to give the wife more than is in the marital-asset pot, it can always go back to that old fiction, lump sum alimony, and give the wife whatever he or she thinks is appropriate, even from nonmarital assets.)

In 1988, the Florida legislature followed the lead of the courts and adopted an equitable distribution statute that was to solve all the problems. It didn't do that, but it did help clarify things.

Under the statute, the basic idea has not changed: both parties share equitably in the assets accumulated during the marriage; nonmarital assets and liabilities are set apart and left with the party bringing them in. Now, however, the ideas are all brought together and articulated in a consistent way.

Factors to Consider. The statute does several things. First, it defines what factors the court should consider in distributing the marital assets and liabilities. While the law doesn't limit the court to the listed factors, it does direct the court to specifically consider the following:
  · the contribution to the marriage by each spouse, including contributions to the care and education of the children and services as homemaker;
  · the economic circumstances of the parties;
  · the duration of the marriage;
  · any interruption of the personal careers or educational opportunities of either party;
  · the contributions of one spouse to the career or education of the other,
  · the desirability of retaining any asset, including an interest in a business, corporation, or professional practice, intact and free from any claim or interference by the other party;
  · the contribution of each spouse to the marital, and nonmarital, income and marital debts, both positively and negatively;
  · the desirability of retaining the marital home as a residence for any dependent child of the marriage, or any other party, when it would be equitable to do so, it is in the best interest of the child or that party, and it is financially feasible for the parties to maintain the residence until the child is emancipated or until exclusive possession is otherwise terminated by a court of competent jurisdiction;
  · the intentional dissipation, waste, depletion, or destruction of marital assets after the filing of the petition or within two years prior to the filing of the petition;
  · any other factor necessary to do equity and justice between the parties.

Marital Assets. The equitable distribution law also defines what marital assets and liabilities are:

· assets acquired and liabilities incurred during the marriage, individually by either spouse or jointly by the both of them;
· the enhanced or appreciated value of nonmarital assets if the increased value results from efforts during the marriage or the expenditure of marital funds or assets;
· interspousal gifts during the marriage;
· all retirement, pension, profit-sharing, annuity, deferred compensation, and insurance plans accrued during the marriage, whether they are vested or not;
·real property held by the entireties, regardless of when it was acquired.

As you see, all real estate held in joint names as tenants by the entireties (that is, held in some form that references the marital relationship, such as "John Doe and Mary Doe, Husband and Wife") is presumed to be a marital asset, regardless of whether the property was acquired during the marriage. The parties are still free to try to prove a special equity in the real property; the proof must be, however, beyond a reasonable doubt, a very heavy burden. (See the discussion of special equity later in this chapter.)

Nonmarital Assets. Nonmarital assets are the assets that belong to one or the other of the parties and that will not be divided between them in making

Considerations in making equitable distribution:

· contributions to marriage
· financial circumstances
· duration of marriage
· lost opportunities
· contributions to other's career or education
· need to keep certain assets intact
· desirability of keeping children in house
· intentional dissipation of marital assets
· contributions to assets and debts

Marital assets are:

· all assets and liability acquired during marriage
· enhanced value of nonmarital assets resulting from marital efforts
· interspousal gifts
· pensions, etc., accrued during marriage
· real estate held by the entireties

A *special equity* is an ownership interest in property titled in the other spouse's name.

Nonmarital assets are assets that are not part of the property division between the parties. They include:

· assets and debts predating the marriage
· assets acquired in exchange for preowned assets
· gifts or inheritances from outside marriage
· income from non-marital assets
· assets and debts that the parties agree are nonmarital

the property division. Nonmarital assets are:

· assets and debts existing before the marriage and anything acquired/incurred in exchange for those assets or debts;

· assets received by one spouse from gifts or inheritances from outside the marriage;

· income received from nonmarital assets unless the parties treated it as marital income;

· assets or debts that the parties agreed in writing would not be treated as being marital;

· liabilities incurred by forgery by one spouse or the unauthorized signing by one spouse of the other's name.

Unless the judge thinks another date is more just and equitable, property is classified as marital or nonmarital by its status on the earliest of the following dates: the parties' signing of a separation agreement, the filing of a divorce action, or any other date the parties agree upon in a separation agreement. The valuation date is the date the judge thinks is fair under the circumstances. The usual dates are the dates of separation, filing of the action, and trial date.

All property acquired by either party during the marriage is presumed to be marital but can be shown to be nonmarital by the greater weight of the evidence.

The equitable distribution law brings us closer to being a community property state, but Florida property still must be divided by the judge and not by a mechanical rule that ignores the parties' contributions.

Property vs. Alimony. The judge must decide on the distribution of the property before considering alimony. This allows the judge to consider each party's post-marriage assets in determining how much, if any, alimony is appropriate.

The judge can order that the property division be evened out by the payment of money in one lump sum or in payments. For example, if the major assets of the marriage are a store (worth $250,000) and the marital home (worth $100,000), it would be easier to give one spouse the store and order him or her to pay the other spouse $75,000 than to leave them joint owners of both or to order both the store and the house sold.

Once the judge divides the property, no deeds or transfers are required. If the Final Judgment contains adequate descriptions (legal descriptions, VINs, etc.) it has the effect, when recorded, of a deed (on real property) and a power of attorney (for cars, boats, etc.). Most attorneys will still require the usual conveyances signed so that the public record and their client's titles are clean.

The judge can rule on and distribute any property in the state of Florida even if one of the parties lives outside the state and doesn't participate in the case. Likewise, property outside the state can be awarded to one party or the other (but not partitioned) if both parties participate in the case or have been properly served.

Military Retirement Benefits. Military retirement and retainer pay are both marital assets. If the holder is a ten-year military veteran and the marriage lasted at least ten years, the court can order that the other spouse receive direct disbursement from the federal government.

The Future of Property Division. As with all laws, the equitable distribution statute is not the final word. Rather, it is like a blank page with the words "Chapter One" at the top. Over the years, the seemingly plain words of the law will be interpreted, explained, and construed. Lawyers will expand the language until it covers ideas and approaches that the legislature never dreamed of.

Complexity is inherent in any situation where so many equities must be considered. Difficult property decisions will always be part of a fair divorce system. When minor children are involved, for example, the judge must still decide if it is fairer to allow the custodial parent to stay in the house or to allow both parties to immediately receive their interests by selling it.

Valuations of certain assets will remain difficult. A store producing a certain annual income is pretty easy to value. A professional producing the same income may not be. The reason is that a practice usually depends exclusively on the professional himself. Another example of the professional practice problem is that some practices are salable and some are not. A dental practice can be sold and its market value can be determined on very objective standards but medical practices seem to be particularly difficult to sell. For property division purposes, do you assign different values to the two practices even though they may be producing the same income?

Other types of property, such as real property, pensions (except State pensions), and furniture, are subject to relatively easy valuation.

Special Equity

The Supreme Court of Florida caused some confusion in the case establishing equitable distribution. It used the term "special equity" to refer to the interest of a nontitled spouse in marital assets. This was correct since the court was establishing a new circumstance under which one party would have a property interest in property titled in the other's name. However, the use of the term creates problems because a body of law has been developed about the term "special equity" that has nothing to do with equitable distribution. Florida lawyers have, by and large, not used "special equity" when talking about equitable distribution. I will, therefore, use the term only to mean the traditional concept of special equity. Even though special equities are very rare today, let me discuss some of the concepts that apply in those rare instances when it applies.

A "special equity" is an interest that one spouse has in the property titled in another's name as a result of contributions from sources clearly unrelated to the marriage, or as a result of extraordinary contributions to acquiring or enhancing such property beyond the ordinary marital duties. That's a mouthful but not a difficult concept.

Suppose, for example, that you came into the marriage with $100,000. When you bought some gold after marrying, your good-for-nothing spouse (whom you then loved) told you to have the gold held by your broker in joint names. Now that you are about to divorce the reprobate, your spouse wants half of the gold. Is he or she entitled to it?

Unfortunately, the answer is maybe. The law presumes that jointly titled property is marital property and you have the burden of proving that no gift was intended. Of course, you have the initial burden of proving that you paid for the gold with non-marital funds; that part should be easy but it is always difficult to prove a negative and you may find it impossible to prove no gift was intended.

Now suppose that you didn't buy gold. Instead, you bought stocks and bonds and traded them over the years. If you cannot clearly trace your preexisting money through the exchanges and convince the judge, beyond a reasonable doubt, that the same $100,000 (or funds directly resulting from the $100,000) still exists, you have no special equity. Even if you met that burden, the enhanced value of the stocks and bonds would be marital since they resulted from your trading efforts during the marriage. Only passive appreciation would be considered non-marital.

Now suppose that your spouse brought in $10,000 and put it into joint names but made it clear that she did not intend to make a gift of it. The money remains intact. Suppose further that you put your $100,000 into a joint bank account and used the money for living expenses, and the money was frittered away over the years. Your spouse has a very good chance of getting a special equity for that $10,000. You have almost none for your money. Your spouse's funds can still be identified; yours cannot.

A special equity can also be created by extraordinary efforts exceeding normal marital duties. As an example, a husband who builds all or part of the marital home by hand may be granted a special equity in the property. Do husbands ever really build a house by hand? Yes, they do. Do they get their special equity in that house? Usually not. In practice, a special equity will only be recognized for clearly demonstrated cash (or its equivalent) or property contributions. Exceptions are rare.

Appreciated Special Equity. Your special equity will grow along with any passive appreciation in the asset. For example, if the gold cost you $100,000 but is now worth $135,000, you are entitled to the full amount. This was true under the case decisions and it is true under the new equitable distribution statute.

For the rest of this discussion, keep in mind that real property held by the entireties is presumed to be marital and you would only be entitled to a special equity if you could prove that no gift was intended, such as by a notation on the deed that your initial contribution was not to be considered a gift.

When the special equity covers only part of the property, the determination of the amount of the special equity's appreciation is not always easy. Your lawyer will refer to the calculation as a Landay calculation, referring to the case that established how to handle appreciation. Let's take the most common example: You invest your nonmarital $10,000 into the marital home, just bought for $100,000.

The rest of the house is mortgaged for $90,000; your spouse contributes nothing originally. Your entitlement in the beginning is clearly 10% (really a special equity of 5% in your spouse's share).

It is easiest to talk in terms of your receiving, upon divorce, the first 10% and splitting the rest, giving you 55%, (100 minus 10 = 90; 90/2 = 45; 45 + 10 = 55). The calculation is exactly the same whether the property appreciates or depreciates but, when depreciation occurs, Landay can give strange, and seemingly unfair, results.

Let's look at some examples of what happens, first when there is appreciation and then when there's a loss. Let's assume, for the appreciation side, that the house is ultimately worth $250,000 and the mortgage has been reduced through payments during the marriage to $50,000. You get the first 10% off the top and split the rest, giving you $25,000 plus half of the rest of the net equity (half of $175,000 or $87,500). You would end up with $112,500 and your spouse with $87,500. Your $10,000 has grown along with the appreciation of the house.

That's fair and easy. However, when there's a loss you could end up with less than you started with. Suppose again that the mortgage has been reduced to $50,000. However, instead of appreciating, the house has lost value so that the gross proceeds are only $90,000. You are entitled to 10% off the top, or $9,000, and half of the balance of the equity ($31,000), or $15,500. This gives you a total of $24,500. Your spouse, who made no initial contribution, realizes $15,500. After deducting your initial contribution, you realize only $14,500!

It doesn't seem fair. The reason it works that way is that your spouse shares in neither the appreciation nor the depreciation of your nonmarital $10,000; when your $10,000 shrinks to 90%, along with the house depreciation, that's your loss and not your spouse's.

Remember that a special equity must be derived from assets that are clearly unrelated to the marriage. Neither of you can claim a special equity for property purchased with salary earned during the marriage. The traditional macho argument, that it was bought with "my money—I went out and earned it," carries no weight with the courts.

Professional Degrees

Some states include the value of a party's professional degree in making equitable distribution. If one spouse put the other through medical school, a court in those states might reward this by giving that party a percentage of the net income of the practice for life, not as alimony but as a property distribution.

The Florida Supreme Court has rejected that position, primarily on the ground that the value of the contribution to the degree is speculative. The justices found themselves unable to distinguish how much of the income results from the education and how much from the efforts after medical school, particularly the efforts after the divorce occurs. Suppose, for example, the divorce occurred very shortly after the doctor became licensed. Certainly, almost all of the doctor's income at that point could be attributed to education. The same could not be said for the doctor's income ten years down the line; although the education remains an essential element, the efforts and professional reputation the doctor developed over those ten years would be a considerable factor also. Faced with an impossible allocation task, the Florida Supreme Court says that you don't even consider the education. A degree has, in effect, no value in a Florida equitable distribution.

Lump Sum Alimony

Lump sum alimony is now, and always has been, a form of property division. It arose as a legal fiction when courts couldn't impose property divisions on divorcing parties. Now that they can, it should disappear, and it has for all I can see. I do not recall the last time I saw a lump sum alimony award.

Although lump sum alimony is discussed in detail in Chapter 7, let me mention it here briefly. Regardless of the rationale given in any particular case, a lump sum award is almost always a property division. It has all the attributes of a property division: it is final and unmodifiable; it must be paid even if either party dies before payment; it is not deductible by the payer for income tax purposes (nor includable by the recipient); its enforceability is not dependent upon ability to pay (although to award it, the court must find ability to pay it, as well as a "special need" for the lump sum form); and it can be discharged in bankruptcy.

Suffice it to say that lump sum alimony is alimony in name only. Think of it as part of the property division in your case.

Third-Party Creditors

We know that the court can assign the debts of the marriage as part of an equitable distribution. Let's look at one problem related to the assignment of marital debts. Assume that your spouse is ordered to pay all the credit card bills even though both of your names were on all of the cards.

You may think you're free of worry about those bills — until the bank calls you and demands payment. When you tell them about the judgment, they don't want to hear it. How dare they! They dare, and they're right.

Since the bank was not part of the divorce action, they are not bound by its rulings. Between you and the bank, you are just as liable for the payments as your spouse. If your spouse fails to pay, the bank is going to try to get its money from whomever it can. If you have to pay any of it, however, you have the right to sue your ex-spouse and get a judgment.

What can you do? Not much. You can write to all the credit card issuers and notify them of the divorce. Ask them to relieve you in writing of any obligation for the debt. That probably won't work with most banks. With a few banks, however, you can get released if your spouse signs a statement that he or she will be exclusively liable for the outstanding amount.

If a bank refuses to release you, you can demand that the account be canceled. You must notify the issuer in writing that you will be liable for no further charges on the card. That should be effective to limit your liability to the outstanding amount at the time of your notice. Just to be sure, send the notice by certified mail and request a return receipt. Do the same, of course, with department store credit cards.

The situation is much the same for the house mortgage. If one party gets the house, the mortgage usually goes with it. That doesn't release the other party from possible liability if the mortgage goes into default.

Again, most banks will not release the other party from the mortgage. The exposure is not the problem in the case of the mortgage; the house usually has more than enough equity to cover the outstanding mortgage if a foreclosure occurs. Your problem is the information that appears at the credit bureau.

First, a foreclosure would be filed against both parties and would damage both of them for years to come. That is a potential problem. Another is that the credit bureau will continue to show the outstanding mortgage on both spouses' records. In many cases, the outstanding mortgage will prevent the "nonliable" spouse from getting a mortgage on another house. Sometimes, however, a subsequent lender will approve a loan after reviewing the judgment.

The problem with continuing credit liability results from the fact that the creditor was not a party in the divorce and, therefore, not bound by the Judgment. There may be a way around the problem: join the creditor as a defendant in the case. I have never seen it tried (nor, of course, have I tried it), but there seems to be no reason why the creditor could not be joined. I have seen banks joined in partition actions without any objection.

The bank or credit card company could be heard on the issue of liability for the debt. The court could not, of course, release you simply because you want your spouse to pay; there would have to be a legal basis for assigning exclusive liability to your spouse, such as the fact that only he ever used the credit card. There may be traps in the idea; for example, it is possible that joining such a creditor could make you and your spouse liable to the bank or credit card company for the attorney's fees under the mortgage or credit card contract.

Nonetheless, I would not be surprised in the slightest to see this idea tried.

Line of Credit. A line of credit in your name or an equity line of credit on your property is like a blank check. You must take steps to limit your exposure for more debt by cutting them off or limiting access to them once a divorce starts.

Effect of Death during Action

If either party were to die during the divorce, that is, before the final judgment was entered, the divorce action would stop and the estate would be distributed as if the parties had never filed for divorce. If a settlement agreement had been signed, its terms are probably effective even though no divorce occurred; a provision for property division in it would be enforceable.

A Final Judgment of Divorce nullifies all bequests in both parties' wills to the ex-spouse. The Judgment also removes the ex-spouse from serving as personal representative under a will made during the marriage. Pending the action, however, the entire will remains in effect. For that reason, when the action is filed, you might want to consider making a new will, just in case. You can't totally cut out your spouse since he or she can still elect to take a spouse's (or elective) share if you were to die during the divorce. Since that's basically about 30%, that's still better than your spouse getting your whole estate.

Frankly, however, a new will during a divorce makes little difference in most cases. Most married people own most of their property as tenants by the entireties. The property could remain titled in that way until a divorce judgment ends that joint ownership. If you died during the divorce, all property owned as tenants by the entireties would automatically go to your spouse. There's nothing you can do about that. Except not die. I recommend that course of action.

Even with equitable distribution, we are not there yet. Property divisions are still not always fair in Florida. But we're moving in the right direction. Florida is fairer than it used to be; and, tomorrow, it will be fairer than it is today.

9

ENFORCEMENT

What you will learn in this chapter:

- why the judge needs your help to make the judgment work
- why the Final Judgment is rarely the end of your case
- why support is referred to as the "first mortgage" on income
- why payment through the court registry eliminates liars' contests
- how often a nonpaying spouse goes to jail
- how and why civil contempt proceedings sometimes become criminal contempt
- why a judge will sometimes refuse to help you in enforcing a judgment
- why you shouldn't wait too long to enforce support
- what remedies exit for not allowing visitation
- how often women go to jail for refusing visitation
- how you can get the Department of Revenue to enforce your child support for free
- how you can enforce a foreign decree

A judgment is merely words on paper. Those words only have force if the obligated party believes that a court will enforce them. The real power of the court is as much in enforcing judgments as making them.

You are, however, the essential partner of the court in exercising that power. With only rare exceptions, you must ask the court's help before it can enforce its rulings.

A judgment could provide for custody, child support, alimony, and property division. Every one of them can be enforced. Using a hypothetical situation, let's look at each one and see what can be done.

Assume that you are a woman with two children and the judge gave you primary residential care of them. Based on the state guidelines, the judge ruled that your ex-husband has to pay you $700 per week as child support. The judge also awarded "guideline" visitation and ordered your husband to sign over the new car to you. The judge split the house down the middle but gave you exclusive use until your youngest child, now 14, turns 18. Finally, you were granted rehabilitative alimony of $2,000 per week for one year.

The Final Judgment is signed and you hug your attorney, saying good-bye for the last time. You're very pleased knowing that your life will be comfortable and happy from now on.

Sorry, you're in for a big disappointment. Your husband, George, is angry about the judgment and he is going to violate every single ruling. Let's see what can be done about it.

Child Support

Child support can be enforced in several ways. The most common methods are through motions for civil contempt, criminal contempt, and judgment. Let's look at each of these methods.

Civil Contempt. Your attorney wanted to give you some protection on the child support; he told you that the judge would order an income deduction from George's paycheck and the payments would be sent to you by the Florida Disbursement Unit (FDU). However, George said that he wanted to make the payments directly to you; you agreed with George and told the judge that payments through the FDU weren't necessary. (Payment through the FDU is discussed in more detail in Chapter 6.)

You were sure that payment through the FDU wasn't needed and, God forbid, you didn't want his boss involved in your child support through income deductions. Reluctantly, your attorney and the judge gave in, and you are to receive your payments directly from George. Nonetheless, the judge entered an Income Deduction Order but provided that it would not take effect right away. (The judge can only delay its effect if he/she finds good cause for doing so and explains why in the judgment.)

And receive you do. For the first week. He paid you, in cash, $700 the first week, $400 the second, and, when you called him after he missed the third payment, he angrily told you that he had money problems. He had remarried and his new wife was sick. You have a problem.

The solution is to make it George's problem. First, you call your attorney and tell him what's going on. He will probably send a demand letter to George (or write your ex's attorney) telling him of the need to comply strictly with the judgment. If you don't call your attorney at that point, your problem will get worse and your ability to enforce the support may actually decline.

Let's assume that George still doesn't pay. He cries to you that he'll pay when he can. Not good enough. The law is that any support owed to you (whether child support or alimony) is the "first mortgage" on his income. No other bill comes ahead of you, and certainly not his new wife's illness. If you're smart, you instruct your attorney to go back to court.

Your attorney can seek contempt or judgment, or both, and, of course, the immediate application of the already existing income deduction order. And he or she can seek attorney's fees from your ex for these efforts. Your attorney files a motion for contempt, which will advise the court and George of five things: the remedies you seek, the default in payment you say occurred, the name of the judge who will hear the motion, and the time and place of the hearing. A typical motion for contempt will usually simply state:

> YOU ARE HEREBY NOTIFIED THAT the Wife will apply to The Honorable **William Arthur** on **January 22nd, 2008** at **10:00 a. m.** in Courtroom 7 of the **Elegant County Courthouse**, 722 Ritz Boulevard, **Posh, Florida**, for an order adjudging **George Dephition**, the **Husband**, in indirect civil contempt of the Court for violation of the *Final Judgment of Dissolution of Marriage* entered by this Court on October 10th, 2007 by failing to pay the full child support payments due on November 1st, 2007 and all payments thereafter. **30 Minutes** have been reserved.
>
> At said hearing, the undersigned will seek attorney's fees and costs and entry of a judgment for the arrearage.

The form and the procedure are what all legal procedures should be: efficient. The only drawback, and it is a small one, is that, in calling up the hearing quickly (and most of us do it as quickly as possible), your attorney won't have a chance to take George's deposition to find out his defenses, if any. If you and your attorney act quickly, that won't be much of a problem. If, however, you waited for six months, you might be surprised to find George telling the judge that he lost his job and your attorney would not have enough information to effectively cross-examine him about how and why he lost his job. For all you know, George quit his job two weeks earlier just for spite.

Since the court did not make the Income Deduction Notice effective immediately, your attorney will also serve a notice of delinquency once George is at least one month in arrears. George will have 15 days after receiving the notice to contest the income deduction order; he can only contest on the following grounds: error in the amount payable or in the amount of the arrearage, or mistaken identity. If he does contest, a hearing must be set within 20 days and the court must rule within 10 days after the hearing. Contests and hearings are very rare in this area.

If you have acted quickly, the amount of unpaid support is relatively minor and you show up at the hearing ready to win big. You come in with a big advantage: the presumption that George is capable of paying the support and the purge amount the court may set. Because of that, all you need to do is testify that he hasn't paid since October and that you have incurred attorney's fees in this proceeding. Unless a valid defense is made, your testimony is sufficient to (1) find George in willful contempt since he (under the presumption created by the judgment) has the present ability to pay, (2) sentence him to jail until he brings himself current or pays a different purge amount set by the court, (3) enter judgment for a reasonable attorney's fee and (4) enter judgment for the amount of the arrearage.

Your agreement to allow direct payments has already hurt you; the payments could have been deducted from George's paycheck. It's about to get worse.

Now George testifies that he did pay you; he paid you in cash. In fact, he says that he gave you some extra!

As you can see, the judge is presented with a liars' contest. Because the payments did not go through the FDU, there is no proof for either side. That is the big advantage of using the FDU: it keeps a record that is accurate and admissible in court as prima facie (that is, sufficient without any other evidence to prove your case) evidence of the status of payments.

Fortunately, the judge doesn't believe George and, after taking testimony, is about to act. What options are open in this case?

First, let's restrict ourselves to the contempt citation. Contempt is a frightening thing, to George anyway. Theoretically, the judge could send George to jail immediately upon an order of contempt stating that the sheriff shall keep him in jail for up to 30 days subject to releasing him if he pays the full arrearage.

Judges rarely do that. Instead, they will usually grant a "purge period," that is, a period (usually 10 days) in which George can pay the arrearage and avoid going to jail. If he doesn't pay during that period George will go to jail (but only after another hearing). Some judges will enter an order that he is in contempt; some will withhold the actual contempt citation until the purge period passes. With those judges, George would have no record of contempt if he paid up.

If George does go to jail, he can get released by paying the amount found by the judge to be owed. For this reason, George is said to have the "key to the jail cell." He can open the door simply by paying. The judge must set a purge amount that is within George's ability. Because he came into court with a presumption that he could, he would have to prove that he cannot pay the purge.

Thirty days is a typical contempt sentence. At the end of the 30 days, the sheriff is sometimes ordered to bring George back before the judge to give George another chance to comply. If George refused, the judge could sentence him immediately to another 30 days, etc. Of course, he can obtain his release during any of these periods by paying up.

This is theory. What is the reality of jailing for contempt? Few instances, very few, and far between. Some judges are tougher than others, but few judges (thank goodness) like to send people to jail. Of course, another reason for so few jailings is that most men will use the purge period to save themselves.

In many cases, to avoid sending someone to jail, the judge will order that George make up the arrearage by paying extra money for several weeks or months until the full amount is current. The rule of thumb is that George would pay an additional 20% of his ongoing obligation against his arrearage. This is the preferred ruling of some magistrates, but not of many lawyers.

Support Due After Majority. As we will see, child support can continue to be paid for a child over 18 if he or she has not graduated from high school but can reasonably be expected to graduate by 19. That obligation is enforceable by contempt. Any other support for the child, such as college tuition, is considered a contractual obligation, not true child support, and cannot be enforced by contempt. Either the child or the recipient parent can seek a judgment if it is not paid.

Criminal Contempt. Maybe your case takes another turn. Instead of claiming that he made cash payments, we find that, when George comes into court, he has no lawyer, just a big grin on his face. One of his friends confided in him that the judge could only hold him in contempt if he had the present ability to pay the arrearage. Thinking he's got you, George doesn't tell the judge about his "sick" wife; instead, he shakes his head "sadly" and tells the judge that he just doesn't have any income. He quit his job because it was too hard. And he doesn't have any money in the bank and his car is pledged to the hilt.

"Sorry, Judge, but I can't pay her."

Sorry, George, that won't work. In addition to ordering George to sell his car (or other property) to pay the arrearage, the judge can convert the proceeding to one for criminal contempt. When George convinced the judge that he did not have the present ability to comply, the judge, as George had heard, lost the power to put George in jail until he paid. As you can see, without the present ability to pay, George didn't have the "key to his jail cell." Therefore, no civil contempt.

To change the proceeding from civil contempt, the judge will read George his rights, including his right to have counsel appointed in his behalf. The judge will adjourn the hearing until a later specific date to allow George to prepare a defense. To criminal contempt. This turn will not make George happy.

To convict George of criminal contempt at the later hearing, the judge must find, beyond a reasonable doubt, that George had the ability to pay the child support and that he intentionally divested himself of that ability. George cannot be compelled to testify at this hearing; just like any criminal defendant, he can invoke the Fifth Amendment against self-incrimination. However, I can think of no reason why his statements at the civil contempt hearing could not be used against him in this proceeding.

Laches is the equitable equivalent of the statute of limitations. If a party has a right to bring an action or to otherwise enforce a right, knows that he or she can enforce it, and doesn't do so, that right can be lost if the delay results in injury to the other party. In such a case, the court can dismiss the action without the right to refile it on the grounds of *laches.*

If George is convicted, his sentence will be for a specific period. He will be sentenced to 30 days (usually), no purge period, no "keys to the jail cell."

Judgment. In addition to contempt, or in the alternative, if George really doesn't have the ability to pay through no fault of his own, the judge can enter a judgment for the arrearage.

A judgment for arrearage is exactly the same as any other judgment. It goes in the public record. It can be docketed with the sheriff. And execution can be obtained to have the sheriff seize and sell any of George's property to pay your judgment.

The Option of Doing Nothing. There is one other option open to the judge: to do nothing. The judge cannot, upon finding that any child support is unpaid, excuse the arrearage. But he or she can, if the equities are extreme, refuse to take any action to enforce the support.

Judges rarely do nothing. Under certain circumstances, however, it may be unfair to do anything else. For example, suppose George had a serious illness, he lost his job because of it, and he obviously needed all of his meager savings just to survive. And suppose, also, that you have remarried a wealthy man.

Under those circumstances, if you were so callous as to try to enforce the child support, the judge could turn a deaf ear and enter an order to the effect that, although the court found arrearage, no action would be taken for the present.

Alimony

There is no real difference between enforcing alimony and enforcing child support. Everything I said about child support applies to alimony; even the motion for contempt would read much the same. Since there is nothing new to add to that side of the case, let's look at the other side and see what other defenses George could raise. Remember that every defense available for alimony is equally available for child support.

George might assert that you were guilty of "laches." To be guilty of laches, you must have sat on your right to enforce the support (i.e., done nothing) during a time when you knew you had the right to compel compliance and the delay caused him some injury.

For example, suppose you didn't enforce the alimony for four years (maybe because you remarried the previously mentioned wealthy man), and, as a result, George reasonably believed that you no longer wanted him to pay. In reliance upon the facts that you helped create, George invested all of his money and his future salary into a modest home for his new family.

Sure, the support is the "first mortgage" on his income and he may have a hard time getting the support reduced for the future, but George has an outside chance of the court finding that (now here's the tricky part), although there is an arrearage (which, remember, the court cannot excuse), it would be inequitable to enforce it. The arrearage would technically continue to exist but, unlike the previous discussion where the judge did nothing, the judge, because of laches, could rule that the arrearage can never be enforced.

Another defense would be payment, as George asserted in our first scenario. If the judge believed that George did make his payments in cash, he would, of course, win the hearing. But the defense of payment can be more complex. Suppose, for example, you asked George to do some repairs on your car instead of paying you. That, if proven, might be considered payment that would satisfy some or all of the alleged arrearage. Under rare circumstances, any money spent on you (or, for child support, the children) might be considered as payment. In most cases, indirect or non-cash contributions are not considered to be support payments.

There are some minor and very rare defenses, such as a lack of willful non-compliance. If George were hospitalized and was absolutely unable to write the checks (or to make arrangements to have them written) as a result, that would be a defense to the contempt charge.

More commonly, George is likely to come in and allege that you and he privately agreed that you didn't have to pay. This is a difficult one for the courts. Usually, there is some grain of truth to the argument, at least enough to make you partially at fault. Technically, the order that George pay you still stands despite any such side agreement, but the judge could find that your conduct prevented (estopped) you from enforcing the money.

Formerly, you lost the right to enforce support by contempt (but not by judgment) at the end of the support period. For example, if George owed you $8,000 in alimony when your year of rehabilitative alimony ended, you could not have him held in contempt for that money if you didn't file your motion for contempt before the year ended. Likewise, you could not enforce child support arrearage after your last child has reached majority. Now, however, you have the right to use contempt to enforce child support after your last child reaches majority; it would seem that alimony should remain enforceable by contempt after it has expired.

Custody and Visitation

Now let's assume that George is accusing you of not being a good girl either. He might do so by filing his own motion for contempt in response to your motion or he might have filed on his own. It really doesn't matter since the two are unrelated. George cannot say that he didn't pay because you weren't allowing him contact with the kids; and you can't interfere with visitation because he isn't paying.

The issue on George's motion is, of course, your interference with George's right to visit with the children. You could be doing it in several ways: by denying contact on his days, poisoning the children's minds against him, always turning them over to him late, always needing to change his visitation days, etc.

Let me tell you what George can do, and it isn't much. If the judge finds at the contempt hearing that you did interfere with George's contact, there is little that the judge can do to help him. Let's look at the choices, none of which are exclusive to the others:

First, the judge could give you a very stern lecture, possibly even telling you that continued interference could lead to a change of custody. (In fact, the judge cannot change custody solely for that reason; he or she would have to find for other reasons that the best interests of the children required the change.)

Second, the judge could give George extra visitation to make up for the time lost through your interference. This is not done as often as you think; it probably should be done more.

Third, the judge could impose rigid visitation that you must observe without exception and without excuse. This could later be the foundation for a criminal contempt citation.

Finally, the judge could convert these proceedings into criminal contempt proceedings and go through the same procedures that I mentioned above. To do anything effective, the judge would have to go to criminal contempt because there is no equivalent in criminal contempt to the "keys to the jail cell." There is nothing you could do to obtain your release except in the highly unusually circumstance where you have hidden the children from George and refused to tell him or the judge where they were. Civil contempt coerces future action; criminal contempt punishes past conduct.

You might guess that the jailing of a woman for criminal contempt as a result of visitation matters is even rarer than men going to jail over support. And you're right.

Enforcement of custody is sometimes needed when a father simply refuses to return a child after visitation. This doesn't occur often because there is rarely even a color of an argument that the father could make. He would be seriously jeopardizing future contact.

He might escape the extreme wrath of the court if he were to allege danger to the children. The remedy, under such danger, is not to simply withhold the return of the children, but rather to file to modify custody and seek emergency intervention to protect the children pending the action.

There is no law that I know of in Florida that would force George to see the children. Consider if George refused to exercise his visitation and you believed that it was hurting the children; could you ask the court to order George to visit? You could ask, but I think the judge would simply shrug. Even though the children clearly need their father's presence in their lives, it isn't practical to make him see the children if he doesn't want to.

Florida law does, however, allow the court to increase the child support payable by a nonvisiting father. George's failure to take the children would certainly increase your expenses; meals alone would be increased by almost 40%. The increased child support is even made retroactive to the date when the father first stopped seeing the kids.

Fines. There is one remedy for contempt that judges almost never use. They can fine the guilty party.

Judges are understandably reluctant to send people to jail; the jails are too crowded already, you can't pay support if you are in jail or lose your job, and these people aren't really criminals, etc. All the usual explanations.

Maybe attorneys don't ask for fines. Maybe there is rarely enough money anyway. Maybe . . . who knows, but fines are a tool available for either civil or criminal contempt that is rarely used.

Property

Generally, property matters are not enforceable by contempt. However, if the court ordered a specific action by George, he could be held in contempt for failure to carry that out.

Until recently, for example, if George refused to execute a power of attorney to convey the car to you, the judge could hold him in civil contempt and jail him until he complied. In fact, rather than jail George, the judge would have just ordered that title be transferred by the Department of Motor Vehicles and it would issue a new title on such an order. Now, even that isn't necessary since the judge's award of the car to you constitutes an order that title is to be transferred into your name. For this reason, it is important that the Final Judgment contain all legal descriptions and vehicle identification numbers.

Suppose, however, George had possession of the Oriental rug given you by your great aunt. If he failed to return that upon a direct order to do so, George could face a contempt citation for his action.

Garnishment is a procedure for seizing a debt owed by a third party to the paying party before the money gets to the paying party. Although we don't usually think of them as a debt, wages are the most commonly garnished debt.

The court can use *sequestration* to take control of some or all of the paying party's property to assure that it is not removed from the state. There doesn't have to be any unpaid support for *sequestration,* only evidence that the paying spouse has threatened not to make his or her payments and intends to remove property from the state to avoid the court's jurisdiction over it.

Attachment is similar to *sequestration* in that the court authorizes the sheriff to go out and take control of the paying party's property. However, the court can **attach** that property only if there is unpaid support.

Other Enforcement Methods

There are some other means for enforcement of alimony and child support that, while less important, need to be discussed.

Garnishment. Garnishment is still available to enforce child support or alimony. The law has always allowed an ongoing garnishment for this purpose. For all practical purposes, however, the income deduction order is nothing more than an ongoing wage garnishment order and has practically replaced the garnishment procedure.

Sequestration. Sequestration of assets is still available. If there is reason to believe that assets exist but might be made unavailable for future support, the court can take control of the assets to ensure that they are not disposed of.

Attachment. The court can authorize the sheriff to take possession of the paying spouse's property or attach it. Unlike a sequestration, the recipient spouse does not need to prove any intent to remove the property from the state. After attachment, the property will be sold at public sale and the proceeds used to pay the unpaid support. In contrast, sequestered property cannot be sold unless the paying party falls in arrears.

Department of Revenue Enforcement. Historically, the Department of Children and Families (DCF) (formerly the Department of Health and Rehabilitative Services (HRS)) has enforced child support (for its own benefit) in welfare cases. When children were receiving AFDC (Aid for Families with Dependent Children, that is, welfare) for single-parent children, DCF would pursue recovery of the welfare payments from the absent parent. There was never any charge for this since DCF was only recovering money for the state.

For a while, DCF was doing private enforcement also. There was no charge and, unfortunately, the people using its services rarely got more than they paid for.

Currently, the Department of Revenue has authority over all child support enforcement. They contract out the actual work to either the Attorney General's office, the State Attorney, or private contract attorneys.

Foreign Decrees. Florida is the land of immigrants; even the Seminoles originally came from Georgia. Many immigrants bring their divorce decrees with them and want to know how to enforce them.

Florida will recognize a valid divorce from another state. It will usually recognize other aspects of the foreign judgment to the extent that they are final. Unfortunately, the most important parts are not final: child custody and support, and alimony. Congress has mandated that every state recognize and enforce other states' child support orders.

If both parties have become residents of Florida, you can usually convert the foreign decree into a Florida judgment by filing it in Florida and giving notice to your former spouse of your intention to make it a local decree. Once it domesticated, it is treated like any other Florida judgment, and can be modified and enforced here.

If one of the parties is not a resident of Florida, things are more complicated. Even if you are a nonresident, you can domesticate your home-state divorce decree if your husband has moved to Florida. If you have moved here and he has not, there is little to be gained by domesticating the foreign decree; Florida courts have no power over your nonresident ex-spouse. Under those circumstances, you must enforce the judgment in your former home state or, if your husband has moved to another state, in the state where he is presently living.

Uniform Laws. If you are a resident of Florida, were divorced in Florida, and want to enforce a decree against your husband who has left the state, you can use one of two uniform laws. "Uniform" laws are those which have been adopted in the same or similar form in all or most of the states with the intention that the states will assist in enforcing rights across state lines. The two uniform laws that are useful for enforcement purposes are the Uniform Interstate Family Support Act (UIFSA) and the Uniform Child Custody Jurisdiction and Enforcement Act (UCCJEA).

The Uniform Child Custody Jurisdiction and Enforcement Act establishes which state has jurisdiction over a child and his or her custody. Its basic provision is that the most recent six-month residency in a state establishes that state's exclusive jurisdiction. I discuss this act in more detail in Chapter 5.

UIFSA is supposed to enable a wife living in a state other than her former husband's to enforce support obligations without having to go to the husband's state. It is one of the least effective laws on the books and needs a major overhaul.

In practice, the wife's petition for support or to enforce support is filed local-
ly, usually by the Department of Revenue through one of its contract attorneys (or
state agencies), and is then sent to the husband's state. He is summoned into court
in that state to respond to the wife's petition. The State Attorney or the equivalent
in that state generally represents the wife's interests in that proceeding.
Unfortunately, without the benefit of discovery into the husband's income and
assets, the foreign prosecutor has no way of knowing what the husband is capable of paying. Private counsel can be employed to represent the petitioner and discovery is permitted. It is extremely rare, however, that private counsel appear in
UIFSA cases and even rarer that adequate discovery is conducted.

The result in most UIFSA cases is often a very low compromise order that
infuriates the wife and brings joy to the husband's heart. The fault with UIFSA
lies with asking public officials (or attorneys subcontracted to the state) to handle
cases for which they are often untrained, underarmed, and underprepared.

Summary

Keep in mind that all judgments are only as good the courts' ability to enforce
them. The remedies are still somewhat cumbersome. They work for the most part.

Things are changing. Enforcement is getting better as better tools are given the
courts to make their rulings work. In truth, however, the effectiveness of enforcement
will always depend upon the willingness of the courts to act decisively. Currently, the
courts are doing better and we can only hope that their commitment endures. Things
are going to change a lot more. More change will likely take place in enforcement in
the next ten years than in any other area of marital law. Ten years from now, the work
of the courts will be far more effective.

If you can wait ten years before you need enforcement, you'll be better off.
But if you have problems today, don't wait. Justice delayed is justice denied; no
change in the law is going to make the wait beneficial to you.

10

MODIFICATION

What you will learn in this chapter:
- what parts of a final judgment can be modified
- what must occur before a court will modify support
- what changes the court can make to alimony
- whether rehabilitative alimony can be modified into permanent alimony
- when the court loses the power to extend rehabilitative alimony
- what events serve to terminate permanent alimony
- when child support can be modified
- how the remarriage of the custodial parent affects child support
- whether the parties can agree to waive child support
- what happens to child support when one of the children turns 18
- on what date a modification of support is supposed to be effective
- whether unpaid back payments can be modified
- whether a child can decide that he or she wants to live with the other parent
- whether the custodial parent can relocate from the area without the other's consent

Only death is final. Except for property rights, nothing is ever final in a "Final" Judgment of Dissolution of Marriage. Everything is subject to modification.

Let's be more specific. As I've pointed out earlier, divorce involves only a limited number of issues: the divorce itself, child custody and support, alimony, and property division. Obviously, the divorce itself and, as I mentioned above, property rights are not modifiable. The rest can seem like cancer, a lingering death.

There are some rules, however. The basic one is that a court can only modify a judgment if there is a substantial and material change in circumstances. Let's see how that rule applies in the different areas. For this chapter, I will assume that "you" are the husband and that your ex-wife's name is Donna.

Alimony

Let's get the worst part over first. As we know, there are four types of alimony: permanent-periodic, rehabilitative (also usually periodic), bridge-the-gap, and lump sum. We can eliminate lump sum right away. As we saw in Chapters 7 and 8, lump sum alimony is actually a property division and not really alimony. As such, it cannot be modified under any circumstances. Likewise I am unaware of any case in which bridge-the-gap alimony was modified.

Rehabilitative Alimony. Rehabilitative alimony is alimony you pay for a limited period of time with the expectation that Donna will be able to support herself by the end of that period. It is based, of course, on a balancing of her need and your ability to pay.

Obviously, rehabilitative alimony can only be modified if there is a change in one (or both) of those factors. The modification could be in the duration or the amount of the alimony.

To award rehabilitative alimony, the court must find that Donna is presently incapable of supporting herself but that she will probably be able to support herself in the future. The court must also find that Donna has a specific plan to rehabilitate herself.

Let's assume that you have been ordered to pay Donna $1,000 per month for three years; the three years is the time Donna stated at trial that it would take her to get her nursing degree and the judgment specifically stated that she could reasonably be expected to be able to support herself upon receiving that degree.

There are six modifications possible: (1) the amount could be increased or (2) it could be decreased; (3) the duration could be increased or (4) decreased; (5) the rehabilitative alimony could be converted to permanent alimony; and (6) it could be terminated.

The amount could be increased if there was a substantial, material, and permanent change in her needs or your ability. Let's assume that the $1,000 per month was, at the time of trial, clearly inadequate to cover her needs but was all that you could afford. If you got a new, higher-paying job or won the lottery, Donna could seek a modification to better cover her needs. It would help her if the judgment specified that Donna needed more but that you lacked the ability to pay what she needed. Likewise, if you originally had the ability to pay more than the $1,000 per month but she didn't need more, she might get an increase if her needs materially increased. A modification upward is relatively rare.

On the other hand, if you lost your job for reasons outside your control, you might obtain a decrease, despite Donna's continuing need. Or if she obtained a grant or scholarship that reduced her needs to well below $1,000 per month, or if she remarried and her new husband was able to cover her expenses, then you might get a reduction. (Note that, unlike permanent alimony, rehabilitative alimony does not necessarily end on Donna's remarriage.)

If the changes were only temporary, such as Donna's skipping a semester at school, or you being temporarily laid off, the rehabilitative alimony would probably not be modified. The judge might abate it, especially during your layoff, but would then extend the period so that Donna's total amount would not be reduced.

Now, let's assume that despite the expectation that Donna will be able to support herself after three years, she simply isn't able to do so. There are three possibilities. The judge could permit the alimony to expire without extending it; extend it for an additional period; or convert it into permanent alimony.

Donna must petition the court for the extension or conversion before the rehabilitation period ends. If she doesn't, the court loses jurisdiction and the judge cannot award her any further alimony.

If she does file her petition in time, she will win only if she shows that she remains incapable of supporting herself despite diligent effort to rehabilitate herself and that you still have the ability to help her.

"Diligent effort" does not necessarily mean that she must start nursing school immediately after the divorce. The courts recognize how traumatic divorce is and that a reasonable delay may be justified. With that exception, however, the judges expect to see proof of significant effort throughout the rehab period before they will consider any extension.

If the judge is satisfied that the rehabilitation hasn't worked despite Donna's effort, he or she must then consider whether rehabilitation remains likely. If it does, the judge would merely extend the period. If, however, it appears that Donna is never going to be self-sufficient, the judge might make the alimony permanent. He could not, of course, do that if she had remarried. In fact, although conceivable under the law, it is very unlikely that Donna would have any chance for an extension if she was remarried.

Donna must be very careful of the deadline, the date for the last payment. If that passes, she's on her own. No exceptions, no excuses. The court has lost jurisdiction. The significant action is the filing for an extension or conversion. The court will continue to have jurisdiction to hear the petition after the alimony has expired if it was filed on time.

Some people are confused about what ends the court's jurisdiction. It is not the making of the last payment that ends the court's jurisdiction; for example, you couldn't eliminate the court's jurisdiction by making your last six months' payments in advance. The judge would still have jurisdiction for a petition filed up through the end of the rehabilitative period.

This means that the court still has jurisdiction during the month after the last payment. If each payment is clearly prospective, that is, to cover Donna's expenses for the following 30 days, her rehabilitative period would not end on the first of the month when you make your last payment but, rather, would end on the last day of that month since the last day ends the rehabilitative period. I would not, however, recommend that Donna delay filing until the last minute. Until recently, all decisions on point referred to the date of the last payment as the last day to file for modification. Although the law seems relatively well settled on this point, some Circuit Judge might still rely upon the old, outmoded (but not reversed) decisions in his or her district and might conclude that payments are for the month immediately before they are paid and still cut off your right to modify on the earlier date. Donna should make sure she files for modification before the date that the last payment is due.

The last possible modification is early termination. If Donna were to win the lottery or leave nursing school to accept a well-paying job, you could seek to terminate the rehabilitative alimony right away. You would not necessarily win just because she seems to have abandoned her efforts to become a nurse. Remember that, although your Final Judgment recites her plan to attend school, she would not likely lose her support if she chose, instead, to become a teacher.

Donna probably has every right to change her mind and seek to rehabilitate herself in other ways. She could, for example, decide to take a low-paying receptionist position in the hope of working herself up to a well-paying secretarial position. Judges do not like to lock wives into pursuits which they may find unpromising. Thus, just dropping out of nursing school will not be likely to end Donna's alimony.

If the rehabilitative alimony results from an agreement between the parties, it can be subject to certain conditions that the court could not impose. For example, the parties can agree that it will not be modifiable, either in amount or duration, or both. The courts will, except under very extreme circumstances, enforce that. In one recent case, the wife contracted incurable cancer and sought to extend her rehabilitative alimony; since the parties had agreed that the alimony would be unmodifiable, the court was bound by the stipulation and refused to modify.

You and Donna might agree that the alimony will only continue as long as Donna remains in nursing school or as long as she remains unmarried. The court couldn't impose those conditions without agreement from both of you but would accept your stipulation and make it part of the judgment.

One decision states that a provision found in virtually all settlement agreements may carry unexpected import. That case held that a statement in the agreement that it could only be modified "by a writing signed by both parties" divested the court from modifying without consent of both parties. Attorneys should generally add further language that recognizes the right to seek judicial modification also.

Permanent Alimony. The rules for permanent alimony are not very different from those that apply to rehabilitative alimony. Of course, the judge will have to take a longer-range view of changes. The obtaining of a decent job for a wife on three-year alimony might result in the judge ending rehabilitative alimony but might bring about only a decrease in permanent alimony. Without meaning to imply that permanent alimony is anything but alimony, there is some truth to the idea that it is viewed, in a loose sense of the term, somewhat as a property right that is not lightly terminated.

Of course, there is no time limit for seeking to modify permanent alimony. The court has continuing jurisdiction over it since it is ongoing.

Permanent alimony is, of course, eliminated by the remarriage of the recipient or the death of either party. The judgment should recite those conditions; if it doesn't, you might have to get an order terminating it if Donna should remarry. It would be purely a technicality since the law is quite clear on the fact that remarriage always ends permanent alimony.

Your burden in proving your right to modify alimony, whether permanent or rehabilitative, will be no different if you agreed to the support. The cases that said that you carried a higher burden in seeking modification of support resulting from a settlement agreement than you do if the support were imposed by the court have been voided by a 1993 statute that makes the standard of proof the same.

Historically, a husband's voluntary retirement could not be considered as a basis for modifying alimony. That has changed and such a retirement is a factor that the court must consider in looking at the overall issue of whether modification is appropriate.

Modification for Live-in. The legislature has recently addressed a gray area in alimony modification by empowering courts to reduce or terminate alimony if the recipient has entered into a "supportive relationship" with an unrelated person of the opposite sex. The court is directed to consider many factors set out in the statute, including the length of time that they are together, whether they are holding themselves out to be married, whether they have pooled their assets and income, and whether they have purchased property together. Although the law is workable on its face, only caselaw will determine how it is applied in real cases.

Child Support

Child support is treated, in many ways, the same as alimony. It is based on need and ability, and substantial and material changes in those circumstances, or in one of them, are necessary to obtain a change.

There are differences, however. The best interests of the children will always be considered in any attempt to modify. Child support is now determined under guidelines contained in the statutes. (See Appendix E.) Rather than deciding every case on its individual merits, the judge is supposed to consider only the incomes of the parents and the number of children in awarding support, unless extraordinary circumstances exist. These might include unusual physical or emotional problems a child has, independent income of the child, his or her age, extent of visitation rights, and unusual expenses previously covered in that particular family. (The last might be something like violin lessons.)

The guidelines will be a basis for modification if the difference between the existing obligations established before the guidelines came into effect and the guideline obligation is at least $50 or 15%, whichever amount is greater.

Needs. Children's needs are relative. For a poor family, food on the table and Salvation Army clothes might be all the needs. For a wealthy family, the standard of living would be far different; a son turning 16 might "need" a Mercedes Benz. What would happen, however, if your divorce occurred when you were making little money and your family's standard of living was commensurate with your meager ability, but you later start earning $200,000? Do your children still eat pasta five nights a week?

The answer is no. Your children are entitled to share your prosperity; their "needs" will move up with your income.

Of course, your children's needs can change for other reasons. If one child develops a medical condition requiring unusual expense, modification is possible. Likewise, if another child turns out to be a musical prodigy and his training is expensive, modification is possible. Remember, however, that child support will only be increased if you can afford to pay more.

You can seek a modification downward if Donna starts earning more; under the guidelines, the percentage you should provide would need to be adjusted but your bottom-line obligation probably would change very little. If Donna loses her job and her ability to contribute to the children's expenses, your obligation could increase even though you don't earn, and the children don't need, any more.

If your (ex-)wife were to remarry and quit working while her new husband supports the family, that should not affect your obligation. Her income will be imputed to her former level. If she sought to modify, the new husband's income would be relevant to the action and you would be entitled to that information.

Technically, Donna cannot contract away your obligation to pay support or her right to seek modification. Even if she signs a settlement agreement waiving all child support, she can seek it later. There is a "but" here, but not much of one. Case law says that, although the parties can't agree to waive support, such a waiver is effective if the parties' agreement is approved by the court and made part of a judgment.

Even with the court's approval, however, the waiver is not worth much.

Waiver or no waiver, if the children need support and you can afford to pay, the judge is going to order you to pay. It's the old "best interests of the children" standard. The court-approved waiver does no more than increase your wife's burden in proving the children's need. An exception might be if valuable consideration were given for the waiver, such as deeding the house to Donna to cover all future child support. In that event, the court may uphold the waiver of periodic support, especially if the consideration were clearly given as an alternative means of supporting the children.

Inflation alone is not supposed to constitute a basis for modification. However, it is a factor that may be considered if other factors are present. Since the children are always growing older, the double change of older children/greater expense and inflation may get the court's attention.

Although the guideline support is to be adjusted for the independent income of the children, case law encourages children to earn their own money by excluding that from consideration in modification proceedings. You shouldn't be able to reduce your obligation by $45 per week just because your 16-year-old son has the motivation to work part-time. That would kill the motivation very quickly.

If Junior has trust income, however, that can be considered. Obviously, the trust fund won't be affected by whether you pay support; making you pay when the money for support is already there wouldn't make sense. In such a case, it is simply a matter of looking at the child's true needs.

As with all matters involving your ability to pay, your income will be imputed at your highest potential, not necessarily at what you actually earn. So, if you give up your corporate job and become a traveling artist, your support obligation will be based on your former corporate job, not the itinerant income.

Child support terminates when a child turns 18, dies, marries, or otherwise becomes emancipated (that is, is no longer legally considered a child). If one of your three children turns 18, that doesn't necessarily mean that support is reduced by one-third. The housing needs and many other expenses will not be reduced by that much, if at all. Settlement agreements often take that into consideration and provide a formula for reduction at a less drastic scale as each child leaves. The child support guidelines should control in the absence of an agreement; you will note from the guidelines that child support for two children is always more than two-thirds of the support for three children at the same income level. In fact, if you are paying a set amount for the three children that full amount will continue to be due after the first turns 18 unless there is a provision in the Judgment (usually through a Settlement Agreement) or you obtain a modification.

The court may extend child support beyond 18 for a child who has not yet graduated from high school but can reasonably be expected to graduate before his

19th birthday. Although the statute is discretionary ("the court may . . ."), that rule now applies without exception. Almost all child support rulings include the language that extends it. Then it becomes a factual question about the child's likelihood of graduating before 19. Keep in mind that the support does not continue until 19 if he or she will graduate after that birthday. It stops at 18 in such a case.

Child support doesn't necessarily end when a child turns 18. If the child is clearly not capable of being self-supporting in the adult world, Donna can ask the court to extend the support for a limited, or unlimited, time, as circumstances dictate. She must petition the court before the child reaches 18. This is usually done for medically or emotionally disabled children; in one case, however, a court found that a particular child was disabled because he lacked a college education and extended child support through college. It was upheld on appeal but I wouldn't rely on it.

Effective Date of Modified Support. In theory, the court is supposed to make any modification effective on the date that the petition was filed. In practice, increases are usually made retroactively but reductions are often not. The discrepancy results from the courts not wanting to make a recipient repay monies already received.

Arrearage. Neither child support arrearage nor alimony arrearage can be modified. Once the support has accrued, the court is without jurisdiction to reduce it. Therefore, it is important to file for a modification as soon as the need is apparent. The payments accruing after the filing are not vested and can be changed. In practice, the husband who diligently pays his support pending the court proceedings often gets no relief while the one who pays little or nothing probably gets help.

Custody and Visitation

Basically, the same rules that apply to other modifications apply in custody matters: there must be a substantial change in circumstances since entry of the original judgment and it must be in the best interests of the children that custody be changed.

The most common circumstances causing custody battles are remarriage of one party, problems with visitation, and live-in boyfriends or girlfriends. The weight given to each circumstance will be determined, on a case-by-case basis, by looking at the actual effect on the children.

A statute effectively eliminates the children being used as in-court witnesses. No child can be deposed, brought to a deposition, or brought to court to appear as a witness or attend a hearing, or subpoenaed to appear at a hearing without prior order of the court.

To avoid putting the children through any kind of courtroom questioning, judges usually use social investigations, guardians ad litem, or parenting evaluators. Social investigators, guardians, or parenting evaluators can speak with a lot more people than are likely to appear as witnesses, as well as speak with and observe the children in the homes of both parents. The effect on the children is far less traumatic.

The court is ultimately presented with a written report containing the background information as well as the recommendations of the investigator, guardian, or evaluator.

In addition to the investigator's or guardian's report, which may or may not carry the day, you will want to present witnesses who are familiar with your parenting skills. Find people who see you frequently with the children. Use schoolteachers and counselors if they can help. (If the children are doing well in school, of course, that will help Donna; if they are doing badly, that will help you.)

A psychological evaluation of the children or the family as a whole can often be of help. Even more than the social investigation, a psychological study can win or lose the day. For that reason, you must first consider if you want to have your whole case subject to the subjective perceptions of one psychologist. This isn't much different, of course, than having your whole life in the hands of a single judge.

Considerations in Modifying Custody. A custody battle is contested on the relative merits of the parents as custodians. Despite social and legal changes, the wife will still, in my opinion, come into the battle with a certain presumption in her favor. Cases no longer refer to that advantage, but I believe that, although it may be small, it is still very real. Taking that reality into consideration, let's look at the factors that the court must consider in evaluating a possible change in custody.

The first, if custody was initially agreed upon, is the parties' original intentions as shown by the present arrangement. Understandably, the court will want to know why the existing arrangement is no longer acceptable if it was in the beginning.

The judge will also consider the age and sex of the children. The folklore is that, when approaching puberty, a son has greater need for his father, and a daughter greater need for her mother. I'm not sure that there are any studies that support that idea but we all believe it. Thus, if you seek to change custody of your son when he is 12, you have a better chance, especially if he wants to live with you, than you do when he is 8.

The morals and lifestyles of both parties are obviously a factor, but only if they affect the children. A mother having orgies in the house, with the children asleep upstairs, will not necessarily lose custody of the children. If the children are not subjected to the orgies and are not aware of them, as they were not in a famous Florida case, the orgies will not be a major consideration, if the woman is otherwise a good mother.

Live-ins are a more serious problem. Although attitudes have changed about the moral detriment this causes children, courts are still sensitive about children living in or visiting a home where their parents live with a boyfriend or girlfriend. Agreements often restrict the right of either parent to have an unrelated member of the other sex spend the night while the children are in the home. The fact that a live-in is present in either home will not always result in major changes, either in custody itself or in the visitation allowed. This is true even if there is a prohibition in the parties' agreement, although such a provision will make it somewhat more likely. Often, the threat or the initiation of a court proceeding will cause the live-in to either marry or move out.

In general, the existing custodian has a big advantage, primarily because courts recognize that continuity and stability are very important for children.

The parties' ability to care for the children will always be a factor. Although the judge must consider emotional and economic factors, there is little reason why economics should matter. The more advantaged parent can simply be asked to pay more support.

The health of the parties is also considered by the courts; obviously, this is just a part of the parties' relative abilities to care for the children. If the physical or mental health of a party does not affect the children or affect the care they receive, those factors should not matter.

Case law is presently developing for AIDS. Despite widespread skepticism, the medical experts are holding firm in their assertion that AIDS cannot be spread by casual contact. As a result, AIDS-infected parents are generally not losing custody because of the infection alone.

Remarriage often causes custody battles. Perhaps the children don't like their new stepfather, or the natural father remarries and believes that he can provide the children with the stable, family home life they need. In itself, remarriage of either party will not cause a change in custody. The overall effect on the children will be considered, with a presumption in favor of the existing arrangement.

Relocation. One of the biggest problems arising with custody and visitation is relocation. Obviously, your wife's moving the children more than 30 miles from their present hometown seriously interferes with your ability to see the children. The effect is catastrophic if the move is a couple of hundred miles or more.

The law in this area is now quite well established. A new statute eliminates any presumption for or against relocation when the move will materially affect visitation. The statute directs the court to consider six factors in determining if the relocation will be permitted.

Generally, six factors will be considered in determining if the relocation will be permitted:

· Whether the move would be likely to improve the general quality of life for both the primary residential spouse and the children

· Whether the nonresidential parent conscientiously exercised his visitation in the past

· Whether the custodial parent, once out of the jurisdiction, will be likely to comply with any substitute visitation arrangements

· Whether the substitute visitation will be adequate to foster a continuing meaningful relationship between the child or children and the noncustodial parent

· Whether the cost of transportation is financially affordable by one or both of the parents.

· Whether the move is in the best interests of the children.

If the parties have a written agreement that restricts the right to take the children from the area, that will be given weight and make it harder for the custodial parent to convince the court that it is in the children's best interests to move.

Modification Procedures

Now that we know what can be modified and what factors will be considered, we need to discuss how you get before the court. It isn't hard.

If you wish to modify anything — alimony, child support, or custody — your attorney must file a Supplemental Petition for Modification of Final Judgment. The attorney will generally file it in the original divorce case, that is, as just an added part to the already existing file. In the petition, your attorney will allege what the original ruling was, what substantial and material changes have occurred, and what modification you seek.

Your wife then has 20 days to answer and, if she wishes, to counterpetition. Often, a supplemental petition to increase child support will be answered by a counterpetition for a change in custody, and vice versa.

The case proceeds along the same lines as your original divorce. Both parties can do discovery, and, when the discovery is done and the case is at issue, it is set for trial. The trial is in front of the judge—or, for child support, the magistrate—again. No juries are ever involved.

Modification cases can be every bit as difficult and painful as divorce actions. If the amount of support is the only issue, they are not nearly as trying as when custody is at issue. Just as you wouldn't start a divorce lightly, enter into a contested modification only if it is necessary and your attempts to work out a change amicably have failed.

11

TAX ASPECTS
OF DIVORCE

What you will learn in this chapter:
- why you need to know about taxes
- why your divorce lawyer needs help on taxes
- how taxes apply to alimony payments
- what *private ordering* is and how it can help both of you
- what kinds of payments qualify as alimony
- why the IRS doesn't care what name you give support
- what the *three year rule* is and how to avoid it
- why you may have to include your ex-spouse's social security number on your tax return
- who pays the taxes on lump sum alimony
- who gets the tax exemption for the children
- whether the court can award the exemption to the paying spouse
- what tax law applies to child support awarded before 1984
- what special tax treatment applies to transfers between spouses as a result of a divorce
- the advantages of getting the house in the divorce
- the advantages of not getting the house in the divorce
- who gets to deduct attorney's fees

You need to understand a little bit about taxes because your lawyer may not. Divorce lawyers are not tax lawyers. Few are experts even in divorce aspects of the tax laws. You should not rely on a divorce lawyer to provide you with tax advice. If it matters to you, and it certainly should, seek out tax advice from a tax lawyer or a certified public accountant. Your lawyer may advise you to get professional tax advice. If not, go and get it anyway.

Careful tax planning can complicate divorce settlements. The lack of planning can create complex tax situations because the parties never even thought about the tax results of what they were doing.

The treatment of taxation in this book is not meant to be exhaustive. This chapter should serve only to warn you that there are very real tax considerations that you and your lawyer should consider both in settlement and in presentation of your case. What your divorce lawyer may not say to you, I will: go to a tax lawyer (or CPA) for tax advice related to your divorce. Give the tax expert a summary of the finances, the issues, and your prospects (prepared by your divorce lawyer) and get advice on what the effects of the different structures will be on your taxes.

If you enter into a settlement agreement, it should address the status of marital income taxes. If any are owed, the terms should specify who pays

> *Private ordering* is the agreeing between the parties that payments that would otherwise qualify as tax-deductible (by the payer) alimony will not be treated that way. As a result of the private ordering, the payments are not deductible by the payer and not includable by the recipient.

them. If a refund is coming back, you should specify how it is shared.

We're now operating under laws passed in 2001 and 2003. The 2001 changes were not as extensive as the previous changes (1984, 1986) but will have some impact on pre- and post-divorce planning. The full effects of the 2003 changes are not yet clear. The result of change is, of course, greater need to consult with an expert on taxes. The discussion that follows is no substitute for that expert advice and should be treated as no more than an introduction to the areas of interest.

Alimony

Remember that there are four types of alimony: permanent-periodic, lump sum, bridge-the-gap, and rehabilitative. There are variations of the four, such as exclusive use of the home, payment of mortgage or rent payments, and transfer of annuities or insurance policies. The best approach, however, is to understand the general rules regarding taxation of alimony and then look at how unusual types of alimony affect taxation.

Permanent Alimony. As we've seen, this is alimony paid, usually at specified periods, for the rest of either party's life. Such alimony is usually "deductible/includable." That means that the party paying the alimony (assumed in this discussion to be the husband) can deduct it from his income for tax purposes, and the recipient (the wife) must include the alimony in her income.

In order to get alimony treatment (that is, deductibility/includability), the payments need not be periodic (that is, at specified periods), nor need they arise out of any obligation of one spouse to support the other. This makes it easier to get alimony treatment for property transfers. And why would a wife want to have to pay taxes on property she receives? Because she can receive more value without it hurting the husband one bit more.

Let me give you an example: Assume that the husband is in the 28% tax bracket and the wife is in the 15% bracket. If the parties reached agreement that the husband had to transfer $10,000 to the wife, he could simply write her a check for $10,000 and he would be out $10,000.

Now consider what he would be out if he can get alimony treatment for the transfer: To realize $10,000 after paying 15% taxes, the wife would have to receive $11,765. If the husband can deduct his payment of that amount, his net cost is only $8,471!

To induce the wife to accept the transfer on a schedule that will allow it to be treated as alimony, the husband might have to sweeten the offer to offset the possible delay or inconvenience. But, with over $1500 to play with, the parties should be able to work out something to mutual advantage.

To make it even better, the parties are now allowed to "privately order" the tax payments to some degree. That is, they are allowed to agree privately that payments that would otherwise be alimony would not be treated that way. This, too, can make it easier to structure settlements to mutual advantage.

To qualify as alimony, payments must be made under a divorce or separation agreement, order, or judgment. The payments under a final judgment or order qualify as alimony only if the husband and wife are not living together (except for up to one month while the husband prepares to move out) at the time of the payments; they will be treated as alimony if the parties continue to live together under a temporary support order or agreement. Finally, the payments must stop upon the death of the recipient. That is, the payments must really stop; if the parties have some arrangement under which some other payments start when the "alimony" stops, the so-called alimony will not be given alimony treatment. (If the parties remain married at the end of a year, they will lose alimony treatment for all payments if they file a joint return; this seems self-evident, since the payments would wash each other out, but the IRS specifically includes this rule.)

The payments must be in cash, check, or money order. They don't have to be paid directly to the wife; by order or with the agreement of the wife, the husband can make payments for rent, utilities, insurance premiums, etc., that will be considered alimony. If, however, he transfers the right to receive promissory note payments or annuity payments, they will be considered property transfers and he can't deduct their value. He also can't come over and fix the plumbing and deduct the cost of his services; if it's not cash, it's not alimony.

The fact that the payments will end on the death of the wife does not have to be expressly stated in the agreement/judgment. Since, under Florida law, alimony stops upon the wife's death, that condition doesn't have to be expressly included.

I indicated above that, if the death of the wife causes some other payments to increase, that eliminates the alimony treatment to the extent of the new payments. For example, if the wife were receiving $500 as alimony and $500 as child support, and the parties agreed that, if the wife should die, the alimony would stop but child support would increase to $800, only $200 ($500 minus the substitute payment of $300) would be treated as alimony. This would be true from the very start of alimony payments. You must keep in mind that the parties cannot "privately order" the $300 to be alimony; private ordering only goes one way — payments that qualify for alimony can be excluded by agreement but not vice versa.

> The *three-year rule* applies when alimony payments exceed $10,000 per year and the amounts change significantly during the first three years. The purpose of the rule is to unmask property transfers that are designated as alimony.

That "substitute payment" rule cuts both ways. If the parties agreed that, upon the death of a child, the wife's alimony would increase to $600, that extra hundred would be considered as alimony right from the beginning.

If alimony decreases upon the death of a child, the amount is, of course, not considered alimony; it is clearly child support. Before 1984, any amounts not designated as child-support payments were considered alimony; now, we have something called alimony which must be treated as child support.

If there are automatic reductions in alimony that occur at least twice at or around events related to the children, that will cause the amounts to be treated as child support. For example, assume the divorcing parties have two children, one who will turn 18 in 2009 and the other in 2013. Any decreases in alimony payments which "coincidentally" occur within six months of each of their birthdays will be treated as child support from the beginning.

Three-Year Rule. The IRS has kept some rules that inhibit disguised property transfers. The main one is the three-year rule which provides, in effect, that significant changes in alimony payments during the first three years, if alimony is more than $10,000 per year, may result in "recapture" of some of the alimony. Plainly stated, some of the money will lose alimony treatment. This is one of those areas you need to discuss with a tax expert. Suffice it to say that you need advice on the three-year rule if the annual alimony payments exceed $10,000 and they vary during the first three years.

"Overlooked" Income. Historically, the IRS has had fits trying to keep track of who's deducting and who's including alimony payments. Without sophisticated computers, it was an impossible task. Even the most honest people often erred. For example, when a husband deducted court-ordered premiums for insurance owned by the wife, he was legally entitled to do so. In many cases, however, he never notified the wife that he made the payments or how much he paid; she wouldn't, therefore, include it in her income. Tax payments and mortgage payments were other common payments not fully reported by recipients.

Times have changed and the IRS does have sophisticated computers, which can cross-check returns of ex-spouses. To enable the computer to locate the ex-spouse's return, the deducting spouse must now provide the wife's tax identification number (her social security number); he is subject to a $50 fine if he fails to do so. In this way, the IRS hopes to reduce the estimated half a billion dollars annual loss because of overlooked income.

Rehabilitative Alimony. Tax people don't recognize the difference between permanent and rehabilitative alimony. It's sort of a "one size fits all" handling of alimony. If the rehabilitative alimony qualifies as alimony under the rules for permanent alimony, it's alimony.

Lump Sum Alimony. Lump sum alimony is not "true" alimony at all. The IRS basically agrees with this interpretation. The one rule that forbids alimony treatment for lump sum alimony is the requirement that the payments terminate upon death. Lump sum alimony is vested immediately, even if not payable immediately, and the death of neither party terminates the obligation. Thus, if payments are really lump sum alimony, they are not deductible by the husband and they are not includable in the wife's income.

Special Cases. Suppose the husband lacks income to pay alimony but the court awards the wife exclusive use and possession of the marital home. Isn't that clearly alimony since the husband is losing the rental value of his half and the wife is realizing that value? The answer is no! Remember, to be treated as alimony for tax purposes, the payments must be made in cash (or its equivalent).

The result would be different if the husband were required to make the wife's half of the mortgage payments without reimbursement at some later date. To the extent of her half of the payments, he could deduct the payments. I suppose, despite the usual rule that only the party actually paying is entitled to deduct interest payments, that the wife could deduct the interest since she must include the gross payment in her income.

If the exclusive use of the home were clearly tied to the minority of the children, no part of any required payments would be deductible as alimony.

In evaluating your tax situation, your tax expert can refer to the basic rules and, possibly, some IRS or tax court rulings and will generally have little trouble deciding the appropriate treatment. Where a genuine doubt exists as to proper treatment, he or she will generally advise you to give yourself the benefit of the honest doubt and take the most favorable treatment. In such a case, it would be most wise to notify your ex-spouse of the position you are taking on your return so that your ex can take that into consideration. It's not only a matter of courtesy; it might avoid an audit.

Child Support

Child support payments are not deductible. With the exception of the adjustment of child support/alimony at the time of events related to the children's ages or the death of the wife, there really isn't much complexity to the issue.

There are a few rules regarding the dependency exemption that you should know. Let me discuss them briefly. The first is that (under current law) the custodial parent is automatically entitled to the exemption. She or he gets the exemption if the parties are divorced, separated, or not living together for the last six months of the year.

Unless it is waived in writing, the custodial parent has the exemption, no matter how much the spouse contributes to the support of the children. The waiver can be made permanently, for a specified period, or each year, and a copy of the written waiver must be attached to the noncustodial parent's tax return. Generally, it is best for the wife to execute a new waiver each year so that she can be sure that the husband is current in his support payments before she does so.

Courts in some states have awarded the exemption to the husband and forced the wife to execute a waiver. Other states have refused to recognize the authority of their courts to do so, presumably on the grounds that the Tax Code authorizes "voluntary" waivers only. Florida courts now have the power to award the exemption to the payer of child support.

The Tax Code does not define what "support" means but provides a list of expenses that will be recognized as support: including food; shelter; clothing; medical, dental, and educational expenses. Cases have also brought in the cost of summer camp and drama lessons.

For either parent to qualify to take the exemption, the parents (including the parents' new spouses if they've remarried) must jointly contribute more than half of the child's support. If one of the parents takes the exemption, the child cannot claim himself or herself. To cross-check that, all children over five years old must have social security numbers and the claiming parent must list that number when he claims the child.

Regardless of who is entitled to the dependency exemption, either parent who pays child-care expenses can take the credit for such expenses. Likewise, to the extent that they are deductible, medical expenses are deductible by either parent regardless of who has the exemption.

The ***basis*** in a property is essentially the cost to the taxpayer. However, because the IRS has its own definition of *basis* for tax purposes, the actual cost may not always be the same as the *tax basis*. Since the *basis* is untaxed, the seller always wants as high a *tax basis* as possible.

The exemption can be quite substantial for many taxpayers. For 2006, it was $3,300; thereafter, it will be adjusted each year according to the cost of living.

If a husband is required to pay both alimony and child support but pays only a portion of it, the child support is presumed to be paid first. For example, if he were required to pay $100 per week in child support and $200 per week in alimony but only paid $150, only $50 would be treated as alimony for tax purposes even if he wrote on the check "all for alimony."

The "head of household" status for income tax purposes is granted to the party who pays more than half of the support for the household, even if the party is not living in the household! Thus, an ex-husband fully supporting his ex-wife and the children would be the head of that household and he could claim that status on his 1040.

Property Transfers

As we have seen, the tax reforms give parties greater control over their own affairs. It also states, as a matter of policy, that transfers between spouses should not be subject to taxation.

Specifically, Code Section 1041(a) states that:

No gain or loss shall be recognized on a transfer of property from an individual to (or in trust for the benefit of) (1) a spouse or (2) a former spouse, but only if the transfer is incident to the divorce.

A "transfer incident to a divorce" is one which occurs within one year of the end of the marriage or is related to the cessation of the marriage. Put another way, no transfer of property between spouses made within one year will be taxed regardless of why it was transferred, and no transfer that is related to the divorce will be taxed, regardless of when the transfer is made. There is a presumption that a transfer more than six years after the divorce is not related to the divorce but the parties can avoid taxation by showing that it is related to the cessation of the marriage.

As a result, all transfers qualifying under this section are treated much the same as gifts (but it does not affect the unified credit). The recipient receives the same basis as transferor. (Gifts are treated a little differently since, for a gift, the recipient receives transferor's basis or fair market value, whichever is lower.)

The current laws are good, but . . . The "but" is that it contains some traps for the unwary. Take the following example: Leslie and John buy a house for

$100,000 and it is worth $250,000 when they divorce. John agrees to buy out Leslie's half interest for $125,000. It would seem that his basis should be $175,000 (half of the original cost plus the payment to Leslie), but it isn't. The law is, you will recall, that the recipient takes the transferor's basis; this is true even if he pays more than his wife's basis for her interest. As a result, John's basis will only be $100,000, and he may eventually be taxed on all gain over that figure.

Transfers into trust for a spouse or former spouse have some different rules beyond the scope of this section. Again, the best advice is to see a tax expert.

Annuity contracts can be transferred like other property without any tax consequences. Formerly, the recipient paid income taxes on the entire amount of all income received from the annuity, with no deduction for the amount the transferor paid for the annuity. Now, the recipient can deduct a pro rata share of the income for the annuity's cost; that is, the portion of the income attributable to the initial investment is not taxed.

Likewise, life insurance can be transferred without any taxation, either at the time of transfer or when the insured dies. However, if the insured spouse, usually the husband, has to pay the premiums after transferring the policy to the wife, the premium payments are treated as alimony unless excluded by agreement of the parties.

Individual Retirement Accounts (IRAs) can be divided between divorcing spouses by judgment or agreement (some IRAs require a QDRO); to avoid taxes (or penalties), the recipient must place the transferred share into the recipient's own IRA.

Notes or other installment contracts can be transferred without taxation. Taxes will, of course, be due on the interest collected with each payment. In a similar vein, bonds can be transferred with no taxes due on the principal at the time of transfer. If, however, there is any accrued interest, taxes must be paid on that interest for the year of the transfer, even if the interest is not paid until the following year.

If one party ends up with the marital home (let's say the wife), she may receive some substantial tax advantages (as long as she doesn't pay her husband more than his basis). While she owns it, she can deduct all of her interest and real estate tax payments. Under a 1997 change, she will have no tax liability for sale of a home worth up to $250,000.

Pensions can now be transferred in whole or in part. The wife can even elect to receive benefits at the earliest date that the husband could have retired, even if he doesn't retire then. This leads to the incongruous result that a wife could be receiving part of a husband's pension while he is still employed and, because of his continued employment, not yet eligible to receive whatever portion he did not transfer. The transfers are accomplished by a "Qualified Domestic Relations

A *Qualified Domestic Relations Order* is an order issued by a court in a divorce case that directs the administrator of a pension plan to pay all or a portion a one person's pension to that person's former spouse.

Order," commonly called QDROs (pronounced "qwahdros"). There are no taxes on the transfer and none on the principal value transferred, but the wife will probably have to pay taxes on any portion of a payment that is due to appreciation.

The freedom to transfer assets between spouses and former spouses applies to all property, not just marital property.

Attorney's Fees

Generally, attorney's fees in divorces are not deductible. Even if the fees are incurred for the preservation of income-producing property, the fees are not deductible since they are related to a claim arising from a purely personal relationship, the marriage.

You can get some tax advantage out of those fees, however. If you can reasonably identify the fees specifically incurred to protect or obtain income-producing property, you can add the fees to the basis for the property and reduce the taxable profit you later realize when you sell it.

Fees incurred for obtaining or enforcing taxable income (that is, alimony) are deductible. Fees for tax advice are also deductible.

These fees are only deductible if the spouse incurring them actually pays them. If the other spouse has to pay otherwise deductible fees, neither party gets the deduction. Therefore, it might be wise in some cases to pay larger, deductible alimony rather than attorney's fees. Since alimony payments need no longer be on a regular schedule, it doesn't matter how the payments are made so long as they are called alimony. The only possible pitfall is that some of the payments might be recaptured (that is, treated as nondeductible) if there is a violation of the three-year rule explained above.

Another way to preserve the deductibility of the fees is to have one spouse transfer appreciated assets to the other instead of paying the fees. When the recipient sells the assets, he or she will have to pay taxes on the gain, but that gain will be offset by the deductible fees.

Remember that only certain fees (for alimony, tax advice, etc.) can be deductible. No contortions will make the rest of your fees deductible.

Finally, let me return to the advice I gave you at the beginning of this chapter. Don't expect your divorce lawyer to be a tax expert. Instead, assure your lawyer that you understand that he or she can't be an expert in everything and encourage him or her to get the necessary assistance. You will both gain by the tax expert's help.

12

MEDIATION

What you will learn in this chapter:
• why negotiation often fails to resolve divorce cases
• how mediation offers an alternative way to resolve differences
• why you need outside help in negotiating the issues in your divorce
• how the system inhibits complete honesty in mediation
• how mediation encourages cooperation
• how often mediation works
• what happens if you work out all of your differences

In the past, Settlement Agreements were generally reached through negotiations between the attorneys for both parties. A little give here, a little take there, always with an eye (a guess?) toward what a court would do under the circumstances of the parties. There is another way, however. More and more settlements are coming out of the mediation process. Mediation is not a new idea, but its application to resolving marital difficulties has only become common in the last 20 years.

The problem with negotiations between the parties is that, by the time the attorneys know enough about the case to try negotiation, they already identify with their clients enough to have lost much of their objectivity. Besides that, they are expected to get results and feel the pressure not to give much ground on the issues.

On the theory that truth arises from a contest between conflicting positions, our legal system is essentially adversarial. There is nothing wrong with the theory and it works pretty well in practice. But that doesn't mean that we shouldn't try other ways. Mediation is one of those other ways. It assumes that two human beings can resolve their differences through reasoning rather than conflict, if their reasoning can be channelled in the right direction. Mediation aims to bring the parties together at a relatively low cost and with a minimum of pain. Court related mediation may be absolutely free.

Although I am not a certified mediator, I have been retained as a mediator on several occasions and I have gone through the process numerous times with clients. Based on this, I can give you my perspective from both sides.

How Mediation Works

In the mediation process, a skilled person helps the parties identify the issues and look for reasonable solutions. Since the mediator does not represent either party, he or she can look at the facts objectively. The process rarely works well if the mediator isn't well trained and reasonably skilled.

> **Mediation** is the non-adversarial resolution of issues with the assistance of a neutral third party.

Mediation can also fail if one party can out-talk or out-maneuver the other. If both parties don't come into the process committed to listening to each other, the process runs into difficulty. A skilled mediator can, however, recognize the personalities early and direct the parties into productive conduct. If a mediator finds that the parties are not suitable for mediation, he or she can withdraw from participation and leave the parties to fight it out in court.

Finally, the process needs people to be open and frank. I believe that this is the biggest dilemma of mediation. If one party is completely honest and makes admissions that are damaging, those admissions are going to come back and hurt that party if the mediation fails. Sure, the law provides that no statement made during a mediation session can be used in a subsequent court proceeding; but that's pure fiction. If John admits during mediation that he had an affair with Cynthia G. Laiggs, and mediation fails, what do you think will be the first question asked during the later deposition? Right: "Did you have an affair with Miss Laiggs?" When he admits it during the deposition, it is obviously admissible in the case. If he denies it, he knows that he has lost all of his credibility and everything he says thereafter on any aspect of the case will be disbelieved.

I don't know that this dilemma is as much of a problem as it was in the past. Most mediators now separate the parties and there is only a very limited exchange of information in the presence of the other. For this reason, there is less chance than in the past of damaging disclosures occurring.

Role of a Mediator. The mediator's first responsibility is to make both parties feel comfortable; he or she must gain their confidence and respect. Next the mediator must educate the parties about what mediation means, how it works, and how any decisions will be implemented.

Then, the parties and the mediator reach an understanding of what issues will be mediated (and which ones exist but will not be mediated). The mediator will try to have the parties reach agreement on the order in which the issues will be considered. It's no secret that mediators sometimes use the need to establish an agenda as a device to establish immediately whether the parties can work together at all, even if only on a procedural matter. From there, he/she will often address relatively easy issues first so as to continue the momentum of accomplishment.

The mediator will write down the agenda, thereby showing that something has already been accomplished. As the mediation progresses, each little agreement will also be reduced to writing. The writing serves to close out the discussion on that point, allowing the parties to move on to new areas. Many mediators issue memos of progress after each meeting and send copies to the parties and to their attorneys.

The parties are instructed at the outset that they are bound by nothing, that all agreements are preliminary and will be reviewed at the end before they are established firmly as undisputed points. This allows the parties to reach tentative agreements more easily, free of the fear that they can't retract the assent. In theory, they can; in practice, the mediator knows that even a tentative agreement is very difficult to retract. Any assent, no matter how conditional, is progress.

Effective mediation requires that the parties limit discussions to relatively narrow areas without significant digression and that the exchange be as free of emotion as possible. If the mediator can distract the parties from their emotions and persuade them to deal with the facts, that is, to reason together, the mediation has a pretty good chance of some success.

Sometimes, because the parties seem irreconcilably opposed on a specific issue, such as custody, a mediator will avoid that issue and have the parties deal with tangential aspects, such as how each relates to the children; how much time each can spend with them; and possible visitation, vacation, and holiday schedules. After dealing extensively with those aspects, the parties sometimes find that it is apparent who should have custody.

At the end of each session, the agreements, no matter how minor, will be read from the mediator's notes. The mediator will generally ask the parties to confirm that those points were agreed upon. This increases the parties' commitment to the agreements and closes the session on a positive note. In many cases, the mediator will obtain the signatures on a summary of agreements if the parties are willing to commit to resolution of isolated issues without the whole case being resolved. The final step in many sessions will be to agree on the subject matter of the next session. The parties can then leave feeling that they have accomplished something and can free their minds of those matters. They can also start to examine the next issue in the light of the successes of the session just completed.

At the end of the whole process, the parties will be presented with a typed report of all of the agreements and a list of those items not successfully mediated, if any.

When mediation is successful and all terms are resolved, either of the parties can take the report with its still tentative terms to an attorney for review. If the attorney does not see major defects, he or she will generally be able to reduce the terms to a formal settlement agreement that will be expeditiously incorporated into a Final Judgment. It is increasingly rare to see this "tentative terms" stage since my experience is that attorneys are almost always present throughout the process and there is either agreement or there isn't. If the attorneys are present, the signatures of the parties to any agreements are final at that point. For this reason, I have sometimes refused to have my client sign anything that day; my reasoning is that, if the terms are good today, they will be just as good tomorrow. I would prefer that my client be able to review them again in the light of a new day rather than sign anything after many stressful hours of mediation. Of course, there is the risk of losing valuable gains in doing so and, therefore, I don't often use this "let's look at it tomorrow" procedure.

The success or failure of the mediation process can often be determined by the quality of the attorneys representing the parties. If both parties have good attorneys who care about the children, success is much more likely.

A Little Reality. Let me not mislead you about the mediation process. There are negatives, as you might expect. First, mediation is not always successful even with willing and able people. Considering that the mediator is usually dealing with the hardest issue of all, custody of children, he or she should feel good about keeping any number of couples out of a custody battle. Nonetheless, for those who fail to reach agreement in mediation, the effort would seem to show little tangible results.

It is impossible to determine other factors, such as how many of the successful mediating parties would have resolved their differences without mediation. Even if a large number of those would have settled anyway, the process certainly makes the settlement easier for them and probably settles a reasonably high number of cases that would not otherwise have settled.

Courts routinely order the parties to submit to mediation on either certain specific issues (such as custody) or all issues and some courts require the attorneys to participate. Since both attorneys and the mediator (unless court-employed and paid) must be paid, the process can be very expensive. The attorneys' presence can sometimes make the process adversarial and lower the chances of success. Nevertheless, the courts are finding that wholesale mediation is likely to reduce the trial dockets enough to justify the costs. For this reason and because it often narrows the issues in even the unsuccessful efforts, the courts seem committed to ordering it in every case. The process is also somewhat mechanical and manipulative. That's certainly not all bad. People going through a divorce usually need structure, and they usually also need help in bringing out their better nature. The question is whether the process overcomes its methods to achieve a real commitment from the parties.

I believe in mediation. Reasoning together can do no harm. If you are the right people, if you want to avoid a custody battle, and if you are having trouble communicating with your spouse, mediation is for you. If litigation is better than violence, then certainly mediation is better than litigation.

If mediation may be of help to you and your spouse, talk to your attorney about whom he or she recommends. If you don't have an attorney, contact the court administrator at your local courthouse. Ask if they have a mediation program. A court-related mediator may be the least expensive one available, and possibly the best qualified. Finally, if the court does not have one, look in the Yellow Pages under mediators, counselors, marriage counselors, etc.

Mediation in the private sector can be expensive. If the mediation is effective, however, your money has been well-spent.

13

ROLES AFTER DISSOLUTION

Your relationship to your children and your former spouse after a divorce is both social and legal. Laws have become more sophisticated as our understanding increases about the difficult relationships after a divorce. The latest advance is shared parental responsibility.

Shared parental responsibility is the legal phrase that sums up the roles of the ex-spouses. In effect, it says that both parents retain full rights to their children. There is no longer "custody" and "visitation" in a technical sense (although the terms are still often used). The children live most of the time with the "primary residential parent" and have "contact" (rather than visitation) with the nonresidential parent. The contact should be frequent.

You would expect truly concerned parents to share equally in the major decisions about their children's lives: where they go to school, what doctor treats them, what religion they practice, and where they live. Unfortunately, such equal sharing is rare in divorces, probably even rarer than it is in marriages. It is an ideal the law sets out and the best parents strive for it.

The Custodial Parent
What are the respective roles for the parties under the law? Let's look at the wife/mother first, assuming that she has primary residential care (custody) of the

Shared parental responsibility is the sharing by divorced parties of all important decisions about their children.

children. Ideally, she provides a safe and secure home for the children while encouraging a strong bond between the children and their father. The mother is in a position to make the children's contact with their father easy or difficult. Being on the scene, she can make all the decisions and only notify the father after the fact, if at all. It takes a strong and caring woman to place her children's interest above her own and include the father in all important decisions.

Some women fear that fostering a strong father-child relationship will give the father a better chance of obtaining primary residential care in the future. They may be right but they are probably wrong. To change primary residential care, the father must prove that a substantial change has occurred since the divorce that makes it in the children's best interests that they reside with him. If the father can show that, despite the mother acting unselfishly, then the children should be with him. If, on the other hand, he only gains "custody" of the children because she showed herself to be an inadequate custodial parent by, among other things, interfering with visitation, he might just be the lesser of two evils.

The point is that you should always try to do what is best for the children. Few fathers are so unfit that they shouldn't share fully in decisions about their children or see them frequently. Any mother who charges the father with being unfit or asserts that he shouldn't see the children must be presumed to be wrong and bears a tremendous burden to defend her position.

The primary residential parent can usually sway the children to take any attitude that parent wants. Not all prejudice is created by openly hostile comments. In fact, the influence is usually subtle. Children are influenced by exasperated looks, by defensive and hostile body language, by indirect comments on lifestyle, and by hundreds of other clues of the custodial parent's true feelings. They sense the tension their other parent feels when he or she comes to pick them up. If the custodial parent, usually the wife, feels deep hostility and anger toward the other parent, the children will know it. And they will do one of two things: share those feelings or grow to distrust the feelings of the custodial parent. Either way, the sympathy with the custodial parent's feelings or the distrust seriously interferes with child-parent relationship. Both are bad for the children.

Some anger and hostility is inevitable in most divorces. Deep and lasting anger is not, and it can be very destructive for the children. Where it exists, the party should seek counseling to reduce or eliminate those feelings. Such counseling will yield benefits for both the parent and the children.

If you are the custodial parent and you find that your children are becoming more and more distant from your former spouse, you should make an honest appraisal of yourself first before looking for fault elsewhere. If you know that you can't be objective about your conduct and attitudes, and few people can be, spend the money for at least one counseling session to get a professional opinion. If, after your evaluation, you are satisfied that you are not causing your children's behavior, try to talk with your ex-spouse about what may be bringing about the distancing. Don't do it in a judgmental way and don't force it on your spouse but open the door to try to work things out for the best interests of the children.

The Noncustodial Parent

What about the father's role, assuming that he is the noncustodial parent? First, he must pay his child support. There's no excuse for not doing that. Even if he is having financial difficulty and can't pay it all, he should pay what he can. (Paying part of it won't relieve the unpaid part; eventually he will have to catch up.)

Next, he must participate in his children's lives as much as possible. He must exercise all the visitation he can, subject, of course, to the contact schedule agreed between him and his wife. Regular visitation is extremely important; predictability makes the children feel more secure and safe. Visitation on a regular basis also reduces the need to negotiate time with his ex-wife and the conflict that so often accompanies such discussions. Both parents are better off saving their energies for dealing with any real problems their children may have.

The father must encourage his ex-wife to discuss important decisions about the children. He cannot sit back and wait for her to come to him. If he doesn't ask, she might assume that he doesn't care or doesn't want to be bothered. He must let her know that he is interested and will make the time to discuss the children.

If he senses a distance developing between himself and the children, he should try to work it out with the children, but not by questioning them incessantly about what is bothering them or by asking if something is wrong. He must open himself up to them and talk about his feelings. He can even talk about his feelings about the divorce if, and only if, he can do so without criticizing his wife. The children are probably afraid of many things. They can feel the powerful emotions bottled up in their father and don't know if he is angry at them. They might feel guilty about the divorce and think that their father should be mad at them; this is very common among children of divorced parents. The children may also be trying to adjust to loving two people who seem to hate each other so much; they don't yet know how to handle it. The father needs to get to know his children all over again. He has become a different person, almost a stranger, as a result of the divorce: he doesn't live in the house any more, he doesn't love their mommy, and he doesn't sit in his favorite chair. All of those things were the things that made him seem familiar. With so many everyday things changed, the children have a tremendous adjustment to make with him. He must work with them through the adjustment.

Suppose he tries all these things, and nothing works. And suppose he becomes convinced, after honest reflection, that his wife may be, intentionally or inadvertently, aggravating the problem. He must make the effort, again in a non-confrontational manner, to discuss it with his wife. He must express his concern for the children and ask for her assistance in helping the children. There is risk in starting such a conversation, and it may not be welcomed the first time. But the children need a strong relationship with their father. That relationship is worth a lot of risk and a lot of effort.

Most of all, a father must make sure that his children know he loves them. That is often hard in even the best of divorces: the kids are living with their mother and he may be tense when he has to face his ex-wife to pick them up; the children are aware of the tension and are uncomfortable themselves. It's up to the father to break the ice with the children and encourage them to open up. That's not easy, but it will get easier with practice.

What do you do during visitation? You should do the same things you would do if you were living with your children. No, that does not mean that you lie on the couch and watch television. It means, above all else, that you must provide your children with a home in which they feel welcome and one that they feel a part of. Even if you live in an apartment, make them feel that a part of it is theirs. If you can, provide them with a room or rooms of their own where they can keep their toys and clothes when they are with you. Cook for them and wash their clothes. Play catch out in the back yard and even have them do minor chores around the house.

We've all heard of "Disney World" daddies, those fathers who make every contact an occasion for a special trip. That's overreacting. I don't think that's what the children really want and I don't think that it forms the right relationship with the children. Sure, it's nice to take the kids out to eat or to the movies sometimes, but it's not good to do it all the time. You don't buy kids' love any more than you buy their respect. Talk to them in advance about what they want to do; talk to them and let them be part of the decision. If they know that they'll be asked for their ideas, they'll learn to plan in advance and the decisions will get easier and easier. But don't give in to every selfish whim; kids will be kids and some of them will eat candy all day long if you let them. Give them some guidance and structure.

Responsibilities of Both Parents
Both parents will face some problems in common. The first is, as I've discussed,

encouraging (as hard as it may be) love and respect for the ex-spouse. The second is discipline; any two parents will differ, in the degree and method, about proper disciplining of children. To the extent tolerable, each parent must respect the other spouse's methods and philosophy. If they don't, the children will, at best, become confused; at worst, they'll become manipulative.

Children are going to become manipulative anyway. Your battle will be to recognize it and deal with it. They'll play the two of you against each other. Don't believe everything your children tell you about your ex-spouse. As hard as it is to believe, they will lie to you, about the most unbelievable things. Kids are a lot smarter, and certainly a lot shrewder, than we want to admit. Remember that they are fighting to survive the divorce, and they'll marshall all of their defenses and shrewdness to do that, often to your detriment. Children learn social responsibility from you. By being a bit skeptical about their ploys, you discourage selfish behavior and help the children learn to cope in appropriate ways.

At the same time, you must tolerate your children's unexpressed grief and turmoil. Their anguish may not be apparent, but it can come out in indirect ways, such as fights with their friends or poor school performance. Be alert to behavioral changes and consider counseling if you think your child is having excessive trouble.

During or just after a divorce is the wrong time to be excessively tough on your children; it's a time of adjustment. On the other hand, don't abandon discipline entirely. Your children need guidance and they need it from you. If anything is worse than buying their love, it's trying to win them over by giving them complete freedom. Be flexible, but let the kids know that there are limits.

Parenting is difficult. Even in a good marriage, few parents are highly skilled in dealing with their children and their problems. Take this time of adjustment to improve your skills. Look for good books on the subject and work on the skills they teach. One very good book is *P. E. T. (Parent Effectiveness Training)* by Thomas Gordon. It's dated and quirky in places but overall, it will give you some excellent insight into your relationship with your children.

Relationships with Family and Friends

In addition to an ex-spouse and children, a divorced person will still have to deal with the people around him or her, most of all friends and relatives. Relatives shouldn't be much of a problem. They should be told what they need to know; their help should be accepted when it is offered and, within limits, asked for when it is needed.

In-laws may create a different problem. Some people have been very close to their in-laws during the marriage and don't want to lose the relationship. This can be touchy. In many cases, the ex-spouse will resent any continuing relationship of the other spouse with his or her relatives. Fortunately, it isn't the ex-spouse's decision. I can only suggest that contact with the in-laws at an appropriate time will open the door. The in-laws can then show whether they are interested in continuing the relationship.

Friendships can be even more difficult. Most friends will be friends of both spouses. Again, all one can do is open the door and show that he or she is interested in continuing the friendship. Under no circumstances should the friends be enlisted to take sides. That will end friendships faster than anything else. On the other hand, if your friend expressly seeks to talk about the divorce, take the opportunity to talk. Everyone needs someone to talk to, especially during and after a divorce. Don't abuse such a friend by talking about nothing except your divorce, but be open to the help that friend is offering.

Your friends are very important during your divorce. Keep in touch with them and let them know that you want to remain friends. Even mutual friends can, in some cases, remain friends of both parties. Preserve all of the friends you can.

Everyone is somewhat neurotic during and just after a divorce. If you find you can't trust your decisions, get professional help. It's not the crazy person who gets help; if you need help, you've got to be crazy not to get it.

14

What you will learn in this chapter:
- why nuptial agreements are used and what they do
- what types of nuptial agreements exist
- what such agreements usually cover
- whether a court can save you after you signed a bad agreement
- when and how much disclosure of finances is required
- why the protected spouse must make sure the waiving spouse is well advised before signing the agreement
- whether you can have an oral nuptial agreement
- whether you can draft your own agreement

NUPTIAL AGREEMENTS

Nuptial agreements have become popular because nuptial bliss is not guaranteed and because more people are entering into second and third marriages with children and assets. Nuptial agreements reflect the reality, not the romance, of marriage.

A *nuptial agreement* is an agreement that alters the legal relationship that a marriage otherwise creates. Throughout history, society and the law have defined the relationship between a husband and wife; the law provides for duties and responsibilities that exist during the marriage and after it ends, whether the end occurs by death or divorce. This legal definition of the marital relationship is the nuptial relationship that will exist if the parties don't agree otherwise; by marrying without a formal nuptial agreement, the parties are adopting the law's provisions as their nuptial agreement. As a result, a formal nuptial agreement is used only for two purposes: (1) to change the law's provisions or (2) to eliminate uncertainty about how the law's provisions will be applied.

There are two types of nuptial agreements — antenuptial (also called prenuptial) and postnuptial agreements. The only difference is that antenuptial agreements are signed before the wedding; postnuptial after the parties are already married. With one difference, the law treats both exactly the same.

Essentials of Nuptial Agreements

Nuptial agreements are contracts. Simply stated, there must be definite terms, understood and voluntarily accepted by both parties. All nuptial agreements are within the statute of frauds which, among other things, requires that the agreement be in writing and signed by the parties.

Prenuptial agreements are now controlled by the Uniform Premarital Agreement Act (UPAA), which went into effect in Florida on October 1, 2007. It does not change much that applied under caselaw. It eliminates the need for consideration (which, formerly, was based upon the marriage itself).

The UPAA says that parties can contract with respect to: (1) any and all property owned by either or both of the parties, (2) the parties' rights to deal with property, (3) rights upon separation, divorce, or any other event, (4) alimony and waivers of alimony, (5) wills and trusts to carry out the agreement's terms, (6) life insurance, (7) choice of law (that is, what state's law govern the agreement's interpretation), (8) "any other matter" not in violation of public policy.

Although the act expressly prohibits any provision that limits child support (but not a provision that expands it), it does not mention anything about custody or visitation. I am confident that the courts will retain the power to decide those issues no matter what the parties may put in an agreement.

An agreement can only be amended or revoked in a writing signed by both parties. No agreement will be enforced if it (1) was not voluntary, (2) was the product of fraud, duress, coercion, or overreaching, (3) was unconscionable when it was executed. An "unconscionable" agreement will be enforced if there was full financial disclosure, a waiver of any further disclosure, and the challenging

A **nuptial agreement** is a written contract in which one or both parties waive certain rights that they would otherwise have under law.

A **prenuptial agreement** is one entered into before the parties marry. It is also called an **antenuptial agreement**.

A **postnuptial agreement** is one entered into during the marriage. For this reason, divorce settlement agreements are actually just postnuptial agreements.

Consideration is anything exchanged for something else and is essential to make most contracts enforceable; bare promises, without any consideration from the promisee, are unenforceable under law. Consideration does not usually need to have any financial value to make a contract enforceable.

Intestate rights are rights that a survivor would have if his or her spouse were to die without having made a will.

Pretermitted rights are rights that a survivor would have if his or her spouse were to die having made a will before the marriage and without revising it after the marriage.

spouse had (or reasonably could have had) adequate knowledge of the other party's property and financial obligation.

Perhaps the most important provision in the UPAA is the provision that says that a waiver of alimony can be overridden by a court in a divorce action if the effect of it is to put the waiving spouse onto public assistance. Some courts had exercised that power in the past, although very rarely. An interesting aspect of the reservation of that power to the court is that it limits the court to ordering only so much support as is "necessary to avoid that eligibility (for public assistance)." If applied literally, the court would have to determine the minimum support needed to disqualify the recipient and award not one penny more.

Subject Matter. Under the "any other matter" clause of the UPAA, nuptial agreements may provide for any aspect of the marriage, from who takes the garbage out to who drives the Porsche. Usually, however, such agreements are used to provide one party or the other with financial protection. Thus, most agreements provide certainty if either a death or divorce occurs by covering one or more of the following: (1) how much alimony, if any, will be paid if a divorce occurs; (2) how property accumulated during the marriage will be divided in a divorce; (3) how the parties will share in each other's estates upon death; and (4) how the children will share in each party's estate.

Usually, parties enter into a nuptial agreement only if one of them is far wealthier or better employed than the other. Nuptial agreements are also used to provide financial protection for children of a former marriage. Let's consider some examples of how and why agreements might be used.

Consider first a very simple example. A wealthy middle-aged doctor marries a 22-year-old blonde whose only assets are visible when she walks into a room. To reduce the chances that the blonde isn't just gold-digging, our doctor might require a nuptial agreement protecting his existing assets and limiting the amount of alimony she would get upon divorce. Often the amount of alimony will be on a sliding scale tied to the duration of the marriage; she might get $1,500 per month for 24 months if the marriage is less than two years or $4,000 per month for 60 months if it lasts ten years. Provision could also be made if children are expected. Unless the doctor had close relatives (as in our next example), there might be no provision limiting the blonde's share in the doctor's estate.

Now suppose that both parties had been previously married and both have children; assume also that they both have significant estates. If they have no nuptial agreement and one of them dies, the surviving spouse would be entitled to no less than a spouse's share, that is, 30% of the entire estate after taxes and expenses of administration. This is true even if the deceased made no provision for the survivor in the will. To avoid this, the parties can agree to each maintain a will making certain provision (or no provision) for the survivor and expressly waiving all other rights against the other's estate. This agreement will be effective. The waiver of "all rights" to the other's property or estate is a waiver of spouse's share, family allowance, exempt property, homestead rights, intestate rights, and pretermitted interest, but it is better to expressly waive each of them.

In this example, since both parties have significant assets, both might waive the right to seek alimony if a divorce occurred. They would generally agree that each party's assets coming into the marriage would remain that spouse's sole property and that any increase in the value of that property would remain that party's. Provision is usually made for division of property acquired during the marriage. Likewise, because of case law, it may be necessary to specify that both active and passive increases in value remain the spouse's property.

Disclosure. Basically, there must be a fair, full, and open disclosure of assets and financial obligations by both parties before they enter into a nuptial agreement. This gets complicated because there are exceptions. First, if the provision for the spouse is fair (not "unconscionable" under the new UPAA), the absence of full disclosure will not matter. Second, the disclosure is not required if the spouse already knows or should know generally ("adequate knowledge") about the partner's finances. Third, for probate purposes only, no disclosure is required if the agreement is entered into before the parties marry. Thus, if the agreement is entered into before the marriage and only covers death benefits, no disclosure is necessary. Under all other circumstances, disclosure (or adequate provision) is required to give greater assurance of enforcement.

Since few agreements cover only death and since the adequacy of the provision will only be determined later, there is only one way to be sure that your agreement will stand up: make a full, fair, and open disclosure.

Effectiveness of Nuptial Agreements. The freedom to contract includes the right to make a bad bargain. Thus, an unconscionable provision for the wife (or for the husband) will not necessarily void an agreement. A disproportionate provision does, however, raise the presumption of coercion and the husband must then prove disclosure (or knowledge) of finances and a voluntary entry into the agreement. Independent legal advice is not necessary but gives the agreement a better chance of surviving.

There are some interesting cases that illuminate what this means. In one, the husband, who happened to be an attorney, claiming to be overwhelmed by his love for his wife-to-be, imposed an agreement on her that, upon divorce, gave her his previously owned house and a lot more. When they divorced two years later, he sought to void the agreement. The court noted her indifference to the agreement and his expertise as an attorney and upheld the agreement, stating, however, that, if she had been the one who was an attorney, the result might have been different.

In another case, the wife, facing an inadequate provision, asserted that she had only a short time to look over the agreement before signing it, she lacked advice of counsel, and she was unsophisticated in business. The court held, however, that none of that proved either coercion or other involuntariness; the agreement was upheld.

The granting to the court of the power to (partially) throw out an alimony waiver carries forward a developing trend to review the provision for alimony in light of its fairness at the time of the divorce, rather than looking at the circumstances existing at the time of the execution of the agreement. Of course, many agreements that are fair when the parties marry are not at all fair when they divorce. Some of the benefit to the wealthier party of nuptial agreements has been lost because of the change. On the other hand, it is far more likely that neither party will go from prosperity to misfortune.

With regard to death benefits, the issue of fraud has been clarified. In a noted case concerning an antenuptial agreement, the husband willfully and materially misrepresented his assets; he lied. When he died, the wife learned of his wealth and asserted fraud. Even though he had no duty to disclose his finances since the agreement was before marriage, she argued that, once he did disclose, he had to be honest. The courts disagreed and upheld the agreement, stating that nondisclosure in any manner had no effect on an antenuptial agreement; it wouldn't be fair, the court said, to punish someone who made some disclosure when someone who made none was protected. With regard to the fraud issue, the court held that the only type of fraud that would void the agreement would be the type that misled the wife into believing that she was signing some other type of instrument, such as a wedding license application. (This reasoning accords, you will note, with the type of fraud that will void a marriage.) I doubt that this will remain good law under the new UPAA.

There is a degree of coercion in almost every nuptial agreement. Most are entered into with either an express or implied "sign this or I won't marry you." You can do that, but you can't do it right before the wedding.

In one case, the groom picked up the bride-to-be to go to the church. He picked her up early because he had a stop to make — at his lawyer's office. Once there, he presented a take-it-or-forget-the-big-wedding agreement that made her an indentured servant for life (or similar terms); he gave her the opportunity to get legal advice — from his attorney. This poor woman was given three pitches, all strikes: last-minute agreement, unfair terms, and no independent legal advice. When the inevitable divorce occurred, however, it wasn't she who was out; the agreement was thrown out. I suspect that the wife's ultimate award included something to repay her for the mistreatment in the agreement.

It is important to understand that no single element will invalidate an agreement. If the agreement is a last-minute proposal but it is fair, it will be upheld. If the terms are outrageous but the wife had full disclosure, months to consider the agreement, and the advice of a good attorney, she will probably be held to its terms. Thus, an agreement will be upheld if it is either (1) fair, even if no disclosure were made, or (2) unfair and the wife knew all the husband's assets and income.

Keep in mind that a disclosure of assets is required for death provisions only if the agreement is made after the wedding.

One tricky situation has been resolved by the court. Suppose the parties orally agreed upon death benefits before the wedding without disclosure but didn't write the terms down or sign them until after the wedding. Is the agreement antenuptial or postnuptial? Remember, first, that an agreement waiving death benefits can only be made in a writing signed by the waiving party. Second, keep in mind that a waiver without disclosure can only be made before marriage. Here we have non-disclosure and a writing after marriage. Is the waiver valid? The court held that it was since the documenting of the oral agreement was not a new contract made after the wedding; the essential agreement was made before marriage and the later reduction to writing satisfied the requirement that it be in writing.

Some other difficult timing questions have come up. In one case, a valid nuptial agreement provided that the wife would get $150,000 if the husband died. The husband, however, made a later will that gave her $250,000. The wife sought the $150,000 *in addition to* the $250,000, claiming that she was a contract creditor for that additional amount! The court let her have the $250,000 but no more.

In another case, the will preceded the agreement. Since the will, which was never changed, was more generous than the agreement, the wife sought to receive the bequest in the will. The court refused to allow her to do so, holding that the language of the agreement waived her right to take under the will.

Discretion of the Court. In divorce actions, we are in a court of equity. That will affect the result more than any written rule or statute. The judge generally has tremendous discretion to do what is right. If the effect of a nuptial agreement is to cast a former wife of a millionaire onto the welfare rolls, the judge will now award support. If an agreement will wipe out a good and decent husband to the benefit

Suit money is an award of attorney's fees and costs to the less able spouse at the beginning of the divorce to enable her or him to retain an attorney.

of a greedy wife, that agreement is in trouble. The court does not, at least historically, have as much latitude with nuptial agreements as it usually would in divorce matters since, as stated above, the right to contract includes the right to make a bad bargain.

For example, a lump sum amount agreed between the parties to replace all support and alimony cannot, according to case law, be modified by the court. Consider, however, that the court has the power to review the support provisions for two purposes. First, the judge can consider whether a change of circumstances has occurred which would make it inappropriate to enforce the terms originally agreed. For example, suppose a healthy wife of 22 agreed to accept $10,000 in lieu of all alimony if divorce occurred; 30 years later, immediately after a crippling automobile accident, her husband divorces her and wants to pay her just the $10,000. Obviously, under the UPAA, he's looking at permanent alimony.

Suppose, on the other hand, the agreement provided for $5,000 per month in permanent alimony if divorce were to occur. And suppose that the wife immediately made an avocation of marital misconduct which resulted in a divorce less than a year after marriage. Would the misconduct constitute failure of consideration and permit the court to void the agreement? There is no Florida case on this point but other states have held that the agreement can be voided if the wife is guilty of material misconduct.

Basically, a nuptial agreement proffered in a divorce action is subject to being treated like any settlement agreement. After all, a settlement agreement is really nothing more than a postnuptial agreement. Nonetheless, the vast majority of all nuptial agreements are upheld when challenged. It takes extraordinary circumstances to invalidate (factually or legally) a properly prepared agreement.

Miscellaneous Points

Because of their great importance, nuptial agreements must be carefully thought out, well drafted, and detailed. Even small errors can invalidate them. Nothing in this book is going to prepare you enough to draft your own agreement. You are, however, in partnership with your attorney in the representation and it helps if you understand why your attorney must do certain things. Let me, therefore, finish this chapter with a few points that relate to nuptial agreements.

Statute of Frauds. As stated earlier, a nuptial agreement is subject to the statute of frauds. It must be in writing to be enforceable.

Separation/Attorney's Fees. Most nuptial agreements deal with alimony (or the waiver of alimony) upon divorce. This does not affect the wife's entitlement to temporary alimony, suit money, or attorney's fees. Even if the wife specifically waives alimony during a separation, she may still be entitled to seek it from the court; Florida courts have taken the position that a waiver of temporary alimony does not alter the husband's obligation to support the wife so long as they remain married.

Even though attorney's fees are in the nature of alimony, they are not waived by a general waiver of alimony. In one case, the wife did waive attorney's fees in the agreement, but her waiver was held to be limited only to the divorce action itself and not to any post-judgment proceedings.

Public Policy. Many public policies bear upon divorce proceedings. One policy forbids any agreement that encourages or facilitates divorce. No one knows what that means since every settlement agreement and every nuptial agreement seems to do just that. Nevertheless, nuptial agreements are not such agreements under case law; therefore, they are presumptively valid.

Another public policy is that parties who are unable to act at arm's length because of their close and confidential relationship must act with a high degree of candor and fairness. Unfortunately, in this area, they must act either with candor or with fairness. As we have seen, no candor is needed if the provision is fair; no fairness is needed if there has been a disclosure.

It would seem that public policy would nullify the waiver of rights to unknown assets. While that is true in divorce actions, where disclosure is required, it is not true for waivers of death rights if waived before marriage. Obviously, a valid waiver effected without disclosure is a waiver of rights to unknown property.

Advice of Attorney. Although the advice of an attorney is not, as we have seen, absolutely essential to an effective waiver, it is foolish to rely upon an agreement entered without such advice. Both parties must have separate and independent advice. If the wife lacks the funds to hire her own attorney, the husband should give her enough money to do so and give her complete freedom to choose her own attorney. The use of one attorney for both parties or the selection of the wife's attorney by the husband are two ways to create a very shaky agreement.

Improper Transfers. It is improper to transfer property to another for less than full consideration to avoid that property being available to creditors. Under certain circumstances, a transfer of individually owned property into joint names as part of a nuptial agreement might seem to be such a transfer; it does effectively make that property unavailable to creditors without any individually owned property replacing it. Nevertheless, if there is a good reason for the creation of the joint marital estate (and there will generally be one), such a transfer is valid.

Cohabitation. It is common for nuptial agreements (as well as settlement agreements) to provide that alimony payable to the wife shall terminate upon her cohabitation with an unrelated male. The courts have held that a mere romantic interlude in which the wife spends several nights at a man's house will not end the alimony. Courts will undoubtedly use the considerations in the recent cohabitation statute. (See Modification for Live-in, page 109.)

Drafting. Courts don't like waivers of alimony. They will find any valid way to nullify such a waiver if it doesn't seem fair. In one case, the wife was granted 30% of the income from husband's property if he died; the agreement also provided that, if a divorce occurred, the husband would be released and discharged from any further obligation to the wife under the agreement. The court held that this was a valid agreement to settle the wife's entitlement if a death occurred but it was not intended to cover alimony rights if a divorce took place. The husband had to pay alimony because the agreement did not waive alimony by name. The message is clear: make sure the agreement is crystal clear and without any ambiguity as to both its scope of coverage and manner of dealing with all matters.

If you wish to have a nuptial agreement that has the best possible chance of being enforced, you need independent legal advice for both parties, adequate time for both parties to consider the terms and negotiate changes, full disclosure, and reasonably adequate provision for the less-advantaged spouse. Some courts may enforce agreements without all of those elements present; don't take a chance. Virtually every agreement executed with those four elements will be enforced. You are seeking certainty and you can only get that by following the rules. Be fair and everything else will fall into place.

Appendix A

CHOOSING AND DEALING
WITH LAWYERS

The public has mixed feelings about lawyers and understandably so. Although I believe that lawyers as a group are extremely honest and dependable, any mistake by a lawyer, whether a misuse of funds or the commission of a crime, makes headlines which creates unjustified mistrust toward all attorneys.

Accepting that lawyers must meet a high standard in the conduct of their lives and practice, there are good lawyers and there are bad lawyers. Because of the nature of our work, it really isn't hard to place a lawyer in one of those two categories. One easy criterion is whether the attorney upholds and respects the system. If an attorney doesn't show respect for the system he or she has sworn to uphold, there is no likelihood that that attorney will show any respect for you or your case. You should be able to gauge this during your first interview. Before that, however, you should gain some insight from the reputation the lawyer has. If the scuttlebutt is that he or she is a "sharp" lawyer or very aggressive, that lawyer may very well be walking close to the line. "Very aggressive" lawyers are often less than aggressive in protecting the integrity of the system. These generalizations are not always true, but such descriptions should put you on notice to be careful.

Finding a Lawyer

It isn't always easy to find a lawyer. There are, however, some ways that will increase your chances of finding the lawyer you need.

Recommendations. One of the best ways is on the recommendation of someone you know and respect. People generally use attorneys who reflect their own values; if you know someone with good values, good judgment, and with a high recommendation for a lawyer, that lawyer may very well be the one for you. Make sure, however, that the lawyer is recommended as a marital lawyer. Always use a specialist for major matters, especially for divorces.

Another excellent way to find a lawyer, probably the best way, is on the recommendation of another lawyer. Although lawyers usually recommend their friends when asked, a competent lawyer will rarely refer clients to a friend who is not also highly competent. We know that our reputations will be affected by the referral.

Probably, the worst way to choose a lawyer is through an advertisement. Former Chief Justice of the U.S. Supreme Court Warren Burger said: "My advice to the public is never, never, never, under any circumstances, engage the services of a lawyer who advertises." Why? Because good lawyers don't seek their clients through the advertising section of the newspaper; their practices are perpetuated by the recommendations of satisfied clients. If you ever consider hiring a lawyer because of an advertisement, ask yourself why the lawyer is advertising; then make your decision.

Referral Services. Another way to find a lawyer is through a lawyer referral service. If you are new to an area and have no other resources available, this may be a good bet. There are two types of public service referral services in Florida: local and statewide. The Florida Bar operates a statewide service that refers clients to attorneys in any county where there is no local referral service.

The problem with referral services is that you have no choice about the attorney; he or she may be a good lawyer, and he may not be. The attorneys are assigned cases on a rotation basis.

If you do not find a lawyers' referral service listed in the Yellow Pages among the attorneys' listings, call 1-800-342-8011 or go to the Find a Lawyer service on the Florida Bar site (http://www.floridabar.org) for help. You will be given the name of an attorney who will consult with you for up to a half hour conference and charge no more than $25. (If you qualify, you may even be able to obtain the services of an attorney for a reduced fee or no fee at all. Most attorneys are very generous in providing free services to indigent citizens.) The fact that you are referred to an attorney by a service does not guarantee that you will get a highly qualified attorney; however, many referral attorneys are highly qualified.

You need to be somewhat careful in using referral services. In the past, all referral services were operated by either the Florida Bar or a local Bar Association. Recently, however, some referral services have popped up which are no more than brokers. In exchange for a subscription fee paid by attorneys, they refer callers to their paying clients (that is, the attorneys paying them for the referral service). These outfits are not seeking to assure the public access to legal services; they are only interested in brokering callers to their customers. Before you accept a referral, ask very specifically if the "referral service" is sponsored by the Florida Bar or a local bar association. If it is not, you might want to reconsider using the referral.

Both the American Bar Association and the Florida Bar publish material to assist you in finding an attorney. The ABA puts out a pamphlet entitled "How to Choose and Use a Lawyer"; it can be obtained free of charge by writing to the Consumer Information Center, Dept. 612M, Pueblo, Colorado 81009. The Florida Bar publishes several free pamphlets including "Selecting a Lawyer for your Special Needs," "Lawyer Referral Service," and "Legal Aid in Florida." These pamphlets can be obtained by writing to Public Information and Bar Services, The Florida Bar, Tallahassee, Florida 32301-8226.

How Lawyers Do It. Finally, let me tell you how attorneys find counsel to assist them in another city or state. Assuming that they don't know anyone in the other city, they turn to a set of books found in every library. It is called *Martindale-Hubble* and it lists virtually every lawyer in the country. What's more, it rates them from "C" to "A." Actually, the ratings are shown as "CV" to "AV." The "V" indicates that the attorney is recognized by fellow attorneys for high ethics; no one gets any rating unless he or she earns the "V" first. Every attorney is subjected to being rated every year by the lawyers in his or her community. A "C" rating means that colleagues rate a lawyer's legal ability as fair to high. A "B" rating equates to "high to very high" legal ability. Finally, an "A" rating means a lawyer's legal ability is recognized to be "very high."

There are many, many lawyers with no rating. Fewer than 25% ever achieve a "B"; fewer than 10% ever receive an "A." The seriousness with which attorneys rate other attorneys is reflected in both the low percentage of lawyers with high ratings and in the fact that lawyers rely upon the ratings to find strangers in distant places to represent their clients.

One final note about *Martindale-Hubble*: Lawyers are permitted to place a biographical card in a separate section of the book. For each such lawyer, the card will list the lawyer's college and law school, any law school honors, bar offices held, publications and books authored, and, most important to you, his or her board certification, if any, and chosen areas of practice. *Martindale-Hubble* is probably as good a source of information and ratings on lawyers as you can find.

Board Certified Marital Lawyers. For the past two decades, the Florida Bar has been certifying lawyers in 15 areas or practice including: taxation, civil trial, criminal law, estate planning/probate, real estate, workers' compensation, and, most importantly to you, marital and family law. Before certifying a lawyer in marital and family law, the lawyer's experience, especially trial experience, is reviewed by the certification board. Because the trial experience must be so extensive, certification in marital and family law may be the most difficult to obtain.

Trial experience alone is not enough. If the lawyer proves to have enough trial work to meet the board's requirements, and there are no significant questions about his or her ethics, he or she may then be permitted to take the board's test. Many are tested, but few are chosen. The end result is that you can be sure that a board-certified marital and family lawyer is highly qualified.

Qualifications of a Good Lawyer. You need a lawyer that fits your needs. Keep that in mind. Some lawyers develop attitudes and preferences that may not be right for you. For example, if you are a woman, you shouldn't choose a "man's" lawyer; you won't be comfortable with each other. Likewise, men shouldn't go to a "woman's" lawyer, one, for example, who has earned a reputation representing doctor's wives.

Most marital lawyers don't get polarized by gender. But every lawyer with any experience has developed a style that reflects his or her attitudes. For example, some lawyers like to try cases, whether it's justified or not; a few will settle any case rather than try it. Neither extreme works well.

You need a lawyer with a well developed sense of fairness. A lawyer must be willing to try a case if it can't be settled, but he must know which cases can and should be settled. Without a sense of fairness, a lawyer cannot negotiate well.

You may consider having a "bomber" represent you. A bomber will fight no matter what — when it is in your best interests and when it hurts you. He will cost a lot of money. The result may be favorable but it may be disastrous. My experience with bombers is that, when the case is over (if it is ever over), the battlefield is littered with the crippled remains of both parties. There is rarely a winner when bombers are involved.

Interviewing Lawyers. It would seem to make sense to interview lawyers before hiring one. It just doesn't seem to work out well in practice. My experience is that clients who interview, or shop for, a lawyer tend not to make good clients; they tend to be compulsive, overcontrolling people with little faith in their case, themselves, and, ultimately, in their lawyer.

This does not mean that clients should feel obligated to hire the first lawyer they consult. Nor should they hesitate to change lawyers if they are unhappy. The problem with "shoppers," if there is one, may simply be that they think that they can evaluate a lawyer after 30 minutes in the office. Perhaps some can or, at least, they can decide whether the lawyer's reputation (which should have brought the shopper to the lawyer in the first place), is deserved.

You should be aware, however, that, through experience, lawyers have become leery of "shoppers." Fortunately, lawyers don't have to accept every client who wants to hire them, and "shoppers" are often talked out of hiring a lawyer by the lawyer himself.

Attorney's Fees. Talk about fees as soon as you think you may want to hire a lawyer. But don't make your decision on that alone.

The attorney with the highest hourly rate may be the cheapest in the end. He or she may, and should, be very efficient and knowledgeable. The initial retainer may put you off, but you must understand that the initial retainer is rarely the total you will pay him. Wouldn't you prefer to pay your lawyer a $6,000 retainer and end up with total fees of $6,500 than start with a $500 retainer and end up paying $10,000? Don't be fooled into thinking that there is any relationship between the size of the retainer and the final fee.

You generally get what you pay for. Marital lawyers are usually pretty famil-iar with the hourly rates other lawyers are charging. If one lawyer is out of line, charging more than he or she is worth, that will be recognized pretty quickly among other lawyers and among people seeking a divorce lawyer. An excessive-ly expensive lawyer will lose business and be brought back into line within a short time.

To some extent, you will control the cost of your divorce. Your lawyer will be charging you on an hourly basis and will charge you for all time spent on your case. You will be charged for the time you spend talking with your lawyer, for research, and drafting of pleadings, for time on the telephone, and for time spent reading material you provide. Most wasted fees are wasted on the last two items. Some clients call their lawyer about every little thing or drown their lawyer with papers. They pay for it in fees and by preventing their attorneys from dealing with the real issues of the case.

Dealing with Your Lawyer

Before you choose a lawyer, make sure that you are comfortable with him or her. You will have a very personal relationship with your attorney, so this is important. If you aren't comfortable, both you and the attorney will be well served by your going on to a different attorney right away. Unless the matter is very small, the cost of changing your attorney at the beginning will be less than the potential expense of continuing with the wrong attorney.

Be frank with your attorney. Tell him the truth about everything he or she needs to know. Your lawyer is required to keep your disclosures confidential.

Don't hide an affair from your lawyer; your spouse already suspects it. If your attorney doesn't know, you've already handicapped him or her.

You must be prepared to defer to your attorney's advice unless you are convinced, after the lawyer's position is explained to you, that he or she is not exercising good judgment. If you can't reach agreement on a course of action that is comfortable for both of you, get a new lawyer, don't try to make this one fit your ideas.

Keep in touch with your lawyer. This doesn't mean that you should overdo it, since you will be charged for all time he spends on your case, including telephone calls. You must understand that your lawyer represents many people; each client of them is a "boss" in a sense and your lawyer has to be responsive to the needs of each different personality. Your continuing contact will help keep your lawyer's attention on your particular needs while also keeping him or her informed of developments outside the case itself. Every case has an appropriate level of communication; work with your attorney in finding the level that fits your case. Both too much and too little communication can make your lawyer's representation of you less effective.

Don't listen to "street lawyers." Practically, everyone you know will want to give you advice about your divorce. Each of them has some experience with a personal divorce or with a close friend who just went through a divorce. Your friends mean well, but their experience is limited. They will worry you at a time when you don't need any more worries. Let your lawyer advise you; if you don't believe that your lawyer knows more than your next-door neighbor, you better get a new lawyer.

Counseling. Your lawyer is not a psychologist. He or she can do little to help you with your anger and your frustration. Your lawyer needs to know the facts about your spouse but doesn't need to listen to how you have been wronged for so many years. Lawyers are not trained to be psychologists.

Every person going through a divorce needs a lot of emotional support. Your lawyer will give you a great deal of support by being there and helping you through your case. But your lawyer cannot be your counselor. Use a mental health professional for that. See your minister, a marriage counselor, or a therapist, but don't waste your money by trying to make your attorney into one.

Don't expect your lawyer to be quite this frank with you. Your lawyer is concerned about you and wants to help you through your divorce. And your lawyer might be reluctant to tell you when you're using him or her for inappropriate emotional support. Don't put your lawyer in that position. Keep in mind the help you need from your lawyer and get the emotional support and advice from a professional qualified to give that.

A Special Relationship. Your relationship with your lawyer will be very much (but not entirely) "us against them." Your lawyer must be your trusted friend and advisor. You must feel free to express your feelings about the case and you must be willing to accept his or her opinion that you may be wrong. There is probably no greater service a lawyer performs for a client than to tell that client when he or she is wrong. When the relationship between you and your attorney is such that differences can't be aired, your opponent is the only possible winner.

When you find the right lawyer, you may be establishing a lifetime relationship. Your attorney will be listening to you and advising you on matters that will affect your life. A good relationship with your lawyer is one of the most important relationships you will form. Your lawyer can save you money, save you from worry, and ease your life in the future in ways you do not now expect. Be assured that a lawyer who fits your needs can be found if you make the effort.

Final Caveat

Let me give you one word of warning. The average layman has great difficulty in evaluating a lawyer's work; great skill often goes unnoticed and mediocre work is praised. Some of the worst lawyers have large and worshipful clienteles; some good ones barely keep their heads above water. A large practice does not mean that a lawyer is good. It only means that the lawyer is satisfying his or her clients.

Studies tell us that most people care less about whether they win or lose than about whether their lawyer believes in their cause and fights strenuously for them. I can confidently tell you that the vast majority of lawyers really do believe in their clients' causes and work hard to achieve success. The difference between successful and unsuccessful lawyers is often no more than the ability to convey conviction and dedication. Since lawyers are so reluctant to feign false praise for each other, you can rely upon statements made by other lawyers. If you ask a lawyer about a colleague and he or she says nothing or "Yeah, I know him," that's often damning with faint praise. If more than one attorney damns a colleague outright, that lawyer has probably done something to bring disrespect upon the profession. Don't believe anyone who defends such a lawyer by saying that the others are just jealous; I have never seen an ethical, skilled, and successful lawyer who drew any jealousy from the Bar as a whole. Such lawyers are a credit to our profession and there can't be enough of them.

You have to choose a lawyer with a few aids, a few guidelines, and a lot of intuition. I hope that this book will help you make a good selection. I can only encourage you with the proudest reference to lawyers in all of literature: "The first thing we'll do, let's kill all the lawyers," spoken in Shakespeare's King Henry VI (Part II) between two anarchists in acknowledgment of the fact that only lawyers protect society from anarchy.

Appendix B

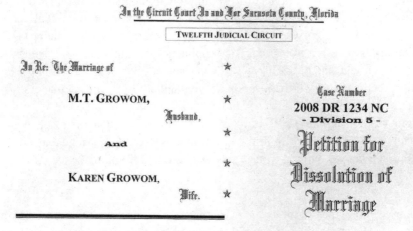

In the Circuit Court In and For Sarasota County, Florida

TWELFTH JUDICIAL CIRCUIT

In Re: The Marriage of

    M.T. GROWOM,
        Husband,

    And

    KAREN GROWOM,
        Wife.

Case Number

2008 DR 1234 NC
- Division 5 -

Petition for Dissolution of Marriage

The **Wife** brings this action, stating that:

Count I

1. **NATURE OF ACTION**. This is a petition for dissolution of the bonds of marriage between **M.T. Growom** and **Karen Growom**.

2. **RESIDENCE**. The **Wife** has been a resident of the State of Florida for more than six (6) months next before filing this Petition.

3. **MARRIAGE/SEPARATION**. The parties were married to each other on May 19th, 1983 in Sarasota, Florida and remain co-habiting to date.

4. **GROUNDS**. The marriage between the parties is irretrievably broken.

5. **CHILDREN**. There have been two (2) children born of this marriage: **GoAnna B. Growom**, born February 3rd, 1995; and **H.T. Growom**, born October 10th, 1998.

6. **PRESENT CUSTODY**. The said children are in the custody of both parties in the State of Florida and have been for more than six (6) months before the filing of this Petition.

7. **PRIMARY RESIDENCE**. Although both parents are fit, the best interests of the children will be served by having them reside primarily with the **Wife** and by entrusting her with the day-to-day and emergency decisions concerning the child.

LAW OFFICES OF GERALD B. KEANE

Florida Bar No. 156572

Suite 5 ★ 46 North Washington Boulevard ★ Sarasota, Florida 34236

941 366-7255

152

8. **F.S. 61.522**. In compliance with F.S. 61.522, the **Wife** avers that:

    a. The children have lived at the following location for the past five (5) years:

        1. 1865 Peachtree Boulevard, Sarasota, Florida from February 1999 until present.

    b. The names and present addresses of the persons living with the child during said period are, respectively:

        1. **M.T. Growom** and **Karen Growom**, 1865 Peachtree Boulevard, Sarasota, Florida.

    c. I do not know of, nor have I participated (as a party, witness, or in any other capacity) in any other court decision, order, or proceeding (including divorce, separate maintenance, child neglect, dependency, or guardianship) concerning the custody or visitation of the minor child in this state or any other state.

    d. I have no information of any pending proceeding (including divorce, separate maintenance, child neglect, dependency, or guardianship) concerning the custody of visitation of the child in this state or any other state.

    e. I do not know of any person who is not already a party to this proceeding who has physical custody of the children or who claims to have custody or visitation rights with respect to the child.

9. **CHILD SUPPORT**. The **Husband** is able to provide, and the **Wife** requires, both temporary and permanent support for the minor children of the parties.

10. **ALIMONY**. The **Wife** needs, and the **Husband** has the ability to pay, temporary, rehabilitative, bridge-the-gap, lump-sum, and permanent periodic alimony.

11. **REHABILITATION**. In order to increase her earning power and be able to contribute to her own support, the **Wife** is in need of additional education, training, work experience and is in need of rehabilitative alimony to enable her to secure the said education, training, and work experience.

12. **AUTOMOBILES**. The **Wife** drives a jointly-owned 2003 Lexus 430SC and is in need of same both permanently and pending this action; the **Husband** drives a jointly-owned 2000 Toyota Solara.

13. **USE OF MARITAL HOME**. The **Wife** is in need of exclusive use and possession of the marital home pending this action. The said property is located at 1865 Peachtree Boulevard, Sarasota, Florida.

14. **JOINT OBLIGATIONS**. The parties have jointly incurred financial obligations to third parties which are currently outstanding.

15. **CONTRIBUTIONS TO MARRIAGE/EQUITABLE DISTRIBUTION**.   Both parties contributed to the marriage as a whole and to the acquisition of the assets of the marriage.

16. **ATTORNEY'S FEES**. The **Wife** has retained **Gerald B. Keane** to represent his in this action and has agreed to pay him a reasonable fee for his services.

17. **INABILITY TO AFFORD FEES**. The **Wife** lacks the financial ability to pay the said fees and the costs of this action; the **Husband** has the ability to pay the said fees and all costs related to this action.

18. **MILITARY SERVICE**. The **Wife** has personal knowledge that the **Husband** is not in the military service at present.

Therefore, the **Wife** prays that:

a. Her marriage to **M.T. Growom** be dissolved.

b. She be awarded temporary and permanent custody of **GoAnna B. Growom** and **H.T. Growom**, the parties' minor children.

c. She be awarded temporary and permanent child support for the minor children.

d. She be awarded temporary, rehabilitative, bridge-the-gap, lump-sum, or permanent periodic alimony, or a combination thereof.

e. She be granted exclusive use and possession of the marital home pending this action.

f. She be granted temporary, permanent, lump-sum, or rehabilitative alimony, or a combination thereof.

g All questions between the parties relating to the respective debts and obligations to each other and to third persons be adjudicated.

h. The assets of the marriage be equitably distributed between the parties,

i. She be awarded attorney's fees and suit money both pending this action and for the entire action.

j. She be granted such other relief as the Court may deem appropriate.

k. Jurisdiction be retained by the Court for enforcement of the *Final Judgment* and otherwise.

Count II

The **Wife, Karen Growom**, sues the **Husband, M.T. Growom**, for partition, stating that:

19. **NATURE OF ACTION**. This is an action for partition of real and personal property.

20. **PARTITION**. The Wife seeks partition of real and personal property, hereafter described, which is owned by the parties and is incapable of division.

21. **REAL PROPERTY DESCRIPTION**. The property is fully described as:

> **Lot 1, TARA ESTATES**, as recorded in Plat Book 63, pages 6-8 of the Public Records of Sarasota County, Florida.

LAW OFFICES OF GERALD B. KEANE

Florida Bar No. 156572

941 366-7255

Suite 5 ★ 46 North Washington Boulevard ★ Sarasota, Florida 34236

22. **PERSONAL PROPERTY DESCRIPTION**. The personal property is fully described as: the furniture and furnishings of the marriage.

23. **INTERESTS OF PARTIES**. The **Husband** and **Wife** are presently owners by the entireties of the above-described real and personal property and, upon the granting of this dissolution, will become, according to the best knowledge and belief of the **Wife**, tenants in common in the said property, each owning such interest as the Court may find.

24. **ADDRESSES**. The names and places of residence of the parties are: **Karen Growom** and **M.T. Growom**, 1865 Peachtree Boulevard, Sarasota, Florida.

25. **VENUE**. The above described property is located in Sarasota County, Florida.

26. **ATTORNEY'S FEES**. The Wife has retained **Gerald B. Keane** to represent her in this action and has agreed to pay him a reasonable fee for his services.

Wherefore, the **Wife** prays that the above-described real and personal property be partitioned and sold, that the proceeds be divided between the parties in such proportions as this Court finds the respective parties' interests to be, and that the **Wife** be awarded a reasonable attorney's fee and the costs of this action.

> *I acknowledge a continuing duty to advise this Court of any custody or visitation proceeding (including dissolution of marriage, separate maintenance, child neglect, or dependency) concerning the child in this state or any other state about which information is obtained during this proceeding.*

KAREN GROWOM

GERALD B. KEANE
Attorney for **Wife**

LAW OFFICES OF GERALD B. KEANE
Florida Bar No. 156572   941 366-7255
Suite 5 ★ 46 North Washington Boulevard ★ Sarasota, Florida 34236

V	E	R	I	F	I	C	A	T	I	O	N

State of Florida
County of Sarasota

    Before me, the undersigned authority, this day personally appeared **Karen Growom** who ☑ is to me well-known or ☐ identified herself through her Florida Driver's License, and who was first by me being duly sworn, says that she is the **Wife** in the above styled cause and has read the *Petition for Dissolution of Marriage* and has personal knowledge of the facts and matters alleged in it, and each of these facts and matters is true and correct.

    Sworn to and Subscribed before me this _____ day of **September, 2008.**

Commission Expiration

Notary Public 9 GERALD B. KEANE

LAW OFFICES OF GERALD B. KEANE
Florida Bar No. 156572
Suite 5 ★ 46 North Washington Boulevard ★ Sarasota, Florida 34236
941 366-7255

Appendix C

PREPARING A FINANCIAL AFFIDAVIT

In concept, a financial affidavit is a simple document. It is a sworn statement of your income, expenses, assets, and liabilities. The form for the affidavit is prescribed by the Florida Supreme Court.

Both parties must file and serve a financial affidavit in a divorce case. If you are seeking support, you must serve it on your spouse (or his or her attorney) along with your notice of hearing on temporary support. Your spouse's affidavit must be filed no later than 5:00 P.M. two days (or seven days if provided by mail) before the hearing.

The standard interrogatories also require you to provide a financial affidavit along with the answers. If there is no temporary support hearing and no interrogatories are sent, both parties must file and serve their affidavits at least ten days before the final hearing.

Despite the use of financial affidavits in almost every divorce case, no one knows exactly what must be reported. Income, assets, and liabilities present minimal difficulty. Expenses are the problem. No rule states what expenses are to be reported; no case has ever said. And, for certain, lawyers don't know. Fortunately, developments in the law and particularly the requirement that child support be established using guidelines (which rely solely upon income), expenses are of little significance in the vast majority of cases.

Let me give you some ideas about what different expenses might seem appropriate and then I'll tell you why each of them is defective:

1. Past history. If you reported your expenses for recent past history, say for six months or a year, those expenses would show what you and your spouse expended together; they will have little relevance to what you need as a separated individual.

2. Future expenses. If you reported, instead, your guess of expenses for the foreseeable future, you could not support the figures with any documentation whatever; you could face a withering cross-examination on the affidavit.

3. Interim expenses. If you used the expenses you had immediately after the separation, your figures would, among other problems, be significantly exaggerated, since every move or transition necessarily involves a lot of unusual expense. Although useful for a brief period, possibly two months, this is probably the least reliable method of doing the affidavit.

What does that leave us? It seems that the best affidavit is one that merges all three. It considers past history and projects expenses for the foreseeable future, and reports interim expenses as nonrecurring. The only alternative, a cumbersome but often necessary one, is to file several different affidavits as the circumstances require.

Supreme Court Forms

At the end of this appendix, you will find a copy of the short form of the prescribed Florida Supreme Court financial affidavit. (The long form differs only in requiring more details about assets and liabilities, most of which is irrelevant.) I've filled it in for a hypothetical wife employed at a local establishment in her neighborhood. Skipping expenses for the time being, let's look at the different aspects of the form:

Employment Information. There's nothing complicated here. "Rate of pay" could cause some confusion. Since the affidavit is based on monthly income and expenses, some people think that the rate must be stated that way. It needn't; if your income is based on an hourly rate, you should insert the hourly rate.

Income. The income section requires you to report your "current" income and has prompts for a variety of other possible income sources. This, is obviously to avoid the previously common excuse, "Oh, gee, I forgot that I get a $10,000 bonus every year."

This section is not without its loopholes. For example, is a Christmas bonus part of your current income in July, especially if there is no guarantee that there will be a bonus this year? After years of recommending that you put it down anyway, I believe now that you should make an objective evaluation of your chances of getting it. If you are certain that you will get it and can make a safe estimate of its amount, list it. If, however, you have only a 50/50 chance of getting it, or the amount has fluctuated significantly, it would be unwise to put it down.

Overtime is another loophole. Some husbands develop "RAIDS" during a divorce. (RAIDS is "Recently Acquired Income Deficiency Syndrome") One of the ways they get it is by refusing to work any overtime. Even if an average of 20 hours of overtime was available each week for the last ten years, it always seems to disappear during divorces. And it seems like he'll never have overtime again.

Sometimes, attorneys inadvertently encourage that type of conduct. I'd like to believe that judges see through it and impute the overtime income in the absence of compelling evidence that work conditions have truly changed. I think it has to be reported and that you shouldn't change your overtime work pattern unnecessarily. (It sometimes can't be avoided because separations often impose schedule changes on fathers because of contact with the children.)

Assets. The affidavit requires you to report all assets, even those only in your husband's name, and split the value of marital assets. Because marital property will be presumptively divided equally, this presents an accurate picture of how division will occur.

Valuation can be difficult at times. For example, the house or vacant land probably hasn't been appraised in years. The cars may be too old to appear in the "blue book." A privately owned company is of very disputable worth. Honest guesses, however wrong they may be, rarely cause any problems. Disputes can be easily resolved through appraisals.

Assets are frequently overlooked, often honestly. But an overlooked asset will make you look worse than any other error on your affidavit. I'll tell you later how to minimize the risk of doing that.

Liabilities. Debts are just as frequently overlooked. Such omissions almost never make you look bad, but they can hurt your case.

Everyone wants to load up on liabilities and be weak in assets; think of it as the opposite of a financial statement with your bank. (That, incidentally, is why bank financial statements are the best source of impeaching information; no one ever underestimates assets, or overestimates liabilities, on a financing statement.)

Gifts/loans from parents probably present the biggest problem in this area. Was the $10,000 from Dad a loan or was it a gift? Often, there is no documentation and the parties honestly remember events differently. If your parents provided you with the money, you would have accepted it, like most adults, with the attitude that you would repay the money as soon as you could. Your spouse, on the other hand, would think that your parents owed it to you. Even if you had never repaid a dime in the last fifteen years, you would still retain your conscientious intention to pay it back. Hot disputes arise from such unwritten transactions.

Expenses. You need help to do the expenses well. But I think it is unwise to work with your attorney on the initial effort. Remember, you're paying your lawyer between $3.00 and $5.00 a minute (yes, a minute!), and he or she probably won't be as good at this type of work as your accountant or, even, you and your best friend.

We have already decided that your expense listing should be based on your records, your foreseeable future needs, and the immediate expenses related to the divorce. That decided, the task is easier. (Let me remind you again, however, to follow your attorney's directions. If he or she instructs you to approach your financial affidavit differently than I suggest, follow those directions. The only exception: if your lawyer should instruct you to use the affidavit to mislead the court, get a new lawyer. You shouldn't be paying anyone for that kind of advice.)

Steps to the World's Best Financial Affidavit

The Supreme Court tells us what form to use; we have no choice about that. It's what we do with that form that makes it something special. The "world's best" financial affidavit is simply one that is completely honest, accurate, and defensible. Let's go over the affidavit step by step.

Employment Information. Just make sure the information is accurate. Confirm the exact name of your employer and verify the address. If you have any doubts, ask your superior what your exact job title is.

Look on your latest paycheck for your rate of pay. If it doesn't appear there, call bookkeeping and get it. Make sure you know whether you are paid every two weeks or every half month; they are not the same since, over the course of a year, every month contains four and one-third weeks. That might not seem like a big difference, but consider that if you earn $500 every half month, you make $83.33 less each month than someone earning $500 every two weeks.

Income. Your base pay is usually pretty easy to determine. For some people, it isn't, however. For example, suppose you work in construction; weather can cause your weekly income to vary. Or suppose you are a sales representative and you get a draw against commissions.

When your base pay is not certain, you must rely on your income records. Get your pay stubs for the last six months; use a whole year's records if your income varies according to the season. If you don't have your pay stubs, ask bookkeeping at your company for help. Average your gross income (excluding overtime and bonuses) on a monthly basis. Adjust that, if necessary, for any unusual events that might have occurred during that period. Take the following example:

Gary Lugbacker, a carpenter, loses a lot of work because of rain days during the summer. His current rate of pay is $18.00 per hour. During the last year, he has averaged $650 per week income; however, most of that was before he received a raise from $15.00 per hour. To come up with a legitimate figure, all he has to do is calculate the average number of hours he worked during the last year, regardless of his pay rate, and calculate his current income by multiplying the average hours by the current hourly rate. His monthly income is four and one-third times his weekly average.

Now go down the list of other possible income sources on the affidavit form. That list should remind you of any income you might have forgotten. Just to make sure, however, go to your tax return for the last couple of years and make sure that you haven't overlooked anything.

Your next task is to list the deductions. This may involve some calculations. For example, you can't just copy the withholding deduction from your paycheck. The form requires that you "normalize" it to your actual status. Does that mean that you treat yourself as (a) married, (b) unmarried, (c) with dependency exemptions for children, (d) without exemptions for children, (e) with dependency exemption for your spouse, or (f) without exemption for your spouse? No one has bothered to explain what the Supreme Court meant.

Since the idea is to put everyone on the same basis for comparison purposes, the only logical answers for the wife (assuming that she has the children during the divorce) are (b) unmarried, (c) with exemptions for the children, and (f) without exemption for the spouse. For the husband, the answers should be (b) unmarried, (d) without dependency deductions for the children, and (f) without exemption for the spouse. Any other answers would make the court compare cherries with coconuts. Actual available funds for each must take into consideration the taxation that will exist after the divorce; current tax law gives the exemptions to the custodial parent unless the custodial parent voluntarily consents to his or her spouse taking it or the court awards it to the other party. (Of course, if the husband is seriously contesting custody, he should also include the children as dependents.) In sum, my advice is for both parties to normalize to the actual status as it will be, or they hope it will be, after the divorce.

FICA and Medicare deductions need to be normalized, too. As you may know, deductions are made at 7.65% (6.2% for Social Security and 1.4% for Medicare) of your gross income up to $87,000. The deductions then stop. You must normalize them if you make more than $87,000; you do it by averaging the $6,655.50 (7.65% times $87,000) over the whole year. (You should get $554.63 per month.) If you make less than $87,000, any paycheck should give you the right FICA deduction.

Most people have their insurance deducted from their paycheck. If you do, just take the amount from your pay stub. Confirm that it is deducted from every paycheck and not, say, once a month or every other paycheck.

Loans from your company's credit union will usually be deducted from your paycheck. Don't forget to list the deductions in the proper place. Loans deducted from the paycheck do not belong here. Even though they may actually be paid by a paycheck deduction, the loan payments should be listed among expenses as payments on bills. In my opinion, the proper place to list them is with the bills and not with the deductions from the paycheck. Your attorney may disagree; if so, follow your attorney's advice.

When you complete your deductions, the amount left over should be the same as you take home each month if you make an adjustment for normalizing the withholding and FICA. Check it to make sure. If you don't come out the same, look for a mistake somewhere.

Expenses. Now we come to the hard part. We can make it a little easier by breaking it down into parts. The parts are going to be (1) documented history, (2) adjustments for future needs, and (3) temporary expenses.

The documented history is made from two sources, income records and your checkbook. Let's deal with the checkbook first. You need to make a "spreadsheet" to start off. A spreadsheet is a large sheet of paper, usually at least 25 inches wide, with rules and vertical columns; you can buy them at any stationery store. You should tape them together in pairs, side by side, because you are going to need a lot of columns. You then write, across the top of the columns, the expense categories listed on the financial affidavit, one to each column. On the left, from top to bottom, list every check you have written for the last six months (or, preferably, the last year) and its amount.

Now comes the easy part. Decide, for every check, which expense category it fits. Sometimes, a check will cover more than one type of expense (for example, if you went to a department store and wrote one check for both a gift and for clothing for yourself). That's no problem; just put the appropriate amounts in each column. Make sure that the total of the separate columns for each line is the same as the check.

The most difficult check to spread is the one you used to make your credit card payment. You really need the credit card statement to break that one down. If you don't have it, make your best guess. With the credit card payment, you also have to make a decision about whether a particular payment belongs in your clothing expenses or in your payments on bills. I'll give you my opinion about how to handle that a little further on.

After you have all the checks spread, add up all the checks and all the columns. The sum of all the columns must equal the total of all of the checks. If it doesn't, you made a mistake somewhere. Once it balances, you have one more step. You must compare the check total with your total disposable income. They won't match unless every paycheck and every interest payment, etc., goes through your checking account. That is rare. Most of us spend a significant amount of cash. Put down the total of the unaccounted-for income right under the checks as if it were another check; call it "cash ($xxx.xx)" Now spread the cash across the expense columns as best you can. This won't always be easy and the result will be a guesstimate at best. Once you've done that, check yourself again by making sure the columns all add up to the total cash listed on the left.

Now you must make some adjustments. First, you must estimate how much each expense would have been different if your spouse had not been living with you. (If you are the noncustodial parent, reduce the amount attributable to the children also.) For example, food is the easiest to adjust: if it was just you and your spouse before the divorce, you might reasonably estimate that your food expense alone would be 60% to 65% of the expense for both of you. Throw out your spouse's clothing expenses and such entirely. Look at every item and eliminate or adjust each one where needed.

Another adjustment must be made for nonrecurring expenses. If your grandmother died last year and you had to travel to Maine for the funeral, that is not an expense that you should include for the future; take it out.

So far you should have no expense listed for credit card payments; you spread each payment to the appropriate column for which the charge was made.

If your health and/or life insurance is deducted from your pay check and you listed it as a deduction in the income section, you shouldn't have that listed as an expense. If you listed the insurance again, you would be taking the expense twice. You might indicate on that line "deducted from paycheck" so that the item isn't overlooked.

Now you need to pull out your crystal ball and estimate what adjustments are necessary to make the expenses realistic for the future. This involves some hindsight. For example, if you spent $35 per month for clothes last year because you couldn't afford more, add an amount that would have allowed you to reasonably meet your needs. If $75 per month would have allowed you to buy the clothes that you reasonably needed, change the $35 to $75 but make notes about why you feel you need the extra money.

Think of other ways that your spouse's absence will affect your expenses. You may need a whole lot less aspirin; on the other hand, you will have to pay for a plumber the next time your sink leaks. Try to think of every item your spouse cost you and everything your spouse saved you. Make notes so that you know where the figures came from. Now you have to do something about the credit cards. As I said, you can't look back at your actual monthly payments and just put them down. Instead, for each card on which you may reasonably be liable to pay, you need to take the outstanding balance for each card and estimate what monthly payment will eliminate the balance within a reasonable time, say a year or 18 months, if you make no further charges. Make sure you include interest. And make sure you understand how and why you did that; you may have to explain it in deposition or in court. You are not double-dipping; you are servicing a debt at the same time that you must buy clothes, etc.

Finally, make estimates of transitional expenses. These are expenses that you will have for the next several months as a result of the separation/divorce but won't have when the divorce is over. List your attorney's fees and be realistic. Either put these expenses in a separate category ("transitional expenses") or list them separately in the appropriate categories with an asterisk and explain them at the bottom of the page.

Let me remind you that your expense itemization is only as good as your ability to defend it. Make good notes and keep them in a neat manner so that you will be able to understand them when you need to refer to them.

Assets. Make a list of your major assets first. Put down your house, your cars, bank accounts, stocks, etc. Then, start putting down every little item you can think of. Your jewelry (item by item), your furniture (as a whole), any collection you might have, any debt owed to you. Put down your pension and any profit-sharing interest you may have. Do it for yourself and your spouse so that you have everything on paper.

Next, pull out tax returns for the last few years and see if you listed all of your income from stocks, bonds, or bank accounts. Check any bank financing statement that you filled out during more peaceful times.

Then, sit down with a friend and ask him or her to start naming things your friend thinks you own. You don't have to show your list; you'll be surprised how often a friend will remember something you've forgotten. If you're in the house, walk through it a few times, looking in every cabinet and closets for things of significant value you may have forgotten. Don't forget the pictures on the wall; some of them may be valuable. If you have a safe deposit box, go to the bank and look through it.

Finally, look through your checkbook to see if there are any relatively large checks for big items.

You will have some trouble with valuation. We all tend to overvalue our possessions and that's generally not to your advantage in a divorce. The criterion is not what an article is worth to you; rather, you must assign the price that an arms-length sale would bring. An "arms-length" sale is one between a willing seller and a willing buyer, neither of whom is under any coercion to sell or buy.

You may love your sofa, but the average person on the street is unlikely to pay more than $75 to $100 for it, even if you paid $1,200 to buy it only a year ago. Antiques are a different matter; they will tend to grow in value. Even so, be realistic about a piece's value. Where the assets justify it, you can obtain a personal property appraisal. Clothing has almost no value. Few people could sell their whole wardrobe for more than $250. Real estate values usually are estimated at the time of the first financial affidavit. Often, in the course of litigation, especially if the parties disagree on valuation, an appraisal will be done. Stocks and bonds have readily determinable values. Don't guess; go to your last statement or call your broker. Many people own time-shares in a condominium. Basically, most of them are worthless. If you think that I'm wrong, call up the company that's still marketing in the same building (they never seem to sell out completely) and ask how much they will offer to buy your week back. If they refuse (and they will), just put down a nominal amount on your affidavit, say $500 for a $3,000 share or $1,000 for a $6,000 share. If you really want the time-share out of the divorce, you don't have to be so cavalier; put down a higher figure. No one will ever criticize you for overvaluing your property. Your spouse may gladly offer it to you in exchange for something he or she wants.

When you enter the property on the affidavit, you must apportion the value between you and your spouse. That really isn't difficult. If the property is marital, you must show it as each of you owning half. If the property was acquired during the marriage but there isn't any title, it's half and half.

Liabilities. Debts are nothing more than negative assets. You find them in much the same places: income tax returns, checkbooks, etc. You can start by listing the obvious ones: house mortgage, car loan, credit card balances, etc. Don't forget to list any debt you owe your attorney. List any loans you still owe to relatives.

Liabilities rarely present problems. Be sure, however, that you check any promissory notes carefully.

Often, a note/mortgage on property owned by one party was signed by both parties. If so, list the debt even if you don't want, or expect to receive, the property. One tricky aspect of this is the fact that while you probably only have rights to half of a joint asset, you are 100% liable for the joint obligation on it. Some attorneys fudge on their client's net worth, not completely without justification, by giving their client only half of a property's value in the assets listing but all of the debt in the liabilities section. It may be technically accurate, but it is unquestionably misleading.

(A less common, and totally unjustified, trick is reporting only the equity in an asset in the assets list and the debt in the liabilities. Since many judges look at the debts and subtract them from the assets, the liability is deducted twice.)

Finishing Touches. At least a few days before the affidavit must be filed, bring your efforts to your attorney's legal assistant or secretary to go over with you. His or her experience can be a great help to you. When both of you are satisfied, your attorney will prepare it in "final" form. Before you sign it, however, your attorney will probably go over it one more time. Your attorney will be looking for anything that looks out of line and will ask you to explain any such items. Do not, however, depend on your lawyer to catch errors. Often, numbers that look normal to him or her will be wrong for you; abnormal numbers, ones that catch your lawyer's eye, may be correct. Ultimately, you will be on your own with the affidavit and your lawyer can only try to make sure that you can defend it.

Tricks to Avoid. Some attorneys like to pad financial affidavits. Let me tell you how they do it. (And then I will tell you not to be part of it.) The first way is to insert "reserves." You see it in various ways: "reserve for house repairs," "reserve for auto repairs," "reserve for vacations." There is a certain allure to such listings; they seem to make sense. They don't.

You should have already listed your historical and foreseeable repair and vacation expenses. Carried to its logical extreme, everyone could list $3,100 per month as "reserve for new house" since the average house costs $185,000 and Americans move on an average every five years. It is nothing short of deceit.

The second trick is to break down listings into smaller and smaller parts. The more categories you list, with a reasonable amount for each, the larger will be your needs. To take a ridiculous example, a meal for four might cost you $6.00 to put on the table; using this ploy, however, you could show a need of over $13.00: salad per person, $0.45; portion of meat, $1.20; vegetable, $0.40; potato, $0.15; butter, $0.11; salt & pepper, $0.02; beverage, $0.25; dessert, $0.48; beverage with dessert, $0.18; napkins, $0.02. No individual item is clearly excessive but, as a whole, the cost of the meal is way out of line. I think you get the idea: an overly detailed affidavit will be misleading.

Finally, an attorney might tell a client to puff each item by a certain amount, say 20%. If the electricity is usually $78 and you listed $93, the other side probably would have trouble picking that up unless he or she used an accountant.

Likewise, food expenses inflated from $325 per month to $380 would not necessarily show up. The bottom line could, however, inflate monthly needs from $2,500 to $3,000.

There are other tricks also. But just using these three, an attorney could double actual needs without any easy way to disprove it, short of hiring an accountant to go through the documentation for each item on the affidavit. That's not practical in 90% of all cases.

If your lawyer tries any of these tricks or otherwise suggests that you misrepresent your finances, get a new lawyer. A lawyer who would defraud the court will certainly defraud you. Why would such a lawyer's bills to you be any more honest than the affidavit?

When you receive a copy of your spouse's financial affidavit, look it over carefully. See if any of these tricks have been used to inflate the expenses. Scrutinize every item carefully and compare the amounts with yours. You may come up with discrepancies that can help your attorney prepare for deposition or final hearing.

Summary
Take care in working up your financial affidavit. Give yourself the benefit of every reasonable doubt, but don't purposely exaggerate any item. Get help whenever you can, but don't let someone else, even your attorney, do the affidavit for you. You must defend it and you must understand it.

The rules are simple: (1) be as honest as you can be; (2) be reasonable and fair in stating your needs; (3) keep good, neat, and usable notes for each item; and (4) keep in mind that the expense list is not really a list of expenses; it is a report of your reasonable needs if the money were available, taking into consideration your standard of living in the marriage.

Your careful preparation of your affidavit will help you in defending your figures. It will also put you in a very good position to assist your attorney in seeing through your spouse's affidavit.

In the Circuit Court In and For Sarasota County, Florida

TWELFTH JUDICIAL CIRCUIT

In Re: The Marriage of   ★

RHETT BUTLER,   ★   Case Number

         Husband,   **2008 DR 6660 NC**
                               ★   - **Division 7** -

And

                               ★   Financial Affidavit

SCARLETT O. BUTLER,

            Wife.   ★

State of Florida
County of Sarasota

     Before Me, This Day, Personally Appeared, Scarlett O. Butler, to me well-known, and, after being duly sworn, deposes and says that the following information is true and correct according to her best knowledge and belief:

EMPLOYMENT AND INCOME:	
Date of Birth: **01/01/1972**	Occupation: **Receptionist**
Employed by: **Stande & Waite, P.A.**	Telephone No.: **941-333-1234**
Employer's Address: **8000 So. Delais Avenue, Sarasota, Florida 34236**	
Rate of Pay: **$2,832/mo**	Paid: **Twice a Month**
Last Yr's Gr Inc (2007): **Wife: $17,000 Husband:**	

SUMMARY			
INCOME	$2,601	ASSETS	$92,200
EXPENSES	$3,050	LIABILITIES	$71,000
NET DEFICIT	$449	NET WORTH	$21,200

		SECTION I: PRESENT MONTHLY GROSS INCOME
1	$2,832	Monthly Gross Salary or Wages
2	$125	Monthly Bonuses, Comm'ns, All'nces, OvTime, Tips, & Sim Paymts
3		Monthly Business Income from All Sources Example: Self-Employment, Partnership, Close Corporations, and/or Independent Contracts (Gross Receipts minus ordinary and necessary expenses required to produce income) ☐ Attach sheet itemizing such income and expenses.
4		Monthly Disability Benefits/SSI
5		Monthly Workers' Compensation
6		Monthly Unemployment Compensation
7		Monthly Pension, Retirement, or Annuity Payments
8		Monthly Social Security Payments
9		Monthly Alimony Actually Received 9a. From this Case: $ 9b. From Other Case(s): $
10	$10	Monthly Interest and Dividends
11		Monthly Rental Income (Gross Receipts less Ordinary/Nec. Expenses req'd to produce income) ☐ Attach sheet itemizing such income and expense items.
12		Monthly Income from Royalties, Trusts, or Estates
13		Monthly Reimbursed Expenses and In-Kind Payments to the extent that they reduce living expenses.
14		Monthly Gains Derived from Dealing in Property (Excl. Non-Recurring Gains)
15		Itemize Other Income of Recurring Nature
	$2,967	PRESENT MONTHLY GROSS INCOME

		$130	Monthly Federal, State, and Local Income Tax (Corrected for filing status, Allowable Dependents, and Income Tax Liabilities) a. Filing Status: b. No. of Dependents Claimed: 2
		$236	Monthly FICA or Self-Employment Taxes
			Monthly Medicare Payments
LESS			Monthly Mandatory Union Dues
DEDUCTIONS			Monthly Mandatory Retirement Payments
			Monthly Health Insurance Payments (Including Dental Insurance; Adult Only)
			Monthly Court-Ordered Child Support Actually Paid (Children from Another Relationship)
			Monthly Court-Ordered Alimony Actually Paid a. From This Case: $ b. From Other Case(s): $
		$366	Total F.S. 61.30 Deductions
		$2,601	PRESENT NET MONTHLY INCOME

	OTHER EXPENSES			ACTUAL $PAYMENTS TO	
70	$30	Dry Cleaning and Laundry	91	$282	Automobile Loan
71	$75	Clothing	92	$45	Credit Cards
72	$75	Medical, Dntl, Presc (Uncov'd)	93	$15	JoAnn Kandew
73		Unreimb'd Mental Health Exp.	94		
74	$25	Non-Presc. Drugs, Cosmetics, etc.	95		
75	$15	Grooming	96		
76	$10	Gifts	97		
77	$50	Pet Expenses	98		
78		Club Dues/Memberships	99		
79		Sports and Hobbies	100		
80	$35	Entertainment	101		
81	$5	Periodicals,Books,Tapes,CD's	102		
82	$85	Vacations	103		
83	$10	Religious Organizations	104	$342	SUBTOTAL
84		Bank charges, Credit Card Fees			
85		Education Expenses			
86		Other:			
87					
88					
89					
90	$415	SUBTOTAL			
105	**TOTAL MONTHLY EXPENSES:**			**$3,050**	

SECTION III: ASSETS AND LIABILITIES

A	Description of Asset [Check Box Next to Item If you Wish Awarded to You]	Current Fair Market Value	Non-Marital	
			Husband	Wife
	Cash (on Hand) ☐	$100		$100
A	Cash (in Banks or Credit Unions) ☐	$9,000		$9,000
	Stocks, Bonds, Notes ☐			
S	Real Estate: Home ☐	$73,000		$73,000
	Business Interests ☐			
S	Automobiles ☐	$9,000		
	Boats ☐			
E	Other Vehicles ☐			
	Retirement Plans ☐			
T	Furniture & Furnishings in Home ☐	$1,000		
	Furniture & Furnishings Elsewhere ☐			
S	Collectibles ☐			
	Jewelry ☐	$100		
	Life Insurance (CSV) ☐			
	Sports/Entrtnmt Eqpmt (TV, Stereo, etc.) ☐			
	Other Assets ☐			
	Total Assets:	**$92,200**		

B	Liabilities [Check Box Next to Debts You Believe You Should Pay]	Current Amount Owed	Non-Marital	
			Husband	Wife
D	Mortgages on Real Estate (Home) ☐ — 2008	$58,800		$58,800
	Other Mortgages			
E	Credit Card Accounts ☐			
	Automobile Loan ☐	$11,000		$11,000
B	Automobile Loan ☐			
	Bank/Credit Union Loans ☐			
T	Money Owed (w/o Note) ☐	$200		$200
	Judgments ☐			
S	Other ☐	$1,000		$1,000
	Total Debts	**$71,000**		

C	NET WORTH [Excluding Contingent Assets & Liabilities]	
	Total Assets	$92,200
	Total Liabilities	$71,000
	TOTAL NET WORTH	**$21,200**

D	**Contingent Assets** [Check Box Next to Item You Wish Awarded To You]	Possible Value	Non-Marital	
			Husband	Wife
☐				

Contingent Liabilities [Check Box Next To Debts You Believe You Should Pay]	Possible Amount	Non-Marital	
		Husband	Wife
☐			

E	Has there been any agreement between you and the other party that one of you will take responsibility for a debt and will hold the other party harmless from that debt? ☐ Yes ☐ No
If yes, Explain:	

SECTION IV: CHILD SUPPORT GUIDELINES WORKSHEET

☑   A WorkSheet is being filed in this Case

☐   No WorkSheet is being filed: ☐ Child Support is not an Issue in this proceeding.
                                         ☐ There are no Minor Children

I understand that I am swearing or affirming under oath to the truthfulness of the claims made in this *Affidavit* and that the punishment for knowingly making a false statement includes fine and/or imprisonment.	
Sworn to And Subscribed on **August 23, 2008.** **ID:**	
	Wife
Notary Public:	Certificate of Service
	I Hereby Certify That a true copy of the foregoing *Financial Affidavit* was served on **Arather Side, Esq.** this **23 August 2008.**

Appendix D

CONTACT GUIDELINES

Shared Parental Responsibility Guidelines
The attached visitation schedule is approved by the judges of the Family Law Division and supersedes all other visitation schedules which have previously been used in Sarasota, Manatee, and DeSoto counties.
This schedule is effective August 1, 2002 and is to be applied to all cases pending as of that date.

I. Age Specific Guidelines
    A. Infants 0-10 Months. The parties shall confer and agree upon a schedule consisting of three (3) two-hour time periods per week with no more than two (2) days between visits. If the parties cannot agree, visitation shall be on Tuesdays and Thursdays from 6:00 p.m. to 8:00 p.m. and Saturdays from 3:00 p.m. to 5:00 p.m. Visitation should be exercised regularly and preferably at the same place to enable the infant to become familiar with the surroundings. The primary residential parent should promote consistency in the child(ren)'s nutrition and environment by supplying items such as the infant's formula, clothing, blankets, pacifier, wipes, toys, and infant car seat to the secondary residential parent as may be needed.
    B. Older Infants 10 Months to 24 Months. The parties shall confer and agree upon a schedule consisting of two (2) two-hour periods during the week with no more that two (2) days between visits, four (4) hours every Saturday and four (4) hours every other Sunday. If the parties cannot agree, visitation shall be on Tuesdays and Thursdays from 6:00 to 8:00 p.m., Saturdays from 3:00 p.m. to 7:00 p.m., and every other Sunday from 9:00 a.m. to 1:00 p.m.
    C. Toddlers 24 Months to 36 Months. The parties shall confer and agree upon a schedule consisting of two (2) two-hour periods during the week with no more than two (2) days between visits, four (4) hours every other Saturday alternating with one (1) overnight visitation from Saturday through early Sunday afternoon every other weekend. If the parties cannot agree, visitation shall be on Tuesdays and Thursdays from 6:00 p.m. to 8:00 p.m., every other Saturday from 3:00 p.m. to 7:00 p.m., and every other weekend from 3:00

p.m. Saturday to 1:00 p.m. Sunday.

D. Preschoolers 36 Months to January 1 of the Child's Kindergarten School Year. The parties shall confer and agree upon a schedule consisting of two (2) two-hour periods during the week, four (4) hours every other Saturday, and one (1) overnight visitation every other weekend. If the parties cannot agree, visitation shall be on Tuesdays and Thursdays from 6:00 p.m. to 8:00 p.m., every other Saturday from 3:00 p.m. to 7:00 p.m., and every other weekend from 9:00 a.m. Saturday to 5:00 p.m. Sunday.

E. Children from January 1 of the Kindergarten School Year to 13 Years. The parties shall confer and agree upon a schedule consisting of one (1) two-hour visit during the week and three (3) consecutive overnight visitation every other weekend. If the parties cannot agree, visitation shall be on Tuesday from 6:00 p.m. to 8:00 p.m. and every other weekend from 6:00 p.m. Friday to Monday at 9:00 a.m. or until the beginning of school on that day, whichever occurs first. If school is in session, the secondary residential parent shall transport the child to school.

F. Adolescents 13 Years to 18 Years. The parties shall confer with each other and with the child and the parents shall agree to modify the visitation schedule as may be appropriate, giving due consideration to the child's activities and desires. If no modified schedule is agreed upon by the parents, visitation shall continue as provided for children in the prior age group.

II.   Summer Visitation — General Provisions. Summer visitation shall not begin until the summer between kindergarten and first grade.

Summer visitation shall not be added directly to regular overnight visitation; that is, there should be a break between summer visitation and regular overnight visitation.

Frequent telephone contact with the non-visiting parent and the child is strongly encouraged and daily contact is recommended for all age groups. The parties shall confer and agree upon a schedule for telephone contact during summer visitation which is not less than that provided herein.

Parents are encouraged to arrange their summer visitation schedule by April 15 of the calendar year. This will permit an orderly transfer of the children and minimize disruption in the parents' and the children's lives.

A. Children between Kindergarten and First Grade. The parties shall confer and agree upon a summer schedule for each parent consisting of three (3) blocks of five (5) days with at least seven (7) days in between. The non-visiting parent shall be afforded at least one (1) telephone call per day with the child.

B. Children between First and Fourth Grade. The parties shall confer and agree upon a summer schedule for each parent consisting of two (2) blocks of ten (10) days with at least seven (7) days in between. The non-visiting parent shall be afforded at least one (1) telephone call every other day with the child. **C. Children after Fourth Grade through Age 18.** The parties shall confer and agree upon a summer schedule for each parent consisting of twenty-one (21) continuous days. The non-visiting parent shall be afforded at least one (1) telephone call every three (3) days with the child.

III. Holidays and Special Events.
   A. Age Specific.
      1. Infants 0–10 Months. When the secondary residential parent's regular visitation does not occur on Thanksgiving, Christmas, or Easter, the parties shall confer and agree upon a schedule consisting of two (2) hours on each said holiday.
      2. Older Infants 10 Months to 24 Months. When the secondary residential parent's regular visitation does not occur on or is less than four (4) hours on Thanksgiving, Christmas, Easter, or the child's birthday, the parties shall confer and agree upon a schedule consisting of four (4) hours on each day. If the parties cannot agree, visitation shall be from 4:00 p.m. to 8:00 p.m. on each holiday.
      3. Toddlers 24 Months to 36 Months. When the secondary residential parent regular visitation does not occur on or is less than four (4) hours on Thanksgiving, Christmas, Easter, the child's birthday, Mother's Day, or Father's Day, the parties shall confer and agree upon a schedule consisting of four (4) hours on each holiday. If the parties cannot agree, visitation shall be from 4:00 p.m. to 8:00 p.m. on each holiday.
      4. Preschoolers 36 Months to January I of the Child's Kindergarten School Year. When the secondary residential parent's regular visitation does not occur or is less than four (4) hours on Thanksgiving, Christmas, Easter, Halloween, or July 4th, the parties shall confer and agree upon a schedule consisting of four (4) hours on each holiday. If the parties cannot agree, visitation shall be from 4:00 to 8:00 p.m. on each holiday except July 4th, which shall be from 6:30 p.m. to 10:30 p.m.
      5. Children and Adolescents from January 1 of the Kindergarten School Year through Age 18. Except for the first spring break during the child's kindergarten school year, during odd-numbered years, the primary residential parent shall have the children for spring vacation, Halloween, and the first week of Christmas vacation (ending at 6:00 p.m.

on the seventh day), excluding Christmas Day from midday until midday on the day after Christmas. The secondary residential parent shall have the children for July 4th, Thanksgiving vacation (including the weekend), and the remainder of the Christmas vacation, together with one-half of Christmas Day from midday until midday on the day after Christmas. Memorial Day and Labor Day shall be spent with the parent who is scheduled to be with the child for that weekend. During even-numbered years, the holiday entitlement shall be reversed.

B. Holiday Specific: Unless otherwise specified above in the age-specific guidelines, the schedule is:

1. Thanksgiving. Thanksgiving vacation visitation will begin at 6:00 p.m. on the Wednesday that school lets out.

2. Christmas. Christmas vacation visitation will begin at 6:00 p.m. the day after school has ended. The child will be returned home at 6:00 p.m. two (2) days before school resumes in order to ensure a full day home. Christmas Day visitation for the parent who has the second part of Christmas vacation shall be from noon on Christmas Day until noon on the day after Christmas.

3. Mother's Day and Father's Day. Mother's Day and Father's Day are to be spent with the appropriate parent after the child(ren) is (are) three (3) years old.

4. Birthdays. The child shall celebrate his or her birthday with the parent entitled to contact on that day.

5. Religious Holidays. Religious holidays and other days of special meaning should be decided together, written down, and alternated.

Appendix E

STATEWIDE CHILD-SUPPORT GUIDELINES (Florida Statutes 61.30)

The following schedules shall be applied to the combined net income to determine the minimum child support need:

Combined Monthly Available Income	Child or Children					
	One	Two	Three	Four	Five	Six
$650	74	75	75	76	77	78
700	119	120	121	123	124	125
750	164	166	167	169	171	173
800	190	211	213	216	218	220
850	202	257	259	262	265	268
900	213	302	305	309	312	315
950	224	347	351	355	359	363
1000	235	365	397	402	406	410
1050	246	382	443	448	453	458
1100	258	400	489	495	500	505
1150	269	417	522	541	547	553
1200	280	435	544	588	594	600
1250	290	451	565	634	641	648
1300	300	467	584	659	688	695
1350	310	482	603	681	735	743
1400	320	498	623	702	765	790
1450	330	513	642	724	789	838
1500	340	529	662	746	813	869
1550	350	544	681	768	836	895
1600	360	560	701	790	860	920
1650	370	575	720	812	884	945
1700	380	591	740	833	907	971
1750	390	606	759	855	931	996
1800	400	622	779	877	955	1022
1850	410	638	798	900	979	1048
1900	421	654	818	923	1004	1074
1950	431	670	839	946	1029	1101

Combined Monthly Available Income	Child or Children					
	One	Two	Three	Four	Five	Six
$2000	442	686	859	968	1054	1128
2050	452	702	879	991	1079	1154
2100	463	718	899	1014	1104	1181
2700	588	912	1141	1287	1403	1500
2750	597	927	1160	1308	1426	1524
2800	607	941	1178	1328	1448	1549
2850	616	956	1197	1349	1471	1573
2900	626	971	1215	1370	1494	1598
2950	635	986	1234	1391	1517	1622
3000	644	1001	1252	1412	1540	1647
3050	654	1016	1271	1433	1563	1671
3100	663	1031	1289	1453	1586	1695
3150	673	1045	1308	1474	1608	1720
3200	682	1060	1327	1495	1631	1744
3250	691	1075	1345	1516	1654	1769
3300	701	1090	1364	1537	1677	1793
3350	710	1105	1382	1558	1700	1818
3400	720	1120	1401	1579	1723	1842
3450	729	1135	1419	1599	1745	1867
3500	738	1149	1438	1620	1768	1891
3550	748	1164	1456	1641	1791	1915
3600	757	1179	1475	1662	1814	1940
3650	767	1194	1493	1683	1837	1964
3700	776	1208	1503	1702	1857	1987
3750	784	1221	1520	1721	1878	2009
3800	793	1234	1536	1740	1899	2031
3850	802	1248	1553	1759	1920	2053
3900	811	1261	1570	1778	1940	2075
3950	819	1275	1587	1797	1961	2097
4000	828	1288	1603	1816	1982	2119
4050	837	1302	1620	1835	2002	2141
4100	846	1315	1637	1854	2023	2163
4150	854	1329	1654	1873	2044	2185
4200	863	1342	1670	1892	2064	2207
4250	872	1355	1687	1911	2085	2229
4300	881	1369	1704	1930	2106	2251
4350	889	1382	1721	1949	2127	2273
4400	898	1396	1737	1968	2147	2295
4450	907	1409	1754	1987	2168	2317
4500	916	1423	1771	2006	2189	2339
4550	924	1436	1788	2024	2209	2361
4600	933	1450	1804	2043	2230	2384
4650	942	1463	1821	2062	2251	2406
4700	951	1477	1838	2081	2271	2428
4750	959	1490	1855	2100	2292	2450
4800	968	1503	1871	2119	2313	2472
4850	977	1517	1888	2138	2334	2494
4900	986	1530	1905	2157	2354	2516

Combined Monthly Available Income	Child or Children					
	One	Two	Three	Four	Five	Six
4950	993	1542	1927	2174	2372	2535
5000	1000	1551	1939	2188	2387	2551
5050	1006	1561	1952	2202	2402	2567
5100	1013	1571	1964	2215	2417	2583
5150	1019	1580	1976	2229	2432	2599
5200	1025	1590	1988	2243	2447	2615
5300	1038	1609	2012	2270	2477	2647
5350	1045	1619	2024	2283	2492	2663
5400	1051	1628	2037	2297	2507	2679
5450	1057	1638	2049	2311	2522	2695
5500	1064	1647	2061	2324	2537	2711
5550	1070	1657	2073	2338	2552	2727
5600	1077	1667	2085	2352	2567	2743
5650	1083	1676	2097	2365	2582	2759
5700	1089	1686	2109	2379	2597	2775
5750	1096	1695	2122	2393	2612	2791
5800	1102	1705	2134	2406	2627	2807
5850	1107	1713	2144	2418	2639	2820
5900	1111	1721	2155	2429	2651	2833
5950	1116	1729	2165	2440	2663	2847
6000	1121	1737	2175	2451	2676	2860
6050	1126	1746	2185	2462	2688	2874
6100	1131	1754	2196	2473	2700	2887
6150	1136	1762	2206	2484	2712	2900
6200	1141	1770	2216	2495	2724	2914
6250	1145	1778	2227	2506	2737	2927
6300	1150	1786	2237	2517	2749	2941
6350	1155	1795	2247	2529	2761	2954
6400	1160	1803	2258	2540	2773	2967
6450	1165	1811	2268	2551	2785	2981
6500	1170	1819	2278	2562	2798	2994
6550	1175	1827	2288	2573	2810	3008
6600	1179	1835	2299	2584	2822	3021
6650	1184	1843	2309	2595	2834	3034
6700	1189	1850	2317	2604	2845	3045
6750	1193	1856	2325	2613	2854	3055
6800	1196	1862	2332	2621	2863	3064
6850	1200	1868	2340	2630	2872	3074
6900	1204	1873	2347	2639	2882	3084
6950	1208	1879	2355	2647	2891	3094
7000	1212	1885	2362	2656	2900	3103
7050	1216	1891	2370	2664	2909	3113
7100	1220	1897	2378	2673	2919	3123
7150	1224	1903	2385	2681	2928	3133
7200	1228	1909	2393	2690	2937	3142
7250	1232	1915	2400	2698	2946	3152
7300	1235	1921	2408	2707	2956	3162
7350	1239	1927	2415	2716	2965	3172

Combined Monthly Available Income	One	Two	Child or Children Three	Four	Five	Six
$7400	1243	1933	2423	2724	2974	3181
7450	1247	1939	2430	2733	2983	3191
7500	1251	1945	2438	2741	2993	3201
7550	1255	1951	2446	2750	3002	3211
7600	1259	1957	2453	2758	3011	3220
7650	1263	1963	2461	2767	3020	3230
7700	1267	1969	2468	2775	3030	3240
7750	1271	1975	2476	2784	3039	3250
7800	1274	1981	2483	2792	3048	3259
7850	1278	1987	2491	2801	3057	3269
7900	1282	1992	2498	2810	3067	3279
7950	1286	1998	2506	2818	3076	3289
8000	1290	2004	2513	2827	3085	3298
8050	1294	2010	2521	2835	3094	3308
8100	1298	2016	2529	2844	3104	3318
8150	1302	2022	2536	2852	3113	3328
8200	1306	2028	2544	2861	3122	3337
8250	1310	2034	2551	2869	3131	3347
8300	1313	2040	2559	2878	3141	3357
8350	1317	2046	2566	2887	3150	3367
8400	1321	2052	2574	2895	3159	3376
8450	1325	2058	2581	2904	3168	3386
8500	1329	2062	2589	2912	3178	3396
8550	1333	2070	2597	2921	3187	3406
8600	1337	2076	2604	2929	3196	3415
8650	1341	2082	2612	2938	3205	3425
8700	1345	2088	2619	2946	3215	3435
8750	1349	2094	2627	2955	3225	3445
8800	1352	2100	2634	2963	3233	3454
8850	1356	2106	2642	2972	3242	3464
8900	1360	2111	2649	2981	3252	3474
8950	1364	2117	2657	2689	3261	3484
9000	1368	2123	2664	2998	3270	3493
9050	1372	2129	2672	3006	3279	3503
9100	1376	2135	2680	3015	3289	3513
9150	1380	2141	2687	3032	3298	3523
9200	1384	2147	2695	3032	3307	3532
9250	1388	2153	2702	3040	3316	3542
9300	1391	2159	2710	3049	3326	3552
9350	1395	2165	2717	3058	3335	3562
9400	1399	2171	2725	3066	3344	3571
9450	1403	2177	2732	3075	3353	3581
9500	1407	2183	2740	3083	3363	3591
9550	1411	2189	2748	3092	3372	3601
9600	1415	2195	2755	3100	3381	3610
9650	1419	2201	2763	3109	3390	3620
9700	1422	2206	2767	3115	3396	3628
9750	1425	2210	2772	3121	3402	3634

Combined Monthly Available Income	One	Two	Child or Children Three	Four	Five	Six
$ 9800	1427	2213	2776	3126	3408	3641
9850	1430	2217	2781	3132	3414	3647
9900	1432	2221	2786	3137	3420	3653
9950	1435	2225	2791	3143	3426	3659
10,000	1437	2228	2795	3148	3432	3666

For combined monthly available income less than the amount set out on the above schedules, the parent should be ordered to pay a child support amount, determined on a case-by-case basis, to establish the principle of payment and lay the basis for increased orders should the parent's income increase in the future. For combined monthly available income greater than the amount set out in the above schedules, the obligation shall be the minimum amount of support provided by the guidelines plus the following percentages multiplied by the amount of income over $10,000:

		CHILD OR CHILDREN			
One	Two	Three	Four	Five	Six
5.0%	7.5%	9.5%	11.0%	12.0%	12.5%

Appendix F

TWELFTH JUDICIAL CIRCUIT

In Re: The Marriage of   ✳

ROBERT BEACH,   ✳   **Case Number**

Husband,   **2008 DR 6550 NC**
- Division 5 -

     ✳

and

     ✳   **Petition for Simplified**

KAREN BEACH,   **Dissolution of Marriage**

Wife.   ✳

We, **Robert Beach**, **Husband**, and **Karen Beach**, **Wife**, being sworn, certify that the following information is true:

1. **NATURE OF ACTION**. We are both asking the Court for a dissolution of our marriage.

2. **RESIDENCE**. The **Husband** lives in Sarasota County, Florida, and has lived there since July 1st, 2004. The **Wife** lives in Sarasota County, Florida, and has lived there since July 1st, 2004.

3. **MARRIAGE/SEPARATION**. We were married to each other on May 15th, 1993 in the city of Casper in the State of Wyoming.

4. **GROUNDS**. Our marriage is irretrievably broken.

5. **NO MINOR CHILDREN**. Together, we have no minor (under 18) or dependent children **and** the **Wife** is not pregnant.

6. **PROPERTY**. We have made a *Marital Settlement Agreement* dividing our assets (what we own) and our liabilities (what we owe). We are satisfied with this agreement. Our *Marital Settlement Agreement* is attached. This agreement was signed freely and voluntarily by each of us and we intend to be bound by it.

7. **FINANCIAL AFFIDAVITS**. We have each completed and signed *Financial Affidavits*, which are attached to this *Petition*.

8. **NOTICES OF SOCIAL SECURITY NUMBER**. *Notices of Social Security Number* are filed with this *Petition*.

9. **NAME CHANGE**. ☑ Yes ☐ No **Wife** wants to be known by her former name, which is **Karen Shore Gattem**.

10. <u>FREE AND VOLUNTARY</u>. We each certify that we have not been threatened or pressured into signing this petition. We each understand that the result of signing this petition may be a final judgment ending our marriage and allowing no further relief.

11. <u>FINAL HEARING</u>. We each understand that **we both must come to the hearing** to testify about the things we are asking for in this *Petition*.

12. <u>RIGHTS</u>. We understand that we each may have legal rights as a result of our marriage and that by signing this Petition, we may be giving up those rights.

Wherefore, We pray that:

a. Our marriage be dissolved.

b. The parties' agreements regarding property and obligations be approved by this Court.

c. Jurisdiction be retained by the Court for enforcement of the *Final Judgment* and otherwise.

I understand that I am swearing or affirming under oath to the truthfulness of the claims made in this petition and that the punishment for knowingly making a false statement includes fines and/or imprisonment.

_____
ROBERT BEACH
HUSBAND

_____
Attorney for **Husband**

V E R I F I C A T I O N

State of Florida
County of Sarasota

      Before me, the undersigned authority, this day personally appeared **Robert Beach**, ☐ who is to me well-known or ☐ who identified himself through his Florida Driver's License, and who was first by me being duly sworn, says that he is the **Husband** in the above styled cause and has read the *Petition for Dissolution of Marriage* and has personal knowledge of the facts and matters alleged in it, and each of these facts and matters is true and correct.

      Sworn to and Subscribed before me this _____ day of **August, 2008**.

Commission Expiration	
	Notary Public:

      I understand that I am swearing or affirming under oath to the truthfulness of the claims made in this petition and that the punishment for knowingly making a false statement includes fines and/or imprisonment.

KAREN BEACH
WIFE

Attorney for **Wife**

V E R I F I C A T I O N

State of Florida
County of Sarasota

      Before me, the undersigned authority, this day personally appeared **Karen Beach**, ☐ who is to me well-known or ☐ who identified herself through her Florida Driver's License, and who was first by me being duly sworn, says that she is the **Wife** in the above styled cause and has read the *Petition for Dissolution of Marriage* and has personal knowledge of the facts and matters alleged in it, and each of these facts and matters is true and correct.

      Sworn to and Subscribed before me this _____ day of **August, 2008**.

Commission Expiration	
	Notary Public:

In the Circuit Court In and For Sarasota County, Florida

TWELFTH JUDICIAL CIRCUIT

In Re: The Marriage of   ✶

    ROBERT BEACH,   ✶

               Husband,

                             ✶

        and   ✶

    KAREN BEACH,   ✶

             Wife.   ✶ .

Case Number
2008 DR 6560 NC
- Division 5 -

Affidavit of
Corroborating Witness

A F F I D A V I T	
State of Florida County of Sarasota	

Before me, the undersigned authority, this day personally appeared **W.B. Gow,** who is to me well-known or identified himself through his Florida Driver's License, and who was first by me being duly sworn, says that he has personal knowledge of the facts and matters stated below, and each of these facts and matters is true and correct:

    1. I am a resident of the State of Florida.

    2. I have known **Karen Beach** since 1995 and know, of my own personal knowledge, that this person has resided in the State of Florida for at least 6 months before the date of this affidavit.

    3. I have attached a copy of my Florida driver's license to this affidavit

Further Affiant Sayeth Not.

W. B. Gow 20 Tanglewood Street Sarasota, Florida 34224 941-555-9876	

Sworn to and Subscribed before me this ____ day of **August, 2008.**

Commission Expiration	
	Notary Public:

In the Circuit Court In and For Sarasota County, Florida

TWELFTH JUDICIAL CIRCUIT

In Re: The Marriage of   ✱

ROBERT BEACH,   ✱

Husband,   **Case Number**
2008 DR 6550 NC
- Division 5 -

✱

and   ✱

Final Judgment of

✱

KAREN BEACH,   **Simplified Dissolution**

Wife.   ✱

This cause came before this Court for hearing on the parties' *Petition for Simplified Dissolution of Marriage*. The Court, having reviewed the file and heard the testimony, makes these findings of fact and reaches these conclusions of law:

1. The Court has jurisdiction over the subject matter and the parties.
2. At least one party has been a resident of the State of Florida for more than 6 months immediately before filing the *Petition for Simplified Dissolution of Marriage*.
3. The parties have no minor or dependent children in common, and the **Wife** is not pregnant.
4. The marriage between the parties is irretrievably broken. Therefore, the marriage between the parties is dissolved, and the parties are restored to the status of being single.
5. *Marital Settlement Agreement*
   ☑ a. The parties have voluntarily entered into a *Marital Settlement Agreement* and each has filed the required *Financial Affidavit*. Therefore, the *Marital Settlement Agreement* is filed as "Exhibit A" in this case and is ratified and made a part of this *Final Judgment*. The parties are ordered to obey all of its provisions.
   ☐ b. There is no marital property or marital debts to divide, as the parties previously have divided all of their personal property. Therefore, each is awarded the personal property he or she presently has in his or her possession. Each party shall be responsible for any debts in his or her own name.

_____

Circuit Judge

Copies Furnished to:
  Karen Shore Gattem
  Robert Beach

Appendix G

PARENT EDUCATION AND FAMILY STABILIZATION COURSE

Florida law requires that all parties to a dissolution proceeding with minor children or a paternity action which involves issues of parental responsibility must attend and complete a parenting course before a final judgment can be entered. The course must be at least 4 hours long and cover the following topics:

Legal aspects of deciding child-related issues between parents
Emotional aspects of separation and divorce on adults
Emotional aspects of separation and divorce on children
Family relationships and family dynamics
Financial responsibilities to a child or children
Issues regarding spousal or child abuse and neglect
Skill-based relationship education that may be generalized to parent
ing, workplace, school, neighborhood, and civic relationships.

The courses are available, usually from more than one provider, in every circuit and the cost is rather nominal, in the $25 - $50 range but there must be at least one provider who charges on a sliding scale. The Clerk of the Court can provide you with the names and telephone numbers of the providers in your area.

For good cause, the Court can excuse one or both parties from attending the course.

In addition to dissolution and paternity actions, the court can require parties going through a modification action involving shared parental responsibilities, custody, or visitation to take the parenting course.

The courses are generally given by mental health professionals and educators but the purpose is to educate and not to provide individual mental health therapy. The lecturers cannot, of course, provide any legal advice and they are not permitted to solicit participants to become private clients or patients. That last point does not mean that a mental health professional cannot later treat a participant as long as he/she does not actively solicit them.

If a party refuses to, or for any unacceptable reason does not, attend the course, the court can hold him/her in contempt of court or can even deny that party a sharing in parental responsibility for the children. To avoid conflict, the court can prohibit the parties from taking the course together. This is particularly true if there is any history of domestic violence but the providers generally do not want both parties at the same session anyway.

Appendix H

CHILD SUPPORT WORKSHEET

CHILD SUPPORT WORKSHEET 7 September 2008		Marriage of GROWOM Case No. 2008 DR 1234 NC	
		HUSBAND	WIFE
Gross Income		$2,765	$1,290
Alimony Adjustmt (+ to W/, - to H/)			
Income Taxes		$554	$191
FICA/Self-Employment/Medicare		$211	$99
Mandatory Union Dues			
Mandatory Retirement Payments			
Adult Health Insurance			
Court-Ordered Child Support			
NET INCOMES		$2,000	$1,000
Combined Net Income		$3,000	
PerCentage Responsibility;		66.67%	33.33%
Gross GuideLine Support		$1,001	
Health Insurance Paymts for Children		$200	
75% of Day Care Expense		$300	
Net GuideLine Support		$1,501	
CHILD SUPPORT OBLIGATIONS		$1,001	$500

EXISTING BASES FOR ADJUSTMENT

· Extraordinary medical, psychological, dental, educational expenses
· Independent income of child(ren)
· Obligation for both alimony and child support
· Seasonal variation in either parent's income
· Ages of child(ren): years
· Special needs of child(ren) traditionally met in family budget
· Extraordinary contact exceeding guidelines
· Extraordinary total available assets of either parent or child
· Extraordinary debts of either party
· Other necessary adjustments

Appendix I

DEPOSITIONS

A deposition is one of several ways that attorneys can find out about the other side's case. It may be the most useful. A deposition is the formal questioning of a witness under oath in the presence of a court reporter who records both the questions and the answers. The questioning usually takes place in the office of one of the attorneys in the case. If the other attorney objects to that, they can usually agree to hold the deposition either at the courthouse or at the court reporter's office.

Although I dealt with financial affidavits at some length and your deposition is as important as the affidavit, I will treat depositions more succinctly. I would rather that you learn and follow a few rules than to read a treatise on giving a deposition and forget it all when you hear the first question.

Your attorney will prepare you in advance for what will occur at the deposition. He or she will be present throughout the deposition to ensure that you are not mistreated.

Always follow your attorney's advice regarding your testimony at a deposition. You will find that your attorney's instructions will generally include the following:

· Answer all questions as briefly as possible, giving only the information specifically sought by the question. A simple yes or no is the best possible answer to at least two-thirds of all questions.
· Make sure you understand the question completely before beginning to answer it; ask the opposing attorney to repeat it or rephrase it if you are the slightest bit confused.
· Always let the attorney finish the question before you start to answer.

· Always tell the truth. Telling a lie or falsely denying that you know something is perjury, punishable by up to five years in prison. Quite aside from the ethical issue involved, how many lies are worth five years in prison?

· Answer audibly so that the court reporter can record your answer without interpreting whether your head shake was a yes or a no.

· Don't argue with or try to outwit the attorney. He or she is far better qualified to win any argument with you if so inclined. The attorney may also be more knowledgeable about the facts of the case than you are. You'll only lose if you make the deposition a contest. Nothing is more disarming or convincing than a sincere and courteous attempt to answer every question honestly.

· Don't lose your temper. Your credibility as a witness depends on your ability to provide information in an unemotional manner. Any question that tends to inflame your emotions will be either an improper question or one that seeks damaging information from you. Avoid treating the process as hostile; that will only work against you.

· Don't hesitate to admit when you don't know the answer to a question.

· Don't guess at an answer unless you are specifically asked to do so. If you are asked to estimate, make it clear that your answer is just that.

· Allow your attorney time to object to an improper question; if your attorney does object, he or she will instruct you either to answer or not to answer the question. There is no law or procedural rule that permits you to refuse to answer a question but, under certain extreme circumstances, your attorney will instruct you not to answer. Follow those directions.

· Do not ask anyone else in the room for information needed to answer the question. If you don't know, tell the attorney that. Don't look for papers that might have the answer unless you have been required to produce those papers.

· If you have any doubts about whether you answered the questions correctly, don't hesitate to assert your right to read the transcript. Most attorneys instruct their clients to waive reading and signing, but this can sometimes be dangerous. The rules permit you to read the transcript and correct any error in transcription or any answer that you might have erroneously given.

· Dress decently but don't overdress.

· Don't try to win your case in the deposition. The other attorney will not be swayed by your brilliance but may gain a lot of damaging insight into your position if you try to win him or her over.

In summary, answer each question honestly, briefly, audibly, and only after you are sure that you understand it.

Glossary

For your convenience in understanding unfamiliar terms, I have included this very brief glossary. It is not intended to be all-inclusive nor are the terms exhaustively defined. I have defined one hundred terms that I think you may need to understand at some time or other during a divorce. You will find more complete explanations of most of the terms in the text itself. If you need more information, go to the index to locate the discussion and read more about it there.

Affidavit — A sworn statement in writing.

Alimony — The support paid by one divorced party to the other.

Annulment — The legal determination that no valid marriage ever existed.

Antenuptial Agreement — A nuptial agreement entered into before the parties marry; also called a prenuptial agreement.

Appeal — A request that a higher court reconsider the decision or rulings of the trial court. Generally, only rulings on the law are subject to appeal.

Arrearage — The amount of due but unpaid child support and/or alimony.

Attachment — One way that the sheriff can seize property to satisfy a debt.

Attorney — A law-trained person admitted to the bar to practice law; used interchangeably with lawyer.

Bar — The dividing rail in a courtroom that separates the lawyers and judges from the laymen; now, the formal association of lawyers admitted to practice in the state.

Cause of Action — A term used to mean both the right to bring an action and the action itself.

Chambers — The small room adjoining a judge's office where many divorce cases are heard.

Children — Legally, anyone under the age of 18.

Child Support — The obligation of both parents to support the children after a divorce; the term is usually used only in reference to the payments made by the nonresidential parent to the primary residential parent.

Circuit Court — The court with jurisdiction over marital matters; a circuit is generally made up of several counties.

Complaint — A formal paper filed with the court to state the initial legal position of a plaintiff; generally the term refers to actions at law as opposed to actions in equity, such as marital matters.

Contact — The no-fault term for visitation of the nonresidential (noncustodial) parent with the children; the term includes telephone calls and other communication.

Contempt of Court — Specifically, an act which shows lack of respect for the court or its ruling; in fact, the term usually refers to the procedures used to enforce the rulings.

Court — A term with several different meanings, including: (1) the level of defined power, such a Circuit Court, a County Court, a District Court of Appeals, or the Supreme Court; (2) the specific entity (in the person of a judge) who acts in a specific case; and (3) the setting in which cases are heard (which may or may not be a courtroom).

Court of Equity — Generally, that aspect of the court system that deals with cases involving issues other than, or in addition to, money.

Court of Law — Generally, that aspect of the court system that deals with cases completely determined on money issues.

Court Reporter — Formerly called a court stenographer, a person specially trained on special typewriters to record all exchanges in a courtroom or deposition for later transcription.

Custody — The old term, still very common, referring to which parent has the children living with him or her.

Default — A term with at least three common legal meanings: (1) a failure to respond to a petition or complaint; (2) a failure to comply with an agreement term or court order; and (3) a formal paper entered by a court or clerk cutting off one's right to answer a Complaint or Petition.

Deposition — A method of discovery in which one party's attorney questions the other party or a third party under oath and has the questions and answers recorded by a court reporter.

Discovery — The several means of investigating the facts and position of the other party in a case.

Dissolution of Marriage — The term used in no-fault to refer to the termination of a marriage.

Divided Custody — Another term for joint custody, that is, where the parents share approximately equally in taking care of the children.

Divorce — The old term, but still common, for the termination of a marriage; a more archaic term, divorce a vincula, usually followed by "and not from bed and board," merely means a "true" divorce as opposed to a separation; literally it means "divorce from the bonds (of marriage)."

Emancipation — The legal freeing of a child from the restrictions of childhood.

Enforcement — The procedures used to force one party to comply with the court's orders or judgment.

Equitable Distribution — The dividing of property according to equitable principles, considering such factors as when and how it was acquired rather than looking only to record title.

Ex Parte — A communication with the judge on the subject matter of a case without the other side present; in the absence of authorization from the other side or exceptional circumstances provided by law, such a communication is highly improper.

Filing — The act of presenting a paper to the court for retention in the court file.

Final Judgment — The same as Judgment, the written ruling of the court on the ultimate issues of a case.

Financial Affidavit — The sworn statement of a party's income, expenses, assets, and liabilities.

Findings of Fact — The portion of an order or judgment in which the court states what facts are found to exist based upon the evidence presented in court.

Garnishment — The seizure of an asset, commonly wages, to satisfy a debt.

Guideline(s) —A set of rules, procedures, numbers, or schedules that can be used to govern conduct; in marital matters, child support and contact guidelines are typical.

Habeas Corpus — A writ of the court that directs the recipient to bring a person before the court and show legal authority for holding possession or control of that person.

Hearing — Any appearance before a judge to decide an issue or motion.

Hearing Officer — A qualified person delegated by the chief judge in the circuit to hear certain types of marital matters and make determinations of fact.

Home State — The state in which a child involved in a custody determination has resided for the immediately preceding six months before filing.

Income Deduction Order — An order by the court that payments for support be deducted from the obligated party's paycheck before the party receives the money.

Injunction —A court directive that a person do or not do something.

Interrogatories — A method of discovery that uses written questions which must be answered by the opposing party under oath.

Joint Custody — The equal, or almost equal, dividing of the residential care between both parties; disfavored by the courts because it is perceived as damaging to the children.

Judgment — The ruling of the court on the ultimate issues in a case.

Jurisdiction — A term with several different meanings, including: (1) the type of case that a court may try; (2) the specific power of the court over a particular person or item of property; and (3) the territorial limits over which the judge may exercise his or her power.

Laches — The defense that the person seeking relief has waited so long that the other party is unable to capably defend the action or it would, otherwise, be unfair to grant the relief.

Lawyer — Technically, a person educated in the law; now used interchangeably with attorney.

Lump Sum Alimony — Alimony in a specific amount; may be payable in one payment or several payments over a period of time; may be in the form of property.

Majority, Age of — In Florida, 18 years of age.

Marital Agreement — A settlement agreement.

Marital Misconduct — Generally, any seriously improper act contrary to marital obligations; specifically, almost always used to refer to sexual infidelity.

Marital Property — Property accumulated in the course of, and related to, a marriage.

Mediation — The nonadversarial resolution of issues with the assistance of a neutral third party.

Modification — A change in the judgment after it has been entered.

Motion — A request to the court that it take some action; can be in writing or oral, depending on the nature of the relief sought.

Ne Exeat — A writ issued by the court to the sheriff to take a person into custody until he or she posts a bond to remain within the state.

No-Fault — The concept that divorce is a matter of right and not dependent upon misconduct of any type by the other party.

Nonmarital Property — Property brought into a marriage or developed through sources unrelated to the marriage.

Nuptial Agreement — An agreement between two married, or about to be married, people setting out the obligations of each in the marriage.

Order — A written or, more rarely, oral directive by the judge that sets out his or her decision or requires action be taken or not taken.

Parental Rights — The total of all rights and responsibilities parents have toward their children.

Petitioner — The party who first seeks relief from the court by filing a petition for relief, usually for dissolution of the marriage.

Pleading — A formal paper filed with the court that sets out one's legal position in a case.

Postnuptial Agreement — A nuptial agreement entered into after the parties are already married.

Prenuptial Agreement — A nuptial agreement entered into before the parties marry; also called an antenuptial agreement.

Prima Facie — An adjective that describes evidence that is sufficient unto itself that, if unrebutted, will justify granting the relief sought.

Primary Residential Parent — The term under no-fault for the custodial parent.

Private Ordering — an agreement between divorce parties that payments that would otherwise qualify as tax-deductible (by the payer) alimony will not be treated that way. As a result of the private ordering, the payments are not deductible by the payer and not includable by the recipient.

Process — The court papers that, when served upon a party, make him or her subject to the court's authority.

Production — A method of discovery that compels the other party or, sometimes, a third party, to make documents or objects available for inspection.

Qualified Domestic Relations Order (QDRO) — an order issued by a court in a divorce case that directs the administrator of a pension plan to pay all or a portion of one person's pension to that person's former spouse.

Rehabilitative Alimony — A type of alimony that is limited in time on the expectation that the recipient will be able to support himself or herself in the future.

Relief — A legal remedy that a court can give.

Res Judicata — The principle that matters litigated to a decision between two people are forever resolved and cannot be litigated again.

Respondent — The party against whom an action is filed in a court of equity.

Restraining Order — A court directive that prohibits a party under the court's jurisdiction to take a certain specified act.

Rulings — Any order or judgment of the court; more specifically, that portion of the order or judgment which decides the issue presented.

Separation — Factually, the leaving of a common bed or home; legally, the recognition of the need for determination of mutual legal concerns because accord of the parties has ceased to exist.

Service — The formal act of a designated official, sometimes the sheriff, of giving process to a party to bring him or her under the court's authority.

Settlement — An amicable resolution of the issues in dispute, usually reduced to writing and called a Settlement Agreement.

Settlement Agreement — A written agreement resolving the parties' differences in a case; it is usually submitted to the court for inclusion in the Judgment.

Shared Parental Responsibility — The sharing by both parents after a divorce in the important decisions about the children.

Simplified Dissolution –A procedure for obtaining a divorce without the need to use a lawyer; available only if certain criteria are met.

Social Investigation — A court-directed investigation into the circumstances of both parties in a custody battle.

Sole Responsibility — The entrustment, in no-fault, of custody and full decision-making authority to one parent to the exclusion of the other; rarely granted.

Special Equity — An interest that one party has in property that is in the name of another party.

Split Custody — The dividing of siblings between parents in custody disputes such that some live with one parent and some with the other; highly disfavored but now statutorily authorized.

Stipulation — Any agreement between opposing parties or, more commonly, their attorneys, to the court that it may do something without dispute.

Subpoena — A court-backed order issued by the clerk directing someone to appear before the court or for a deposition.

Subpoena duces tecum — A court-backed directive of the Clerk that a person appear at a hearing, trial, or deposition and bring specified documents or objects for inspection.

Suit Money — A fee awarded to be paid by one spouse to the other at the beginning of a case to enable that less able party to secure adequate counsel; technically refers to money used for out-of-pocket expenses but sometimes is used to include temporary attorney's fees.

Summons — A notice from the court that the person served is subject to the court's authority and must answer to an action filed with that court.

Tender Years Doctrine — The legal principle, supposedly no longer in effect, that presumes that a young child is better entrusted to the care of the mother.

Three-year rule — An IRS rule that applies when alimony payments exceed $10,000 per year and the amounts change significantly during the first three years. The purpose of the rule is to unmask property transfers that are designated as alimony.

Transcript — A typed record of a hearing or deposition that is taken from a court reporter's notes (which are not readable to nonreporters in the form taken down initially).

Trial — The appearance before a judge (or sometimes, in non-marital cases, a jury) for testimony and proof leading to a final decision by the judge.

UCCJEA — Uniform Child Custody Jurisdiction and Enforcement Act, a law adopted in every state (and the District of Columbia) to facilitate interstate enforcement of custody awards; it prescribes where case will be heard.

UIFSA — Uniform Interstate Family Support Act, a law adopted in every state to facilitate interstate enforcement of child support and alimony.

Venue — The geographical area (usually a county) in which it is proper to bring a case.

Vincula, a — An archaic Latin suffix used to signify a true divorce as opposed to a separation; divorce a vincula literally means "divorce from the bonds (of marriage)."

Visitation — The old term, but still common, for contact between the nonresidential (noncustodial) parent with the children.

Waiver — A written or oral release of one's specific rights.

Writ — A special type of directive from the court based on common law principles.

Index

Here are some other books from Pineapple Press on related topics. For a complete catalog, write to Pineapple Press, P.O. Box 3889, Sarasota, Florida 34230-3889, or call (800) 746-3275. Or visit our website at www.pineapplepress.com.

Florida Law: A Layman's Guide (Fifth Edition) by Gerald B. Keane. A practical, readable guide to your legal rights in Florida. Covers property law, family law, business law, and special areas. (pb)

The Condominium Concept (Tenth Edition) by Peter M. Dunbar. An updated, practical guide for officers, owners, and directors of Florida condominiums. Written in clear, concise language, this has been an indispensable working tool for officers, directors, homeowners, managers, realtors, and attorneys since the first edition in 1986. Cross-referenced to the Florida Statutes. Includes sample forms. (pb)

The Law of Florida Homeowners Associations (Seventh Edition) by Peter M. Dunbar and Charles F. Dudley. The only complete and practical guide to help ensure that a Florida homeowners association carries out its responsibilities fairly and effectively under current Florida laws. Cross-referenced to the Florida Statutes. Includes sample forms, a table of cases, and complete subject index. (pb)